WRITER'S CRAMP ■ JOHN BYRNE

'The biggest success of the Festival was the emergence of a new comic talent in John Byrne, a Glaswegian artist in his mid-forties, whose first play, *Writer's Cramp*, met with almost unanimous critical acclaim.' Steve Grant, *Time Out*

LOSING VENICE ■ JOHN CLIFFORD

'A truly outstanding first stage play by an Edinburgh-based writer, John Clifford's *Losing Venice* begins in a stylised "Spain" at some indeterminate time between the Re-conquest and the age of Goya.' Angus Calder, *New Statesman*

THE LETTER-BOX ■ ANN MARIE DI MAMBRO

'The audience was . . . absolutely riveted to the plight of a battered wife, thrown out of the house by her husband and trying to explain the situation to her young daughter through the front door letter-box.' *Inverness Focus*

ELIZABETH GORDON QUINN ■ CHRIS HANNAN

'You expect that a play set in the Glasgow rent strike of 1915 will be a model of dour social realism, but Chris Hannan's new play . . . confounds all expectations. The result is both startling and provocative.' Nicholas de Jongh, *The Guardian*

DEAD DAD DOG ■ JOHN McKAY

'It is truthfully and tenderly observed, original in tone, well made and beautifully performed. A delightful piece of work by a major comic talent!' Joyce McMillan, *The Guardian*

SATURDAY AT THE COMMODORE ■ RONA MUNRO

'Most human of all was Rona Munro's *Saturday at The Commodore*, an accurate and effective picture of social life and sexual attitudes in a small Mearns town.' Quintin James, *The Sunday Times, Scotland*

THE STEAMIE ■ TONY ROPER

'The four Glaswegian biddies who rub, scrub and gossip their way . . . one Hogmanay eve back in the fifties create a clubbable camaraderie from their labours in a way entirely lacking today . . . Hearts are worn on rolled-up sleeves. It is impossible not to adore every rose-tinted minute.' Jack Tinker, *Daily Mail*

SCOT-FREE

■ NEW SCOTTISH PLAYS

WRITER'S CRAMP ■ JOHN BYRNE

LOSING VENICE ■ JOHN CLIFFORD

THE LETTER-BOX ■ ANN MARIE DI MAMBRO

ELIZABETH GORDON QUINN ■ CHRIS HANNAN

DEAD DAD DOG ■ JOHN McKAY

SATURDAY AT THE COMMODORE ■ RONA MUNRO

THE STEAMIE ■ TONY ROPER

SELECTED AND INTRODUCED BY
■ ALASDAIR CAMERON

N
H
B

NICK HERN BOOKS

A Nick Hern Book

Scot-Free first published in 1990 as an original paperback.
Reprinted 1993, 1997, 1999 by Nick Hern Books Limited,
14 Larden Road, London W3 7ST

Typeset in Baskerville by Action Typesetting Ltd, Gloucester
Printed and bound in Great Britain by Cox & Wyman Ltd,
Reading, Berkshire

A CIP catalogue record for this book is available from
the British Library

ISBN 1-85459-017-0

Contents

Introduction

This anthology of recent Scottish drama lays no claim to be a 'best of' selection. Instead, it tries to provide a comprehensive overview of some of the most interesting developments in new Scottish theatre-writing over the last decade or so. It is also an attempt to remedy publishers' neglect of Scottish plays which has meant that, with few exceptions, the work of many of the best young dramatists in Scotland today has never appeared in print.

Writing at the start of the 1980s, the actor and director David Hayman claimed that 'Scottish Theatre – in fact theatre in general – is stagnant and unimaginative'. In one sense Hayman's gloom is understandable. At the end of the seventies there was a feeling that the creative energy of that decade, supported by considerable financial investment from various Scottish bodies, could not be sustained. In the light of this and against a background of pessimism about Scotland's future which the referendum decision to reject devolution had engendered, it was widely felt that the eighties could only bring retrenchment and loss.

During the following ten years, however, Scottish theatre was to prove that it was anything but stagnant and unimaginative. From the creation of the Scottish Theatre Company to 7:84's 'Clydebuilt' season; from the many new theatre companies established to the blossoming of the Edinburgh Festival Fringe; from the creation of Glasgow's Mayfest, to the new women writers who have at last found a voice; from the re-rediscovery of the Scots language in the theatre by companies like Theatre Alba to the establishment of a Scottish Theatre Archive and a growth in research in the field of Scottish theatre and drama – with all these and more, the eighties, in spite of severe financial cutbacks, have proved that Scottish theatre is much more resilient and the various Scottish funding bodies much more enlightened, than Hayman's pessimism might have led one to expect.

But it would be useless to pretend that the 1980s have been a time of unrelieved boom and prosperity for the Scottish theatre. There have been losses, like the Scottish Theatre Company, which lasted only a few years, and the Scottish Society of Playwrights which had to scale down its operations drastically when it lost its Arts Council funding. There has been no expansion of Theatre-in-Education and only a modest increase in community theatre work. But no one writing at the end of the eighties could be as gloomy as Hayman was at the start, in spite of the fact that we in Scotland still 'lack' both a playwright of international stature and a Scottish National Theatre.

But what is a Scottish play, the raw material of so many of these recent developments in Scottish theatre? Are Scottish plays only pale imitations of English models, spoken in a quaint dialect and set in Stirling rather than Surbiton? Can we identify any features which might satisfy those who, like Hugh MacDiarmid and R.F. Pollock, searched for a Scots theatre-craft and a Scots psychology in drama as early as the 1920s? The example of Ireland always looms over us, taunting Scots with the Irish success in finding a distinctive theatre voice and with our apparent failure to do the same. But, given their very different histories, can Ireland and Scotland be legitimately compared? In 1938 Neil Gunn voiced his doubts that 'without a great national conflict Scotland would be unable to produce great drama'. As a Scottish War of Independence seems very unlikely, perhaps it would be more useful to measure our theatre and drama against the experience of other countries who have tried to escape from the shadow of London and create their own theatre and drama.

A recent edition of the Radio 4 Arts programme *Kaleidoscope* featured a report from Zimbabwe, in which dramatists and theatre-workers discussed the problems which arose in trying to create a distinctively Zimbabwean drama. In their post-colonial period their theatre was in essence a copy of the English theatre. The professional stage consisted mainly of touring shows from Britain and two or three repertory companies in the large towns. They and the amateur companies performed plays from the English repertoire. There was no organised theatre for any of the tribal groupings. Those wishing to create a Zimbabwean theatre were engaged in various debates. Which language should they use? Shona was too strongly identified with one tribe; English, though understood by all, was too closely associated with colonial rule. What form should the plays take, given that it was felt the West-End model was unsuitable for Africa? Should actors be trained in a Western way, or was there some other form of training which would better fit them to forge a new style of theatre?

Almost identical questions have been discussed in the Scottish theatre for the last eighty years, but as yet no one has satisfactorily answered, or even faced up to them. For the present, the Zimbabweans have solved their problems by writing mainly in English, by adapting some Zimbabwean festival dances and forms of celebration for theatrical use and by putting the emphasis on community acting rather than on training an acting profession.

Recent histories of the theatre in Australia and New Zealand also devote much space to discussing the need felt by playwrights and theatre-practitioners in these countries to break free from the shackles of London and create a distinctive dramatic tradition. Neither country, however, has, as yet, come up with anything more than English genres transported to an Antipodean setting. A play about Ned Kelly is, give or take the odd kangaroo, not unlike a play about Dick Turpin. A murder-thriller set in Auckland is still a murder-thriller.

Only the Canadian stage has made any successful attempt to break the Anglo-Saxon stranglehold. To do that it has used its French traditions and the linguistic and cultural barriers have been crossed by developing a very visual style of theatre which relies as much on theatrical images as on words. In Quebec Michel Tremblay has also explored the feelings of frustration of a minority culture which, as the recent translation by Bill Findlay and Martin Bowman of *Les Belles-Soeurs* into Scots has shown, also speaks directly to the Scottish experience.

Even if we have yet to create an instantly recognisable Scottish dramatic genre, there are certain features which seem to be shared by most plays which can be described as 'Scottish'. For example, an overwhelming number of plays, from Joe Corrie's *In Time O' Strife* to John Byrne's *The Slab Boys*, seem to belong to a genre which could best be described as 'serio-comic naturalism'. Perhaps this mongrelism stems from the debt which the mainstream Scottish theatre owes to the variety stage and its cheerful mixing of genres. From the late nineteenth century, the variety and pantomime stage was for many years the only place where Scots was spoken as a matter of course in the theatre.

For the same reason, Scottish drama assumes a much greater degree of audience involvement than is usual in most English plays, where the proscenium arch is an impenetrable barrier between actor and audience. But Scottish dramatists delight in breaking down this invisible wall and the audience is welcomed into the play, rather than excluded from it.

There is a further possible debt to the variety stage in the sentimental streak which runs through an overwhelming majority of Scottish plays. Playwright and actor, Roddy MacMillan wrote that 'there is nothing wrong with sentiment as long as it's *good* sentiment'. And indeed the sentiments most used in Scottish plays, like affectionate nostalgia, are warm but unchallenging and are often shared by actor, playwright and audience alike. Few Scottish plays rely on hatred or anger though this is seldom to the benefit of the drama. Even the political plays of Wildcat rely on plentiful helpings of sugar to sweeten their message.

Until recently, the nostalgic glow which seemed to settle on so much Scottish drama was the result of the huge number of Scottish plays which were set in the past and used kindly stereotypes of working-class men and women. This urban Kailyardry is in stark contrast to most new English writing which has a contemporary setting and is fuelled by an intellectual wry angst in which the working classes hardly feature at all.

Perhaps what differentiates most Scottish drama from English drama is its social setting. This is more than just the kitchen table versus the Heals' sofa. The drama of both countries relies heavily on a series of shared assumptions, on a shared culture, and on a shared language. An English play will, usually, be spoken in the accents of the South-East of the country and be written in the language of the rulers and the policy-makers, the media and the Oxbridge intellectuals. Those who, in the main, make up the audience for the West End and National Theatres. The 'movers and shakers' and the majority of playwrights, from Left and Right, share a common background of professional, Oxbridge-educated, RP-speaking, middle-class comfort, though some do have qualms about this.

In Scotland, however, the assumptions made on the part of the playwright are less class-based and more national. It seems safe for Scottish playwrights to assume that their audiences will all understand Scots, of a sort; that they are all from the great maw of the lower-middle/upper-working class; that there are certain historical events – The Clearances – about which the audience will share common feelings; that there is a certain culture – embodied in *The Sunday Post* – and certain political assumptions which they all share. The Scottish dramatist often gets a laugh from a presumed common social background. This might manifest itself in, for example, John Byrne's use of playground language – 'he's got a face like a hawf-chewed penny dainty' – which itself assumes that most of the audience will have gone to the same kind of public – in the Scottish sense of the word – school, or in Byrne's mention of the Co-Op, as his English counterpart might mention Sainsbury's.

Most Scots plays also have an overt political message even if they all don't all end, like *In Time O' Strife*, with the singing of the 'Red Flag'. But if there's a message to be had, the audience will be aware of it. Subtle allusiveness and coded phrases are part of few Scots dramatists' armoury.

These few suggestions as to how to spot a Scottish play are of course generalisations and take no account of, for example, the division of the country between Scot and Gael. They also perhaps describe more readily plays which were written before 1980, plays which betrayed an often uncritical nostalgia for croft and craft, took little account of the role of women in Scottish life and concentrated on sectarian violence, football and party politics, ignoring all the while the existence of a Scotland furth of Glasgow.

The 1980s have pushed the boundaries of Scottish drama further than ever seemed possible in 1979. However, as a reminder of the wealth of Scottish plays which were spawned by the seventies this anthology begins with John Byrne's *Writer's Cramp*, one of the funniest plays of that decade and the play which launched Byrne's successful career as a playwright. *Writer's Cramp* was the hit of the 1977 Edinburgh Festival Fringe, transferred to the Bush Theatre in London and was revived the following year at the Hampstead Theatre.

What makes the play so interesting is that, although it takes a chain-saw to Anglo-Scottish literary pretensions and to the whole notion of 'high culture' as enshrined in literary documentaries on Radios Three and Four, it does so in an elegant and beautifully constructed way. Byrne's model for the play was the work of Alan Bennett and in particular the literary parodies in his *Forty Years On*. Byrne proves himself an able pupil but adds something deeper to Bennett's brilliance, while in the process underlining the near impossibility of Scottish writers taking on and beating the English cultural mafia at their own game. They will be seen at best as heralds of a northern cultural revival, at worst as merely quaint. If McDade had looked to Edinburgh rather than to London, then he might even have succeeded in getting a Scottish Arts Council grant for Speirs to intercept, rather than face a lifetime's rejection.

One of the constantly recurring answers to the Scottish theatre's McDade-style lack of recognition and undervaluing of the native contribution is the creation of a Scottish National Theatre. But although such a theatre would help Scottish drama, the rivalry between Glasgow and Edinburgh, among other things, means it is unlikely to materialise for some time. Meanwhile, Scottish drama will continue to exploit the dramatic traditions – like the folk, the popular political and the popular commercial – which have sustained it throughout the century. Indeed in a country as small as Scotland there is an inevitable blurring of the boundaries between these traditions, and Scottish socialist theatre companies for example constantly cannibalise the Scottish commercial popular theatre tradition.

The commercial theatre in Scotland has, as in the rest of the Britain, experienced a long period of contraction partly due to the rise of television. But recently audiences have begun to return to live entertainment, especially to the 'new variety' and comedy acts which have flourished all over the country. One of the most successful of these was The Merry Mac Fun Co named after the eponymous D.C. Thomson *Sunday Post* humorist. – Sample: Absent-minded burglar, 'Jings! Crivens! I've burgled my ain hoose'. The Merry Macs were politically to the left of *The Sunday Post* and had an ear for the designer politics and lifestyles of the 1980s which one of the company, John McKay, put to good use when he consolidated his career as a playwright with *Dead Dad Dog*.

Dead Dad Dog was first performed as part of the Scottish Accents – 'it's no *ma* accent, it's *your* ears' – Season at the Traverse Theatre in Edinburgh. Its success as part of this modest festival of new writing led to Stephen Unwin's production being revived and toured all over Scotland, finishing up in London at the Royal Court's Theatre Upstairs.

Reviewers who saw the piece at its first performance were enthusiastic about McKay's comic invention and peppered reviews with words like 'zippy' and 'offbeat'. McKay however was keen to stress that 'although it's not an agit-prop play . . . politics inform it . . . there's no division between politics and entertainment as I see it'. McKay also saw how effective humour was in his dissection of Thatcher's Britain and its corrupting effect even on so-called socialists. 'Comedy,' he said, 'is my forte. *Dead Dad Dog* is funny but has serious and nasty bits which are more effective because of their place in a comic script.' One should perhaps take McKay's caveats to heart and be careful about attributing too much political significance to the piece. McKay also says he writes comedy from a performer's point of view, and actors obviously relish this, as praise was also lavished on the performances of Ralph Riach and Sam Graham.

John McKay is only one of the young Scottish writers who has benefited from the careful nurturing and writer-centred approach of the Traverse. Under the recent direction of Chris Parr, Peter Lichtenfels, Jenny Killick and Ian Brown, many new Scottish dramatists have been given their first chance of a public performance. Another valuable function fulfilled by the Traverse is to show new Scottish plays beside a variety of international drama. In recent years the emphasis has been on continental drama, especially on the German playwright Manfred Karge, whose two plays *Man to Man* and *Journey to the South Pole*, the latter spoken in Scottish accents, were successes at the Edinburgh Festival and transferred to the Royal Court Theatre in London.

New writers whose early careers have developed at the Traverse include Peter Arnott, Chris Hannan and John Clifford. Though all three write in different styles the Traverse successfully premiered work by all of them in their 1985 summer season. Arnott, as best shown in his play *White Rose* about the Russian pilot-heroine Lily Litvak, writes in a spare, documentary style and draws great dramatic strength from political debate. However, his recent play at the Tron theatre in Glasgow, the diabolic *Losing Alec*, showed that he is becoming more involved in the human side of politics.

Chris Hannan's great contribution to Scottish drama was to take the 'slum drama' genre and attempt to make it poetic and universal. The genre has had a long and varied life, ranging from Robin Millar's melodrama of slum life, *The Shawlie*, through Paul Vincent Carroll's *Green Cars Go East*, to the work of Glasgow Unity, most notably Robert MacLeish's *The Gorbals Story* and Ena Lamont Stewart's *Men Should Weep*. The key feature of the genre was a heightened realism mixed with a strong vein of social protest. In the 1970s Bill Bryden used these features in plays like *Willie Rough* but whereas the Unity plays had a tough core, Bryden's plays tended to mythologise the working class.

With *Elizabeth Gordon Quinn*, Hannan created a totally unsentimental character, unheroic, conservative, and completely uninterested in working-class mass action. Stephen Unwin's production also consciously steered away from realism to expressionism in an interesting attempt to universalise the play, which didn't quite succeed. Critics of the first performance seemed divided as to whether the play was a celebration or a covert condemnation of a woman who cries memorably 'I refuse to learn how to be poor'. While *The Financial Times* wanted to knock sense into her and the *Guardian* called her a 'monster of working-class false consciousness', many critics wanted to canonise her. This diversity of views was both a tribute to the subtlety of Hannan's writing and a reflection of Eileen Nicholas's remarkable performance in the title role.

The third playwright to emerge from the vintage Traverse season of 1985 was John Clifford, much of whose subsequent work has been translated from or inspired by classics of Golden Age Spanish drama. To date, the most successful of these plays has been *Losing Venice*, Clifford's first full-length stage play which has been toured all over the world. Audiences have both enjoyed the sophisticated wit of its dialogue and warmed to its message about the folly of military posturing and adventuring. Parallels were swiftly drawn between the invasion of Venice in the play and the invasion of the Falklands. But one of the strengths of this undogmatic play is that such historical allusions are never overtly made, and instead the audience is left to draw its own conclusions and analogies.

Clifford was also well served by Jenny Killick's production, which used a spare set and relied heavily on the talents of the actors in the company at the time. In a play which seemed to have no connection with Scotland whatsoever, Killick was also able to use the Scottish panto tradition to lend weight to the Doges, who were represented as a couple of crotchety old figures speaking in Scots. In a possibly unintentional display of Scottish democracy Clifford also had the Duke's servant Pablo speak in Scots, so having both ends of the social spectrum use the same language.

The mainstays of the tradition of socialist and workers' theatre in the 1970s were 7:84 and Wildcat Companies. Both grew out of the work of John McGrath in the early 1970s. He first founded 7:84 (named, famously, after the statistic which showed that 84% of the wealth of the country was in the hands of a mere 7% of the population) with the intention of using straightforward popular theatre techniques to present his political message. In many of his shows the elements of entertainment and music threatened to swamp the message, and in 1978 the musicians in the company, who included David Anderson and Terry Neason, left to form Wildcat.

In the course of an interview for *Scottish Theatre News*, David MacLennan, one of Wildcat's founders, explained the different theories which underpinned each company. Wildcat, he said, offered entertainment and something to think about, and was less concerned about being a solely working-class theatre. He added that Wildcat, like so much Scottish theatre, appealed to a broad spectrum of Scottish society:

> We try to deal with subjects with a class perspective, recognise the existence of classes and that they have a profound effect on the way people are treated. That doesn't mean that we exclude members of the middle class from our audience. Many of the most progressive elements in the labour movement come from the middle class.

In the eighties, 7:84 switched the thrust of their artistic policy from new writing to reviving working-class plays from earlier in the century. These included Ena Lamont Stewart's *Men Should Weep* which she had re-written to devastating effect in the mid-1970s and now has the status of a classic of the Scottish theatre. Wildcat meanwhile built up a reputation for the type of hard-hitting shows that 7:84 had pioneered.

However, their most successful show, Tony Roper's *The Steamie*, was not actually written for the company, but was produced by them when Elaine C Smith, one of the company's leading actresses, heard the play read. In spite of the fact that it had been rejected by almost every theatre in Scotland, she recognised its potential. *The Steamie* was premiered in community venues at the 1987 Mayfest and was such a success that it subsequently toured all over Scotland playing to packed houses.

Because it was performed by Wildcat, many people criticised the play for a lack of direct social comment; although this was not Roper's intention. At a 1989 revival of the play at the Greenwich Theatre, Michael Billington while enjoying the play thought it was 'soft soap'. But to look for political significance in the play is a mistake. It is a warm and affectionate tribute to a community spirit in Glasgow which some remembered and many half-remembered or even imagined had existed. The play's success was a direct comment on the sense of displacement which so many in Glasgow felt after the huge and often insensitive programme of urban improvement which the city had undergone in the 50s and 60s. Glasgow realised its mistakes earlier than most, but by that time many of the old neighbourhoods had been razed and the huge soul-less new estates built on the edge of the city. The failure of this dream of urban planning meant that audiences responded immediately to Roper's recreation of a feature of the city's community life which had disappeared.

Another reason for the play's attraction is that it is set on Hogmanay, a time of the year filled with sentimental associations for every Scot. The mere mention of New Year conjours up visions of black-bun, party turns and family feuds fuelled by alcohol. It is the perfect setting for reflections such as those of Mrs Culfeathers, who never fails to bring a collective lump to the audience's throat with her tearful confession that she'd never seen her great grandchildren who live in England.

The play relies heavily on popular theatre techniques, welcoming the audience in, rather than existing in a vacuum behind a proscenium arch. The joke about Galloway's mince, which quickly entered Glasgow's folklore was a marvellously sustained sequence which was embellished by the immaculate sense of timing of the actresses who first performed it.

The Steamie is also, sadly, still unusual in the Scottish theatre, because it is a play about women and women's lives, though it is of course a man's view of their world. Roper's concern in *The Steamie* is for people and his approach is humanist rather than directly political. Perhaps this is part of its attraction for Wildcat, who, said David MacLennan:

> tend to approach the political matter more tangentially, or perhaps create a series of impressions which taken together add up to a strong political statement ... It's important that political theatre has as many different approaches and weapons in its armoury as other types of theatre.

One of the most successful weapons in the Scottish theatre's armoury is the way in which extensive touring has allowed new plays to be widely seen rather than confined to one or two coterie theatres. In the industrial Lowlands young enterprising groups like Clyde Unity tour to community venues and small theatres, performing new work which deals very directly with the social issues that the people who live near these venues confront daily. Larger companies like Communicado tour their plays extensively to the more established venues in the central Scotland.

But many companies tour all over the country to the most remote regions of the mainland and the islands, where plays are often performed in conditions which are far from ideal. Actors who have performed on these tours tell tales of, for example, Macduff, where the company, after spending a day putting up their set were asked by the hall-keeper, 'Well, fit film're we gettin' the night?' And in Greater Bernera actors are told that the audience shows its appreciation not by applause, but by whether or not they stay behind to help the company stack the chairs.

Such venues, however, are the bread and butter of companies like Theatre Alba, who have performed an invaluable service to Scottish drama by reviving plays in Scots and by developing a new style of ballad-theatre which relies heavily on electronic folk music and on fantasy, magic and imagination: techniques which have assured the success of, for example, *The Puddock and the Princess* and Edward Stiven's *Tamlane*, possibly their most completely successful venture into reclaiming Scotland's ballad and folk tradition for the theatre.

The company who revived Highland touring in the 1970s was 7:84, when they took their play *The Cheviot, The Stag and The Black, Black Oil* around the Highlands and Islands, to the areas most affected by the Clearances which were the subject of the play. 7:84 are still touring extensively but their recent plays have been less overtly political and more concerned with the personal as political. Such plays, written for example from a feminist perspective, were pioneered by Marcella Evaristi and Liz Lochhead and their work had an instant response which other women writers have followed up. 7:84's recent programme *Long Short Story* was a courageous experiment in raising issues and asking questions which are usually ignored or swept under the carpet. The domestic violence in Ann Marie Di Mambro's *The Letter-box*, for example, is often seen as an urban issue, since it is easier to contain in a small town where effects of social stigma are much greater, though people forget that the chances of escape for a woman are that much less.

The Highland audiences for *Long Short Story* were very responsive even though, as one reviewer pointed out, *Saturday at the Commodore* was a 'very subtle tale of lesbianism . . . so tactfully dealt with that the majority of the audience missed the point . . . though the delightful Aberdonian accent put on for the occasion by Patricia Ross more than made up for this'. Rona Munro, however, was writing about small farming communities and perhaps the audience's delight in the accent and failure to perceive the gay woman were an example of art imitating life. The same reviewer also praised Anne Marie Timoney who played the battered wife in *The Letter-box* and deserved, he said, 'The Dingwall equivalent of an Oscar' for her performance.

7:84's programme also contained plays which paralleled the experience of exile on the part of the Gaels with that of West Indians in London, and which explored Central American politics. This growing awareness of Scotland in the world, the experiments with spoken Scots by dramatists such as Iain Heggie, the new willingness to look at Scottish history in a less heroic way, to open up all areas of Scottish life for dramatic treatment – even to the extent of re-considering critically the metamorphosis of Glasgow from urban desert to yuppie paradise – all contribute to a growing feeling that anything is possible for Scottish theatre and in Scottish drama. Whether this optimism is misplaced we shall soon know. But what is certain is that Scottish theatre enters the 1990s in a much more buoyant state than it entered the 1980s. Given the cultural depredations of the last decade, that alone is an astounding achievement.

In the course of compiling this volume, Nick Hern and I have received valuable help from many people, in particular: Joe

Beddoes, Morag Ballantyne, Ian Brown, Anne Bonnar, Mary
Brennan, Robin Cameron, Julie Frazer, Christine Hamilton,
Sally Hobson, Jan MacDonald, Joyce McMillan, Elaine
Navikas, Peter Urbach and Elizabeth Watson: to them we offer
our thanks.

Alasdair Cameron
December 1989

JOHN BYRNE was born in Paisley, near Glasgow in 1940 and worked as a 'slab boy' (colour mixer) at A.F. Stoddard, the carpet manufacturers, before going to Glasgow School of Art (1958-64) where he won a scholarship in painting which enabled him to study in Italy (1963-64). From 1964-66 he was a Graphic Artist at Scottish Television and from 1966-68 a designer back at A.F. Stoddard. He had had his first Glasgow exhibition in 1961 but after his first in London in 1968, he became a full-time painter.

His designs for the theatre include *The Great Northern Welly Boot Show* (Clyde Fair, Glasgow, 1971), *The Cheviot, The Stag, and the Black, Black Oil* (7:84 Scotland on tour, 1972), *Finn MacCool* (Edinburgh Festival, 1974), *Traitors* (Hampstead Theatre, 1980), *The Number of the Beast* (Bush Theatre, 1981), *A Midsummer Night's Dream* and *The Cherry Orchard* (Leicester Haymarket in 1984), *The Marriage of Figaro* (Scottish Opera, 1986) and his own *The Slab Boys Trilogy* when revived at the Traverse Theatre, Edinburgh, in 1982, and *Candy Kisses* at the Bush in 1984.

His other stage plays include *Writer's Cramp* (1977), *Normal Service* (Hampstead, 1979), *Cara Coco* (1980) and *Colquhoun and Macbryde* (1988).

On television he is best known for his BAFTA Award-winning six-part comedy series, *Tutti Frutti* (BBC-TV, 1987). He also wrote and directed an *Arena* programme on himself and his work (BBC-TV, 1988).

Writer's Cramp was first performed at the Calton Studios,
Edinburgh on 22 August 1977 and opened at the Bush
Theatre, London on 1 November 1977 with the following cast:

F S McDADE   Bill Paterson
NARRATOR   ⎫
DR ARTHUR QUIGLEY   ⎬
CHARLES BENTWOOD BRAZIL   ⎪   John Bett
MRS THELMA McDADE   ⎭
DOUBLE-DAVIS   ⎫
READER   ⎪
TRUSTY   ⎬
MRS RIPPER   Alex Norton
MALCOLM   ⎪
FATHER MANNION   ⎭

Directed by Robin Lefèvre
Costumes by Ally Byrne
Lighting by Marek

ACT ONE

Scene One

The hymn 'Be Thou My Vision' played on the bowed psaltery precedes the action.

NARRATOR. Thank you, Sandy. 'Be Thou My Vision' . . .
and vision is what we're here to celebrate, this evening. The
vision of one man . . . Francis Seneca McDade. At the
invitation of the Nitshill Writing Circle, in conjunction with
the Busby Sketch Club, we shall attempt, in the next hour or
so, to bring to you . . . through letters, readings, and some
quite striking 'tableaux vivants', the life and times of their
late, lamented mentor. Not only do we hope to lay the ghost of
McDade but also the egg . . . or, more accurately, the clutch
of eggs from which may be unscrambled the mysteries of this
'rara avis': a bird, so exotic of plumage that it remains a great
bafflement to present-day observers that its presence went
undetected for so long perched as it was midst the dun-coated
doos on the deciduous tree of Scottish literature.

What thought the mother cuckoo as place she did her ovum
ben that nest of twig and thorn? For did not her fledgling son
ere soon outstrip his billet, injest the skinny worm of Celtic
art, and whiles soar off in search of plumper grub? Only to
return that he might herald the dawn of a new epoch in
Caledonian culture. A cry, I fear, his dowdy mates refused to
mark. No letter to *The Times* they wrote though early was his
call. Birds of a feather . . .

Take his masterpiece, 'Feet of Clay' . . . It is in this rich tilth
that the serious student of McDade may turn up, with earnest
plough, the literary legumes sown so lovingly these many
seasons syne. A golden harvest, bountiful, sustaining, the
gleaner's reward this fecund furrow till.

And, to take the agrarian allusion just a little further, might I
suggest that Doctor Arthur Quigley . . . sometime master of
Miss Kibble's College, Paisley . . . Frank's alma mater . . .
played no small part in producing the manure that spread and
nourished those pastures when, as a raw young dominie, he
introduced Quink and stylus to those infant digits.

So it is, ladies and gentlemen, with enormous pride . . .
tempered by a native modesty . . . that we present, for your
pleasure and enlightenment, WRITER'S CRAMP . . . being
the life and times of F S McDade, writer, philosopher, painter,
sage . . . WRITER'S CRAMP.

Exits.

McDADE (*under the bedcovers with torch*).
Miss Kibble's College,
Back Snedden,
Paisley,

14 August, 1934
Dear Brendan,
  I am penning this missive in the linen cupboard next to
Matron's room as it is the only place in Shelley House with a
light bulb. It is a fine evening here despite some heavy snow
showers earlier in the day and one can just catch the twittering
of moth under the windows. If one tries really hard one can
picture the gentle Muse rummaging through her carpetbag of
delights . . . which reminds me, did I, by any chance, leave
behind a pair of brown sandshoes at Windyhill last weekend? I
seem to have lost them, and there will be the most frightful
row if I can't lay my hands . . . or, indeed, my feet on them
for the cross-country on Lady Day. Have a skite under the
wash-house boiler for them, there's a pal.

Tadpole Tierney lent me a book of verse by a chap called T.S.
Eliot this afternoon. I skimmed through it before tea. He's
awfully good you know. I don't think I could do that half so
well even without that blackface make-up . . . or am I thinking
of Hutch? Anyhow, there are some quite gay little rhymes . . .

Knock at the door.

McDADE. Come.

Enter DR QUIGLEY, *a schoolmaster.*

QUIGLEY. Ah, there you are, McDade. Matron said I might
find you here. Wanted a word, d'you see. Busy?

McDADE. Just finishing, sir. Writing home, sir.

QUIGLEY. Good chap. Always nice to keep in touch with one's
people, eh. That's the ticket. Now, what did you want to see
me about?

McDADE. Sir?

QUIGLEY. Come on, boy. Mustn't be backwards ... spit it out. What was it, eh?

McDADE. I thought you wanted a word with me, sir? Least, that's what you said when you came in ...

QUIGLEY. What's that y'say? Mmm? Did I? (*Pause.*) Got you! Yes ... 'bout you and this other fellow ... friend of yours ...

McDADE. Double-Davis?

QUIGLEY. That's our head porter, isn't it?

McDADE. No sir ... that's Spiers, sir.

QUIGLEY. Spiers, y'say? Well, you and this chappie Spiers ... according to your form master ...

McDADE. Double-Davis ...

QUIGLEY. Mm? I understood your form master was a Mr Sproul ... Double-Davis, y'tell me? New man, is he? Tch, tch ... I do wish they kept me up to date on staff changes ... it's bad enough ... Anyway, this chap Triple-Thomas tells me that you and Spiers wish to go on to   er   er

McDADE. Magdalen, sir ...

QUIGLEY. Isn't he our head porter?

McDADE. No sir ... university, sir ...

QUIGLEY. Ah, but which university ... er ... which ...

McDADE. Oxford, sir. You know ... dreaming spires and all that ...

QUIGLEY. Spires? Spires? Dammit, that's our head porter! What's that y'say? Dreaming? Asleep on the job? We can't have that ... Good heavens, no ... did the right thing in coming to me with this disgraceful news, Sproul ... Well done. (*Ushers* McDADE *out.*) I'll take it from here, laddie, never fear. And, remember ... my door's always open ... (*Pushes* McDADE *outside.*) Don't hesitate to bring any little worries to me. I'll see that things are put right.

McDADE *re-enters.*

Ah, Single-Simpson ... this chappie, Double-Davis ... wasn't he severely caned last term for introducing vermin into Cook's under-garments?

McDADE. I expect so, sir.

QUIGLEY. Thank you, Spiers. Like to get things straight, y'see. Collate and deploy, that's the secret. Keep a clear mind ... get everything right up here ... marshall your forces. That's the ticket. Keep up the good work in the nets. McDade tells me you'll make the first eleven, yet. Straight bat, straight bat. Well, goodbye, Quigley ... don't forget the school mag. Bit of a poet, I hear. Don't neglect the scribblings, eh? That's the ticket.

Exit.

McDADE. Phew ... (*Continues letter.*) Baldy Houston's down with mumps and seems pretty poorly. Matron's been forcing buckets of Cascara down his throat for the past three weeks but I don't think it's doing the poor chap an awful lot of good ... 'specially as the nearest latrines are four hundred yards across the quad in Tennyson House. He's bound to catch something pretty nasty on one of these jaunts. I'm surprised the young tike is still with us.

I got a postal order for six shillings this morning. Guess who from? Madge. Yes, Madge. She's not one to bear grudges, eh? I bitterly regret that silly jape Double-Davis and I played on her in the cricket pavilion ... but Matron assures us she's on the mend.

Did I tell you that the school outing to Forfar was a great success again this year? Simes Minimus toppled headlong out of the carriage window of the 2.15 while trying to attract the attention of some Brownies in an adjacent compartment. What a lark! Perhaps it was his insisting on strapping on Bunny's bergen like that that caused him to pitch out so suddenly. He's in casualty at Cambuslang Cottage Hospital should you care to drop him a line. I daresay he can get one of the nurses to read it out aloud to him.

We play Byron House tomorrow at ...

There is a knock at the door. Enter DOUBLE-DAVIS.

DOUBLE-DAVIS. Know anything about a bicycle pump, Frank?

McDADE. Oh, it's you, Double-Davis ... come in. A bike pump? No. (*Pause.*) A silverised Bluemel job with dabbies on it?

DOUBLE-DAVIS. The same.

McDADE. No.

DOUBLE-DAVIS. Only Trev seemed a bit upset about it, last night. Whispered something about a pump before he went under . . .

McDADE. Under?

DOUBLE-DAVIS. Chloroform. Doc had to reset both his arms after that bout with Grimes for the Boxing Shield.

McDADE. How did he get on?

DOUBLE-DAVIS. Lost on points. It was pretty close.

McDADE. Plucky beggar.

DOUBLE-DAVIS. Lucky, Frankie . . . now, about that pump . . .

McDADE. I swear I don't know what you're talking about, DD. Scout's honour.

Pause.

DOUBLE-DAVIS. Was that old Quigley I saw going out of here? What was that swine after?

McDADE. Oh, just something about you and I going on to varsity . . .

DOUBLE-DAVIS. Aw, aye. (*Pause.*) Dying for a drag, Frankie boy. Spiers cadged my last 'Four Square'.

McDADE. The shite! Here, have one of mine. (*Proffers packet of 'Gold Flake'.*)

DOUBLE-DAVIS (*lights up*). Finished that piece for the mag, yet? (*Sticks cigs down trousers.*)

McDADE. Glad you brought that up, DD. Have a read of that.

DOUBLE-DAVIS (*reads silently for a few moments*). You a hundred per cent positive about that pump, Frankie?

McDADE. I already told you . . . twice!

DOUBLE-DAVIS. OK . . . OK . . . I believe you. But I don't think Grimes is going to like this. (*Holds out paper.*)

Pause. McDADE *takes pump from trouser leg and hands it over.*

Still, we might manage to squeeze in onto page three. Bonsoir, old thing. (*Heads for door.*)

McDADE. Cheerio, chin, chin . . .

DOUBLE-DAVIS. Napoo . . .

McDADE. Toodleoo . . .

DOUBLE-DAVIS. Goodbye.

McDADE. Cigarettes?

DOUBLE-DAVIS (*holding up pump*). Grimes won't forget this, Frankie.

Exits.

McDADE. Philistine! (*Continues letter.*) We play Byron House at rugger tomorrow, so I'll have to beetle off soon and see if I can't borrow a pair of sparables from the awful Grimes. He owes me something after ripping out half the preface to my 'Decline and Fall' to line his bloody gumboots. It's a bit thick, honestly. Couldn't he get his guv'nor to send him a copy?

Oops, there goes the bell for prep. Must dash. Will scribble a note to your confessor tomorrow explaining about the scabs. Really must fly. Old Sproul's in a foul mood as he caught me and some of the other fellows biting one of the 'Sprogs' in Vespers.

Please write soon. I do so enjoy your letters.

Pip, pip.

Your brother in Christ,

Frankie.

PS. Should you be sending a tuck-box, this half, don't forget to secure it with stout rope and fix it with a heavy padlock. Several of the chap's hampers have been broken open by that rat-faced head porter, Spiers. That last lot of bangers and Dundee cake you sent got snaffled. Don't let me down, B. Please, do as I ask. Oh, by the way, I've just had a poem accepted for the school mag. My very first. It sets forth the reflections of an ageing philosopher who is cruelly slung into a workhouse for alleged incontinence . . . 'Broad Thoughts From A Home', and it goes . . .

READER. I hear the gently babbling brook,
  The roaring waterfall;
  The crashing waves, the coursing stream,
  The heaving ocean's thrall.
  I feel the thunder in the air,
  The clouds they blot the sun.
  I rise up from my bed because . . .

McDADE (*in obvious distress*). I need a number one! PPS. Dodo
  Inkpen sends her fondest.

Exits.

Scene Two

NARRATOR. We spring forward, now, several years. McDade
  has secured that place at Oxford . . . history does not relate
  quite how . . . and is reading Greats. In his recollections of
  university life, 'Gown and Gout', Frank informs us that he
  shared his rooms with one Charles Bentwood Brazil . . .
  strongly rumoured to be a close friend of W H Auden's
  favourite niece. We can but speculate to the veracity of this as
  we are all aware of how often FS forsook historical accuracy in
  favour of a juicy titbit.

  McDade, as I said, was reading Greats and Chic Brazil . . .
  girls' school stories.

  Over, then, to Magdalen College, Oxford. A balmy summer's
  evening, circa 1938.

  Exits.

McDADE. To Punch McEwan-Ewing,
  'New Writing',
  Peasy Wynd,
  Giffnock.

  3 August.

  Sir,
    I am sending you several poems and stories which I think
  your little mag might be interested in. Some of these tales have
  been penned by me . . . in fact, they all have. Likewise the
  rhymes. The poems ain't half bad, as I've been told by my old
  English master, Doctor Quigley, who was up at Oxford in
  twenty-two. I believe that was the same year as yourself.
  Perhaps you knew him before you were sent down? Perhaps
  not. Anyway sir, the verse about the newts is but a sketch for a

longer poem and the story about the reefer fiend is an outline treatment for a motion picture I have in mind. However, the essay to which I should most like you to address yourself is the one entitled 'The Rising Sap'.

READER. Wendy felt every sinew in her lithe body tighten like so many lengths of string as she heard Rinty approach the settee on the balls of his feet. His eager breath rouged her cheeks and she sensed his strong fingers caress her quilt. 'Are you awake, my darling?' he murmured in that low voice that made her pulses race. 'I've brought something to show you.' And, with that, he pulled aside the heavy blanket that covered, but did not quite conceal, her heaving . . . her heave . . .

McDADE. Once your good lady soaks the manuscript in warm, soapy water the grease stains will come out quite easily and render the script perfectly legible. This piece was especially praised by my tutor, Wallace Quick, DLitt. He seemed to like it rather a lot as he gave me a caramel and invited me to spend an evening with him at the cinema. I should be very grateful for an opinion on this one. The essay, that is.

Should my little efforts meet with your approval and somehow wriggle their way into your publication would you be kind enough to remit any payments to me at Magdalen College, Oxford, taking care to mark the outside of the package, 'Newsprint, No Commercial Value', securing same with sealing wax and several bindings of sticky tape . . . 'Vulcanite' is a good brand. The majority of undergraduates on this staircase have had their personal mail intercepted at the porters' lodge and steamed open. Now, I don't expect the name 'Spiers' to mean anything to you but there is a Scout here who bears an uncanny resemblance to a cove we once had at Miss Kibble's in Paisley. Perhaps you know it?

I do hope my work speaks to you. Please cross any postal orders and put the counterfoils in a safe place. Do not, I repeat, do not, send loose coins.

Thanking you in anticipation,

Your humble servant,

F S McDade.

PS. I believe Giffnock is very pleasant at this time of year. Delivery by hand of any monies would be quite in order.

Enter CHIC BRAZIL.

CHIC. Daders!

McDADE. Chickers!

CHIC. Still sending out the jolly old beggars, eh? I say, guess what?

McDADE. No, what?

CHIC. Anners is preggers! By Dickers. I kid you not. Just got wind of it from Hoggers.

McDADE. Poor Anners!

CHIC. Poor Dickers, more like. He'll have to do the right thing, daft blighter.

McDADE. Well, he is the College Chaplain, after all. He ought never to have taken up that invitation to spend Easter at Twickers with Anners. Small wonder she's preggers . . . silly beggars.

CHIC. I say, Daders, weren't you pretty mooners over Anners?

McDADE. Me? Mooners over Anners? Knickers!

CHIC. Steady on, old chap. Didn't mean to get you madders. Just thought I'd give it a mensh, that's all.

McDADE. Sorry, Chickers, trifle touchy today. Must be this damned heat. I say, how did you get on at squashers?

CHIC. Got beaters.

McDADE. Oh, cheesers! I say, park the botty and we'll have some tea and crumpets. (*Pours tea.*) Camels or dromedaries?

CHIC. Mm?

McDADE. One lump or two?

CHIC. Three, please, old bean.

McDADE. I say, pap on a waxing and we'll dent the jolly old drummers, hm?

CHIC. Super. (*Peruses records.*) I say, wee bit passé. Ain't we got any Glenn Millers?

McDADE. Brokers.

CHIC. Buggers. (*Pause.*) I say, were you on the river this afternoon, Daders?

McDADE. Yes, why?

CHIC. Oh, nothing . . . just wondered if you caught a glimpse of Anners. Hoggers let slip that she and Dickers might be going for a short punt . . .

McDADE. Thought they already had . . . at Twickers? No, didn't see them, Chickers. River was thick with punters.

CHIC. I say, were you with a popsie?

McDADE. Well . . .

CHIC. Come on, Daders . . . who was it? Was it the one with the big . . .

McDADE. How dare you! You speak of the woman I love. And, besides, she hasn't got big . . . well, not 'big' the way you said 'big' . . . they're just right.

CHIC. Didn't mean to be offensive, Daders. Bit of the old teasers. (*Pause.*) Seems a jolly decent sort. Nice . . . peepers.

McDADE. Yes, she has, hasn't she? Oh, Pam . . .

CHIC. Pam?

McDADE. Pamela Chrichton-Capers . . . the most beautiful girl in all the world. Why, only this afternoon she was resting her delicate cheek on this stiff dickie. (*Fingers shirt front.*) I don't think I'll have it laundered again.

CHIC. Chrichton-Capers! Ain't she the popsie with the big hooter? Haw, haw . . .

McDADE. Haw, bloody, haw! You're simply greeners 'cos I've got a popsie and you ain't. And don't call her a 'popsie'. Her name's Pam, Pamela, to you.

CHIC. Ooooooooohhh, Pammers! (*Pause.*) I say, wasn't she the popsie the rowing eight hauled up Great Tom in her pyjammers?

McDADE. Beast! You know perfectly well that was Anners . . . starkers!

CHIC. Bloody wasn't!

McDADE. Bloody was!

CHIC. Bloody wasn't!

McDADE. Was!

CHIC. Oh, shut up! Just because I've got a soft spot for Anners . . .

McDADE. Aha! Thought so, you crumb! Just because Dickers got Anners preggers at Twickers you think you can scoff at my love for Pammers . . . Pamela, I mean. You are mooners over Anners, aren't you, Chickers? Admit it!

CHIC (*breaks down*). Oh, yes, Daders . . . God, yes . . . I'm sorry I went on about Pam . . .

McDADE. Pammers.

CHIC. Pammers . . . but I was so broken up when I heard from Hoggers about . . . about . . . (*Heart-rending sobs.*)

McDADE. There, there . . . don't take on so, there's a good chap. If you ask me you're better off without her. (*Pause.*) How long have you been . . .

CHIC. Mooners over Anners? Ever since I saw her put the winner past Henderson at footer. I tell you, Frank, I can't go on without her! (*Sobs.*) It's driving me crackers!

McDADE. I know how you feel, old bean. Why, if I couldn't marry Pam . . .

CHIC. Pammers.

McDADE. Pammers . . . I'd shoot myself. Blow the jolly old brains out, damned if I wouldn't. Chickers, I'm asking you to keep your chin up.

CHIC. Stiff uppers?

McDADE. Stiff uppers. You'll see, it'll all work out right in the end.

CHIC. Thanks, Daders, you're a real brick!

McDADE (*stretching out hand*). Chickers.

CHIC. Daders. (*Takes hand.*)

TOGETHER. Blackers!

Scene Three

NARRATOR. In 1942, McDade, having come down from Oxford sans degree, was in something of a dilemma. Whilst feeling morally obliged to help his country in her darkest hour he was, like so many of his contemporaries, in an agony of doubt over the entire issue of war. This dichotomy was swiftly resolved when the tea-chest in which he was hiding was removed from the hold of a lugger bound for the South Seas.

Within hours he found himself quartered with other NCOs at an Officers' Training Camp. It was here that Frank got involved with the Post-Proustian Penmen, a club formed by some of the men to help fill the empty hours between manoeuvres. He was invited to compose some free-form verse for their anniversary issue of 'Nissen Times'.

READER. The grains of sand, the clock's tick-tock,
Do each of us enslave.
Look back, the parting's permanent,
Ahead, see Marcel wave ...

NARRATOR. McDade was understandably distressed when this piece failed to appear in the Penmen's organ as promised. The matter was put before the adjutant and he, an old Ampleforth boy, upheld McDade's case and awarded him a lifetime's supply of everlasting nibs from the quartermaster's stores. Frank never really got over his shabby treatment at the hands of his fellow officers and ever after kept himself aloof. He returned to more serious work and began his war diaries, 'The Khaki Titfer'.

Let's join FS in his quarters ...

McDADE. Special Training Unit,
Somewhere in Milngavie,

January 10th, 1943.
22.00 hours.

Dearest Mother,
    This letter will come as something of a surprise to you and Father as I hear from Brendan that Uncle Declan let drop that I was in the jungle with the Chindits. Nothing could be further from the truth and I'm blessed if I know how he got wind of a story like that. As you can see from the top of the page, I'm undergoing officer training ... I expect my time in Oxford helped in getting me here. All is quiet at the moment but I daresay things will hot up next week when the Top Brass come down. The first few days of my course have been taken up with what they call 'Aptitude Tests'. Strictly confidential, you understand, but Beano Henderson, an Oxford chum who is filing clerk at HQ, said I'd made a pretty fair showing in all of them ... especially the one where we were asked to divide a group of stuffed rats into pairs and squeeze them through an assortment of differently coloured holes. I must say I quite enjoyed that. Oh, and talking of rats ... I must chase up

Sergeant Rooney re my supply of everlasting nibs . . . I'm cracking on with 'The Khaki Titfer'.

READER. December 18th, 1943. Came to this morning at 14.00 hours. A heavy drizzle brought me round and made my wounds smart. The pounding of the German artillery in the middle distance has set some of the chaps' nerves on end and the Colonel has asked to stroll round the trenches and keep their spirits up . . . I think I'll take my banjo. Young Captain Boyle has just come into my foxhole and offered me a mug of steaming champagne. He's bound to cop a Blighty before the week is out, reckless bugger. The way he stands atop the gun emplacement, lifts up his kilt, and smiles at the Bosch . . . one of the greatest acts of heroism it's been my privilege to witness. It's courage of this order that gives the enlisted men great heart and not just the extra rum ration as the bumboys back home would have people believe. Play up, lads, and play the game! Let's biff that bastard, Hitler, into the middle of next week! Howzat!

McDADE. I shall draw to a close now, Mother dear, as I'm expecting my new batman any minute. That's one of the perks here though I expect I'll still have to scrub my own feet.

Oh, should you find yourself with a couple of spare ration books on your hands, please pass them on to our Brendan and he'll see that they reach me. Don't, whatever you do, send them by post. Several of the non-commissioned officers have had their kit rifled and their parcels confiscated. The CO is looking into the matter but, as far as I'm aware, it still goes on.

Best love to Auntie Mavis and tell her thanks for the balaclava. It eventually got here via Kuala Lumpur. At least, I think it was a balaclava. Tell her thanks from me, anyway.

Must end. Trust everything's ticketyboo at home.

Fondest kisses.

Frank.

PS. Don't clip out the sweetie coupons.

Knock at the door.

VOICE OFF. Captain McDade, sir?

McDADE. Yes?

VOICE OFF. I'm your new batman, sir.

McDADE. Ah ... (*Rises and goes to door.*)

VOICE OFF. Private Spiers.

McDADE *freezes with hand on doorknob.*

Scene Four

NARRATOR. We come now to a particularly harrowing
episode in our dramatic reconstruction of the poet's life. In
February, 1943, having completed his six-week training
course, FS was drafted into the REME as a driver's mate ...
second class. It was while embarking on the troop-carrier
'Redoubtable' that he was hauled from the cab of his truck by
the civil police and taken to HM Prison, Albany, Isle of
Wight. The charge? (*Pause.*) That of being an undesirable
alien. Up to this time, Frank had no real knowledge of his true
parentage, assuming that the gentleman whom he'd always
addressed as 'Dad' was, in fact, his rightful pater. It was to be
some months and the exchange of several dozen letters and
documents before he learned the truth. St Andrew's House
confirmed that the bard was the illegitimate issue of one Otto
Dusselfurt, a peripatetic 'physician' from The Hague.

The news of his Mother's 'dirty dealings' had a profound
effect on Frank and whilst incarcerated at Albany gaol he set
down, in writing, some eighteen poems bewailing his plight.
Among these heartfelt works the one we know best today is
entitled, 'Oh, Mammy', first published in the Christmas,
1944, issue of 'Jottings' under the pen-name 'Sooty'.

This particular poem marks a turning point in McDade's
approach to verse, containing as it does, twenty-seven lines of
thirteen syllables, one of six, and over thirty-five obscene
phrases. The ignominy of his bastardy spawned a whole new
era in the oeuvre of F S McDade. We, the reading public,
whilst sympathising with the Great Man's unfortunate
nascence, must thank Providence that Mrs Thelma McDade
saw fit to dally in a Wee Storey Street bin-shelter with a quack
who could lay claim to Teutonic antecedents.

Over now to Albany Prison.

McDADE (*unrolls toilet paper*).
Cell 14, D Block,
HM Prison, Albany,
Isle of Wight.

27th February, 1943.

Dear Father Mannion,

As I sit here in this squalid prison cell I think back to happier times spent in retreat at your parsonage in Forfar. I wonder if you recall those halcyon days as vividly as I do? Perhaps my present surroundings have something to do with my conjuring up those warm Summer's evenings playing croquet on the lawns ... in between decades of the rosary ... back in thirty-four. The memories of that idyllic August are a great source of comfort and solace to me in my hopefully erstwhile predicament.

It has taken me quite some time to get round to writing to thank you for putting me up that vac, but I was most eternally grateful for such asylum, believe me. Tell me, did you ever receive the five pounds I sent to help defray the cost of repairing my rooms? I think the water did more damage than the actual fire. How is dear Mrs Crouch? Is she still with you? She must be a good age by now. By the way, did her hair ever grow back in?

Chapter six of my new novel was completed at half-past four this morning. Double-Davis, an old school chum from Paisley, who is in the next cell but one, has promised to run off some copies in the printing shop when it's finished. Would you let me send you a suitably endorsed edition? I think you'll find it jolly good value at only six pounds ten shillings. You may send the money ahead if you so wish and I'll reserve a copy for you. Please feel free to order as many as you want as DD assures me he's perfectly willing to put in some overtime.

By the way, Reverend Father, it's rather esoterically titled, 'Pass the Buns, Dolly'.

READER. Flicking idly at the large boil on his cheek, Peter saw at once that all was not well with Mandy. As she stood by the fire and allowed the flames to lick at her jodhpurs he could tell by the set of her narrow shoulders that Rupert had been up to his old tricks. 'Rough day, old girl?' He put the query as nonchalantly as he was able with the Paris bun lodged under his dentures. The girl turned slowly and stared at him fixedly. Peter dropped his gaze to the floor and in an effort to cover the terrible awkwardness he felt, prised off one of his boots. 'Not especially,' said Mandy icily. 'Why do you ask?' Peter felt the words sting the back of his neck and looked up sharply. Just then the door flew open and a figure sprang into the room. As he turned to identify the intruder, Peter caught a glimpse of Rupert's ferret-like features etched in the glow from Mandy's blazing jodhpurs. Then everything went . . .

Blackout.

McDADE (*strikes match*). I must admit to being particularly pleased with it.

    Yours in fetters,

    Frank McD.

Blows out match.
Lights another match.

    PS. Have Mrs Crouch bake any remittances into one of her Mountbatten cakes and send to me by parcel post, taking care to mark the outside clearly in ink, 'School Clothing . . . Unlaundered'.

Match out.
Lights yet another.

    A box of matches would be appreciated.

Blows match out.
Last match.

    Don't have those baked in.

Match out.
Lights up.
Enter TRUSTY *with slops pail.*

TRUSTY. Slops.

McDADE. No thanks.

TRUSTY. No, stupid, 'ave you got any? Only I'm supposed to collect 'em before they sort of fester, know what I mean?

McDADE. Steady on, old chap . . . you'll not find any festering slops in here. Not unless you count what passes for tiffin. Oh, no . . . I don't think I'll stay the week. Just return my deposit and I'll be on my way, there's a good fellow.

TRUSTY. Here, you the penpusher?

Pause.

McDADE. Penpusher?'

TRUSTY. Yeh, geezer what does the scribbling. Eh?

McDADE. My good man, if you're referring to my skill in the jolly old creative writing stakes . . .

TRUSTY. Yeah, that's it. Got a message for you . . . from your boyfriend.

McDADE. Boyfriend?

TRUSTY. Pansy in number twelve. He says if you don't get a move on and finish that tripey mush what you're a-writing of and get it down to the printing shop double quick, you can stick the whole bloody lot right up your . . .

McDADE. Well . . . thank you very much! Charming! You can tell old Cheekychops from me that he ain't dealing with a Gordon Greene or a Somerset Waugh . . . oh, no. Great literature can't be forced like . . . like roobert. Hummmmmmph. Now, pick up that silly pail and toddle along to number twelve and tell him from me that if he doesn't cut the sarcasm and toe the line viz-a-viz the duplicating when I'm ready then I shall delete the thinly disguised reference to him on page forty-nine. Let's see how he takes that. Now, push off.

TRUSTY. No offence . . . passing on the bleeder's message, that's all. (*Heads for door.*). Silly queen . . .

McDADE. What was that?

TRUSTY. I said 'silly queen'.

McDADE. Sorry, thought you said something else. Didn't mean to be rough on you, old thing. Bit edgy, that's all. Haven't been sleeping well lately . . . got a lot on my mind at the moment.

TRUSTY. That's alright, guv. Know how it is with you toffs. Your lot takes it hard. Ain't done much bird before, have you?

McDADE. Oh, I wouldn't say that. There was one young lady in Aldershot . . .

TRUSTY (*taking bottle of home brew from slops bucket*). No, I mean porridge . . . chokey . . . time . . . prison . . .

McDADE. No . . . no, this is my first visit.

TRUSTY *takes swig from bottle and offers it to* McDADE.

McDADE. No thanks . . . I've just downed a large eggnog. You're very kind but, if you wouldn't mind . . . Delousing took up most of the morning and I'm on boiler house duty in fifteen minutes ... I'd like to get some light reading in ...

TRUSTY. Yeh ... best be on me way anyhow. (*Indicates bottle.*) Got about two minutes before this lot comes scorching down the old dungfunnel.

Exits.

TRUSTY (*off*). Hoi, princess ... visitor for you.

Enter matronly lady in large hat.

McDADE. Mother! Is it really you?

MOTHER. Frank ..? Oh, Frank, my wee baby boy. What have they done to you? Let's have a look. Here, you're looking awful peeky. Have they not been feeding you?

McDADE. Not if they can help it ...

MOTHER. Look at the state of this place. This is terrible ...

McDADE. It is a prison, Mother ...

MOTHER. Why didn't you write and tell your Mummy and your Daddy ..?

McDADE. Oh, 'Daddy'! Has he come back from Berchtesgarten, then? Has he managed somehow to dodge the hail of bullets our lads are pelting Jerry with to be by your side in these troubled times? Well?

MOTHER. Whatever do you mean, Frank?

McDADE. Don't you mean Franz, Mother? Or is it Fritz? All those years spent in Wee Storey Street calling another man 'Dad'. The shame of it! Couldn't you have told me? It's bad enough finding out you're a Kraut but to end up doing chokey ...

MOTHER. Chokey?

McDADE. Bird ... porridge ... to end up doing chokey as a result of ... of ...

MOTHER. Don't speak of it, Fritz ... Frank. The suffering ... oh, the suffering. The number of times I've lived to regret that night of fun ... horror! He lied to me, Frank, he lied to me. He told me his name was Gilhooley ... I swear to God he did, and he was straight off the Belfast boat and looking for cosy digs ...

McDADE. He certainly found them, didn't he, Mother? How could you do it to me?

MOTHER. But you weren't there, Frank.

McDADE. That is precisely the point! Couldn't you have taken precautions? It would have spared me a very great deal of embarrassment.

MOTHER. We were very, very much in love. And, besides, he said he would come back and marry me when the potato crop was lifted in Maybole ...

McDADE. I didn't realize that was in the Fatherland. The dirty Nazi spun you a fanny and you fell for it, Mother, dear.

MOTHER. I was at an impressionable age ...

McDADE. Hang it all, Mum, you were thirty-four!

MOTHER. We were much younger then at thirty-four. One day you'll find out how lonely a woman can get when she reaches thirty-four and finds herself ... (*Sobs.*) ... on the shelf ...

McDADE. Will I?

MOTHER. You will, my son, you will. (*Sobs.*) And then ... then, perhaps, you'll understand ... (*Sobs.*) and even ... even sympathise.

McDADE (*eyes abrim*). Oh, Mother, what have I done to you?

MOTHER. No, Frank, it's what I've done to you ...

McDADE. I don't care ... honestly. Please forgive me, mother. How could I put you through it like that?

MOTHER. Because you're a Hunnish bastard like your father, dear, that's why!

ACT TWO
Scene One

READER. Door dreekit Dormley's dimples hing
  Roon' his knees in wrinklit rime,
  An' aw the Kings graut him a boon
  Fur sic a furry woggle true.
  Fir maun the clachan gates din clase,
  An' Wriggles sclim' abune the wa's.
  Desmond grins a couthy grin,
  Fur ilky pithy wriggles cringe.
  Mickey Moakers an' poakey noakers
  Nickit roon' the knickers' rind.
  Fit gran' creckles bide a'ben
  An' grizzles crackit at the groakit.

NARRATOR. Thank you, Sandy. That poem was entitled
'Dimples' . . . one of McDade's alas, too rare excursions into
the Lallans. Would there were more. It first appeared in the
Smithfield Show edition of 'The Lady'. Up to this point in our
narrative we have made but little note of the role played by the
distaff side of Frank's artistic career. Not a great deal is known
of the ladies to whom FS paid court in the forties. Given that
he was 'otherwise engaged' during this period the omission is
not entirely intentional. There is a mention of a Miss Dodo
Inkpen in one of the Bard's early letters to his step-brother but
to suspect a liaison of a more protracted nature from such a
slight reference would be heinous.

We can but surmise that he set about 'honing his nib' on the
grindstone of journalism . . . the evidence being two short
pieces. The first of these, in the April/May, 1947, issue of
'Lilliput', is entitled 'A Artist's Agony' . . . indicating, perhaps,
that the poet was undergoing something of a turmoil following
his release from prison. The second essay, in the '49 Bumper
Edition of 'Men Only', is to be found on page sixteen . . . next
to the advertisement for Purdies Patent Virility Bombs . . . 'My
Life of Fear', indicating, I feel, a more optimistic frame of mind.

It comes as something of a surprise, therefore, when we find
McDade in 1949 with a wife and child and living in London.
Not quite so surprising when we discover that his spouse is the
lovely Pamela, to whom he swore undying love at Oxford. Let
us to London . . .

Exits.

McDADE. c/o Mrs Ripper,
 17 Septimus Lane,
 Canning Town, E16.

31 December, 1949.

Dear Double Davis,
    Managed, somehow, to get your address from the Cowden-
beath police. Well, old chum, how are you? How goes it in
Nairn? I hear you and Beano Henderson spent a couple of
weeks in Lossiemouth during the Summer. How was the
weather? Did you know his guv'nor's just kicked the bucket
and left him almost five hundred pounds? You don't happen to
know where I could get in touch with him, do you?

    Tell me, how's the linoleum trade these days? Still managing to
scrape a living . . . or what passes for a living in Nairn, eh? I must
say we do enjoy The Smoke. There's nothing quite like a great
city for bringing out the best in one. I'm with the BBC now.
Strictly small fry, you understand, but I do hope to gain a
foothold in Drama when they re-jig the Third Programme in a
year or so. I'm with 'Talks' and it can get extremely hectic. I was
just saying to Sir John the other day that if this television malarky
ever gets off the ground then I'll really be run off my feet.

    Did Beano let slip I'd got spliced? Pamela. You remember
that time she almost came to visit me in chokey? Jolly decent
sort. Good background . . . good family. We've got a dear
little baby now. Name of Polly . . . as in 'put the kettle on'.

Baby starts to howl.

    Pam's awfully keen on kiddies. She's gone off to the flicks in
Pimlico tonight with a girlfriend.

Polly bawls.

    Well I thought the poor love deserved a night out for a change.
She spends all her time playing with little Polly . . . that's short
for Apollinaris, by the way . . . teaching him all sorts of tricks to
show Daddy (*Loud squeals.*) when he comes home from BH. The
poor dear's completely whacked by the time I get home.

Howls of anguish.

Polly's such a bright wee chap.

Extremely loud squeals.

You'd never think ...

Screams.

you'd never ... you'd ... SHUTTIT!!!,

Silence.

The writing's going well, I'm glad to say I've put the finishing touches to the second draft of a blank verse play entitled 'Socks and Trousers', which I hope someone will put on in Edinburgh. The second-year students at the St Thomas Aquinas Domestic Science Academy in Harrogate have evinced an interest in this but we must wait and see if they're quite serious. They did perform one of my works, a rather moving piece called 'Paralysis', at Solihull Tec, last Whitsun and the response from the critics was most heartening. Deirdre Mooney, an apprentice 'saucier' in her teens, took the leading role and she was terrific. Her astonishing display of sand-dancing followed by the splits in Act Two had to be seen to be believed. I had a note this morning from Tadpole Tierney. He has a small but flourishing imprint in Grimsby ... Halibut Press ... and wants to bring out a souvenir edition of my prison writings. I'm damned if I can come across them. I didn't happen to give them to you when you were paroled? They were hand-written on two rolls of Izal. Does that ring a bell? Or pull a chain, perhaps? If you do come across them could you let me know right away as Tadpole has promised me a very generous advance if I can get them to him by the weekend.

Must reluctantly draw to a close here as Pamela's due back any minute and if little Polly's not bathed and changed there'll be one awful row.

Adieu, dear chum. Take care. Trust this finds you as it leave me.

Your comrade in art,

Frank McD.

PS. Did I, by any chance, leave a ten shilling note in the inside pocket of that blazer I lent you in Wick? Should you find it would you send it here by return? It's Pam's birthday on Monday and I'd like to take her out for a jolly good tea. You know the drill when sending lucre. I'm just a trifle suspicious of our landlady Mrs Ripper's current fancy man. Nothing I can place the digit on ... it's just a feeling.

Enter MRS RIPPER *with hot water bottle.*

MRS RIPPER. Ooops, beg pardon, Mr Mac, didn't realise you was in . . . otherwise I should have knocked, shouldn't I? Brought something hot to pop in your bed. Ain't half parky out. Don't want her catching her death, do we? Long as she's got her winter woollies on, eh? Still . . . 's nice and warm at the Palais . . .

McDADE. The Palais?

MRS RIPPER. Do her the world of good, little lovely. Fond of dancing, is she?

McDADE. She hasn't gone dancing, Mrs Ripper . . .

MRS RIPPER. Hasn't she, love? Then who was the redhead our Jack bumped into in the Ladies Excuse-Me if it wasn't . . . Oooooh, didn't you . . . Oooooh, I could bite me tongue off . . . trust me to put me big foot in it. I'm ever so sorry, Mr Mac, I am really. Didn't you know she'd gone . . . ?

McDADE. Err . . . yes . . . of course I did . . . goes to the Palais every Friday . . . with . . . Babs . . .

MRS RIPPER. Babs . . . he a tall dusky gent with gold ear-rings and Brylcream? Only our Jack said . . .

McDADE. Er . . . thank you, Mrs Ripper, that'll be all . . .

MRS RIPPER. Alright, love, if you need anything else I'll be downstairs.

Heads for door. Stops at Baby.

How's baby? Hootchy cootchy coo. Where's a little man, then? Aaaaaahhhhh. Has Daddums been bad to this little cherub? Yeeeeeeeeesss . . .

Howls from Baby.

Never mind, sweetheart. Mummy'll be home soon. S'only just gone midnight, lambkins . . .

Sound of distant clock striking.

Ooooooh, I almost forgot! My friend said he'd come straight round after the bells and me in me pinny. Ooooh!

Rushes for door.

Why don't you and wifie pop down later for a snifter? When she comes home, that is . . . My friend would like that. Ever so fond of company, he is. See you later then? Au revoir.

Exits.

MRS RIPPER (*off*). Oh, Mr Mac? . . . Happy nineteen fifty!

Baby howls.

McDADE *dejectedly whistles bar of 'A Guid New Year'. Takes miniature of whisky and goes to pour out small measure. Baby howls. McDADE puts dummy tit on miniature and gives it to Baby.*

McDADE. All the best.

Scene Two

NARRATOR. Nineteen hundred and fifty-five . . . Frank never did gain that foothold in drama when the planners re-jigged the Third Programme schedules. His sandals skidded on the slippery slope and he found himself propelled pensionless one primula-tinged morn onto the pavement of Portland Place. He fell back upon the only means he knew to try to earn a crust for Pam and Polly . . . Still at Mrs Ripper's . . .

Exits.

McDADE. To the Editor,
Sunday Post,
D C Thompson & Sons,
Dundee.

14th March '55.

Sir,
    Many thanks for the letter commissioning me to write a series of articles on 'Workshy Pensioners in Scottish Hospitals'. I think it will make a compelling feature and throw into low relief the sorry plight of our hard-working medics and staff. I have every sympathy with the British doctor in these troubled times. My brother, Brendan, a fully-trained hospital porter, has told me some hair-raising tales of life on the wards and anything I can do to set matters aright will be little more than my duty. I shall endeavour to produce as objective a view as I am able in the three days I shall be touring the infirmaries. Rest assured, I am no slouch when it comes to investigative journalism as my pamphlet, 'Baden Powell, Scout or Scoundrel', will testify. I daresay you have read it. I know for a fact that some two hundred copies went on sale in Dundee only last year.

    I shall break off here as a TV play of mine is about to appear on the box. (*Switches on TV.*) Perhaps you are even now settling back to watch it? It's due on in about six or seven minutes. 'Tight Lines', a melodrama . . . directed by a good friend of mine from varsity, Tommy Henderson. I wonder if you know him? He was a sub on the 'Beano' for a number of years before he went up to Oxford.

Could you let me have a deadline on the 'Workshy Pensioners' piece soonest as I'm putting in a great deal of work on my current novel and I should like to squash your feature in before I set off for Nairn.

Yours truly,

F S McDade.

PS. Might I congratulate you on the recent series of articles by Crawfie. Will be in touch early next week re expenses. Kindly hold all cheques at your offices in Dundee pending further instructions.

That seems alright . . . now, where are those envelopes . . ?

Enter MRS RIPPER *dressed up and carrying a bottle and two glasses.*

MRS RIPPER. Evening, Mr Mac . . . I've brought up something refreshing for you and Mrs . . . (*Looks around room.*) Gone out, has she, love? What a shame. Never mind, eh? I'll leave it here on the table. My, this is cosy. Is that 'What's My Line?' on telly? (*Sits.*) Oh, I do like that Archie Andrews . . . ever so good-looking, he is . . . (*Pause.*) He's a Scotsman. (*Pause.*) Would you care for a small . . ?

McDADE. Eh? Oh, no . . . bit early for me . . .

MRS RIPPER. Go on, Mr Mac, just a little 'un . . . Keep me company. (*Pours drinks.*) What do you say? Go on . . .

McDADE. No, really, Mrs Ripper . . .

MRS RIPPER. Renee, dear . . . call me Renee. All my friends do . . . and God knows you've been here long enough to count as a friend. Say 'when' . . .

McDADE. Really, I don't think I . . . When! Christ!

MRS RIPPER. Here we are, Mr Mac . . . (*Hands him drink.*) . . . Frank. Ooooh, I am awful . . . Still, when all's said and done . . .

McDADE. Cheers . . .

MRS RIPPER. Cheers, Renee. Come on, now . . . cheers, Renee . . .

McDADE. Cheers . . . (*Pause.*) . . . Renee.

MRS RIPPER. That's better. Bottoms up, Frank. Ooooh, I told you I was awful, didn't I? Oooh ...

McDADE. Shhhhhhhhhhh ...

MRS RIPPER. It's alright, love, I've locked the back door and my friend's on nights ...

McDADE. Shhhhhhhhhhhhhh ... (*Turns up TV.*)

MRS RIPPER. What's up, dear? Something on telly?

McDADE. Oh, just an old play of mine ...

MRS RIPPER. Well, if that's all it is ...

McDADE. Shhhhhhhhhhhhhhhhhh!!!!!!!

MRS RIPPER. Beg pardon, I'm sure ...

ANNOUNCER. We now present a documentary film in our series 'Rude Craftsmen from Swaziland and Beyond'. Your guide is Armand Denis.

McDADE. Eh? Where's that 'Radio Times'?

ANNOUNCER. If you have consulted this week's 'Radio Times' you will see that we were to present a drama entitled 'Taut Thongs' by T P McGlade. Due to unforeseen circumstances transmission of this play has been cancelled. We hope to bring you something similar in the near future.

McDADE. Bloody hell!

MRS RIPPER. Never mind, ducks, we was getting real cosy there ...

McDADE. I haven't even been paid yet! I'll kill that bastard!

MRS RIPPER. Have another sherry, Frank.

Scene Three

NARRATOR. Despite the poet's mother, Mrs Thelma McDade, being an accomplished amateur watercolourist and a past president of Busby Sketch Club, it was not until 1957 that Frank took up the tints, abandoning ... temporarily ... his novel writing. His first formal picture was of one George the Baptist, in oils ... painted on the inside of a kettle using specially designed brushes. Painting for McDade was more than a mere dalliance and in the Spring of that year he applied himself with customary diligence to this testing new art form. We have ample evidence of the extraordinary dexterity he

achieved in just a few short weeks in this, (*Unveils large painting.*)
his magnificent painting, 'Ecce Homo' . . . depicting the
Nazarene, in a delightfully relaxed pose, languishing on a day-
bed in jerkin and bumpers. It was this painting, more than any
other, that established Frank as the 'Giotto Nuovo' of Nitshill.
Here is what the distinguished critic, Denholm Pantalone, wrote
in the September issue of 'Scottish Field' . . . 'I have, this
morning, returned from a studio not far from The Hurlet where
I witnessed the varnishing and framing of a series of paintings
the likes of which I have never in my life seen before. I was
astonished at the vigour and élan. They are the work of a Scot,
Frank McDade, recently come home after a long sojourn in
London. When I quizzed the artist as to why so many of the
pictures were painted on Formica using household brushes his
answer was to pick up a pot of Banana Yellow Deep Gloss
Enamel and proceed to draw the outline of a giraffe on my
overcoat. I left that studio three hours later in the certain
knowledge that we have, in Frank McDade, an artist of
enormous verve and originality . . . a painter whom Scotland
can hold up to the rest of Europe and say, "Wha's like us?" '

A perceptive and, indeed, I think you'll agree, prophetic
critique. Over, then, to 'Bideawee', the Great Man's retreat
following the breakdown of his marriage. 'Bideawee.'

McDADE. October 9, 1957.
   Dear Pam,
   I am writing to you, personally, and not to your solicitors as
directed. Please forgive me, my darling, but I must implore
you to reconsider your divorce proceedings. After all, hadn't
we some happy times together? Remember Mrs Ripper's?
Happy days. How we used to stroll along the towpath, me
pushing the pram and you with your message bags. And what
about that time I pretended to lock you and wee Polly in the
coal bunker and the door jammed and it was over six hours
before I eventually twigged? That was a scream, wasn't it?
Don't those times mean anything to you, dear heart? Tell me,
how is the little chap? He must be almost eight by now. Does
he ever ask about me?

   I'm pressing on with the painting now, and seem to be
making some headway, at last. I have an exhibition coming up
in the Drill Hall in Busby and I'll send you and the boy an
invitation. It promises to be quite an occasion and there is
already a stirring of interest in artistic circles this side of

Hadrian's Wall. I've had to keep my prices a bit low as this will be my debut but if I do manage to get the seven hundred and fifty guineas I'm asking for the portrait of the Princess Marina I'll be quite pleased.

Did you get the cheque for the thirty pounds I owed you in maintenance? Sorry I had to post-date it but it can't be long until Michaelmas.

Did you hear Sammy Fishman read one of my poems on the wireless the other night? It was that sonnet about connubial bliss I penned in Brechin that summer. Do you know the one? But then, I don't expect you get the Scottish Home Service very clearly in Gibraltar.

Well, petal, I'll have to close here as the candle stump is starting to gutter and the pair of boots I set a match to this afternoon in a vain attempt to heat this hovel have long since gone out. I'll say goodnight now, my darling Pam . . . I do hope you have a nice holiday in Antibes with Ralph.

Lots of kisses,

My love to the boy.

Remember me in your prayers,

Your adoring husband . . .

ex-husband, Frank.

PS. Polly's endowment policy is due for redemption on November fifteenth. If you're back in the country by then could you see your way to sending me a few quid? I haven't had a square meal in God knows how long. Thanks.

McDADE *turns around two small pictures hanging on wall to reveal paintings of animals.*

NARRATOR. The cage had hit the bottom of the shaft. Frank managed . . . slowly . . . painfully . . . to extricate himself from the wreckage, crawl along the dimly-lit galleries of his black depression and wipe the dust from the words etched upon the coalface of his psyche . . . Depingo ergo sum.

READER. Sable, hog, and badger,
Camel, squirrel, goat . . .
A zoo . . . at the end of my brush.

McDADE. To The Directors,
    Snorkel Gallery,
    Grafton Street,
    London W1.

Sirs,

Please find enclosed two paintings, 'Ecce Homo', and, on
the inside of the kettle, 'George the Baptist'. They are the
work of a Mister . . . Sconey Semple, a pensioner from Nairn.
I came upon this remarkable man painting in the grounds of
the Temperance Hotel, my port of call when I am in that part
of the world. I was immediately struck by the singularity of his
vision . . . he has but one eye . . . and the fact that 'Ecce
Homo' was executed on Formica. What do you think? Is he
worth a show?

Yours hopefully,
F S McDade.

PS. As there is a conspicuous lack of banking facilities in
and around Nairn would you see that all payments are made
over to me personally at 'Bideawee', Nitshill, and I will see
that Mr Semple gets his share.

PPS. Need I add that I have absolutely no financial interests
whatsoever in Mr Semple's work, I merely wish to recoup my
outlay on the Formica and the kettle.

NARRATOR. At last, the breakthrough!
Not since the Blitz had the Metropolis been so rocked on its
heels. These visual doodlebugs of Sconey Semple's rained down
on Mayfair from distant Nitshill and made a crater so deep that
it took several hundred tons of adulatory newsprint to fill it. A
new star shone in the London sky. Bond Street dealers took to
fighting openly in Cork Street for the very dropping from the
Semple easel. 'Vogue' begged the Snorkel to allow the aged
primitive to model St Laurent across a forty-page spread. Three
fashion-feature editors came to blows in El Vino's over the
relative merits of Sconey and Cimabue. Hampstead was agog.
Frank soon perceived the advantages in laying to rest the
geriatric limner and in a letter to the 'Sunday Times' confessed
that he, F S McDade, acting alone, was responsible for these
astonishing canvases. The fashionable watering holes rang with
the news. Far from being castigated Frank was round feted.
And, when he further confessed to being something of a writer,
he was doubly celebrated. He had arrived!

McDADE. Mother ... stop ... Me telly Sunday ... stop ...
Wow! ... stop ... B reports death-bid ... stop ... your's
... stop ... Christ! ... stop ... Stop! ... stop. Thanks box
figs ... stop ... three hundredweight bit steep ... stop ...
Ring BR re reroute Regent's Park COD. Pam ... stop ...
Ciao,
Frank.
Pee Ess ... Excuse reverse charge cable ... stop ... no
British currency ... stop ... Snorkel dough due soon ... stop
... must dash ... stop ... can't stop ... stop ... must stop
... stop ... love Frank ... stop.

Enter MALCOLM, *TV front man.*

MALCOLM. F S McDade?

McDADE. Present.

MALCOLM. Ah, welcome ... Malcolm ... hi. Glad you
found your way up ... super ... now, here's your m-m-mark
... that's it ... super ... quite at home, are we? ... s-s-
super ... a few ... a few feelers before ... we go on the air,
Frank ... good ... good ... super ... um ... tell me
something of your w-w-working methods ... your m-m-modus
operandi ... Do you work in ... in tempera ... or in ... or
in ...

McDADE (*helpfully*). Nairn ...

MALCOLM. ... or in Nairn ... or are you, like so many of
our younger artists, are you mixed m-m-media? Hm?

McDADE. Er ... um ... yes ...

MALCOLM. Ah, super ... good ... um ... Oh, you'll like
... you'll like this ... um ... Susan ... and I were over at
Andy's place ... the Factory? and he is so ... he is so
laid ...

McDADE (*helpfully*). Out?

MALCOLM. Back, Frank ... back ...

McDADE *steps back.*

MALCOLM. Laid-back, Frank ... um ... laid-back ... He is
really into the whole h-h-h-h-heavy absence trip ... ha ...
ha ...

McDADE. Ha ... yeh ... ha, ha ...

MALCOLM. Bill Burroughs.

McDADE. Ha, ha ... yeh ... ha, ha, ha ... ha ... Eh?

MALCOLM. how much was Bill influenced by your gothic novella, 'Keetch'?

McDADE. Keech.

MALCOLM. Super ... How much was Bill into ...

McDADE. Keech.

MALCOLM. ... before he got round to 'The N-N-Naked ...

McDADE (*helpfully*). Lunch?

MALCOLM. That's a sticky one, Frank. Let me see if Spike's around. (*Shouts.*) Spike! Spike!

McDADE. No, really, I don't want to ...

MALCOLM. It's no problem, Frank, honestly ... Spike! ... no problem at all ... Spike!

McDADE. I don't think you ...

MALCOLM. Listen ... I'll nip downstairs, get a couple of nice pies from Betty and we can heat them up in the ... (*Puts hand to ear-piece.*) Sorry, Frank, n-n-n-no can do ... five seconds we're on ... on air ... Now, just rememb ... remember ... hang loose.

Turns to face camera.

Tonight, in the studio, F S McDade, painter ... poet.

Turns to face McDADE.

Frank ... these stories about your being a transvestite.

Collapse of McDADE.

Scene Four

NARRATOR. Alas, dear friends, McDade's new-found fame was short lived. Hard on the heels of his meteoric rise came the honeymoon period accorded all such overnight sensations. But, Frank, in his eagerness to savour to the full the many charms of Success, charged in too lustfully and watched with mounting alarm as his bride slid over the edge of the bed and vanished. Every dog must have his day ... FS had cocked a leg at Lady Luck and the bitch had turned and bit him. Those

self-same critics who had scented his spoor, galloped up and
sniffed rapturously at his goodies, now savaged him like a pack
of dingos. What flaw in his personality had provoked such an
attack? McDade slunk back to 'Bideawee' and agonised in
reams of foolscap over the likely cause ... using the hero of
'Feet of Clay' as a surrogate ...

READER. O'Dowda leant heavily on the stick and let out an
anguished cry. 'My leg!' he squealed, indicating the withered
thing with a sandshoe on the end of it. 'It's my leg ... mauled
by timberwolves ...' He glanced up at the customers in the
bar. '... in Nairn!' One young woman, a strikingly beautiful
octoroon, detached herself from the throng and loped towards
him. You poor bastard, her eyes seemed to say, as she cupped
Bovril's crooked stump in her dusky palm. 'Is it sore?'

NARRATOR. Yes, it did hurt. No balm nor balsam known to
man could heal the terrible wounds inflicted upon McDade's
ego. No fiscal grafts could ease the pain of lesions that would
never close ... not yet awhile. It was to take Frank many
years before the fingers he had so severely burned could once
again grasp the quill. The final letter, from which, in the
absence of any sound evidence to the contrary, we have put
together the last hours of Francis Seneca McDade ... the final
letter ... from 'Bideawee' to Brendan, bearing the inscription,
'To be opened in the event of my death' ...

McDADE (*in bed*). Dearest Brendan,
   When you read this I shall have quit this mortal coil ... that
is if you have obeyed the instructions on the outside of the
envelope. Knowing you as I do I daresay you could hardly
contain yourself. Well, all to the good. You see, dear brother,
albeit step, my physician, Dr Waters, has informed me, this
very morn, that I am for it. He does not mince words. I think
I could accept it, take it on the chin, so to speak, if I were not
in such straitened circumstances. I am, in a word, skint! They
say you can't take it with you but, believe me, I should enjoy
the luxury of gazing upon a thick wad of tenners ere I slip off
to those Elysian Fields. See what you can do, there's a love.
You know, as well as I do, that if I hadn't got involved in that
disastrous musical adaptation of 'Dr Spock's Guide to Baby
and Child Care', I would be in Easy Street and wouldn't have
to implore you to do me this last favour. Now, I know Mum
was due a substantial sum from Burns and Laird when Dad
... Uncle Dennis, that is ... was taken badly and expired

after sampling those pasties on the steamer to Stromness for
the Shopping Week. She was careful with that cash, wasn't
she? I break out in a cold sweat each time I picture the old bas
... dear ... presenting her pass book at the Post Office and
withdrawing monies. I mean to say, she is fairly comfortable in
that single-end in Busby, isn't she? What more does a woman
of ninety-four want than a night nurse and five grains of
quinine a day? We should all be so lucky. You would earn my
undying gratitude if you could, somehow or other, get Mum to
part with her bank book ... just for an hour or so. It's simply
a case of rolling her on to her side and easing it out from
under the air cushion. Then you can nip down to the General,
draw out the lot and send it to me in a registered letter. You
can easily do a credible forgery of her signature ... let your
pen tremble a good deal. Can you do it? That's all I want to
know. If you can, and for pity's sake don't let me down, remit
the cash post-haste to 'Bideawee', Nitshill. That's where I'll be
for the next few ... days. It would make a dying man so very
happy.

I will bid you adieu, sweet Brendan. We shall meet again
beyond the blue.

Goodbye ... goodbye,

Just clinging on,

Frank.

Pause.

PS. Disregard my instruction per registered letter ... I
don't much care for the postman's squint. Have the dough
delivered by hand. If you cannot come yourself give the bills to
someone I trust. Many thanks.

Pause.

Enter FATHER MANNION *breathing heavily.*

FATHER MANNION. Francis ... Francis ...

McDADE. Who's that?

FATHER MANNION. 'Tis I, Francis ... Father Mannion ...
from Forfar.

McDADE. Father ... Father Mannion ... Good heavens, come
away in. Let's have a look at you. Lor' you've hardly changed
a jot in all this time. How long has it been?

FATHER MANNION. Holy Mother, it must be all of forty years, my son . . .

McDADE. What brings you here, Father? Have you been moved by the Bishop? This isn't your new parish, is it?

FATHER MANNION. No, no, Francis, God love ye, no. I had an urgent telegraphed message from yur brother, Brendan, so I came here as quickly as I could. Sweet Child of Prague, but it's a long ride from Forfar. (*Takes off bike clips.*)

McDADE. Here, let me make you a cup of tea. (*Struggles to get up.*)

FATHER MANNION. Dear St Joe, you stay where ye are, Francis. Sacred heart of Jesus, yur not a well man. I was prepared for ye lookin' a little older but, Holy Mary, ever a Virgin, what kind of life have ye been leadin', at all? The Frank McDade I remember was ruddy cheeked, sound of wind and limb . . . an athlete, a cricketer . . .

McDADE. Ah, that was many moons ago, Father. A lot of water, not to mention other things, has flowed under the old pontoon since then. The ever-increasing insatiability of the Vampire Art has ravaged this poor frame. The Frank McDade you once knew and admired has been sacrificed at the altar of creative writing . . . broken on the Ostwald wheel. The young Horatio has toppled from the bridge. No more will these delicate hands forge pages of molten prose from the base metal of experience. No more these mitts heap coals upon the Sacred Flame. Mars has reclaimed his anvil. The Colossus his torch. Come, Father, unwrap the chrism and dab a few spots on this unworthy brow . . .

Loud snores. McDADE *gives* FATHER MANNION *a dunt.*

A moment, Father . . . you have something for me?

FATHER MANNION (*coming to*). Ah, yes, my son . . . we shall endeavour to provide you with a stout pair of pads when you quit the pavilion and stride towards that heavenly crease . . . a plank of good English willow to smite the Great All Rounder's googlies to the far boundary . . . middle and leg now, Francis . . . In nomine Patre, et Filio, et Spiritu Sancto . . .

McDADE (*exasperated*). No, Father . . . a package . . .

FATHER MANNION. A package? What kind of a Holy Mother and all the saints in Heaven, I meant to give ye the

bloody thing as soon as I came in. Here, ye are, my son.
(*Hands over packet.*)

McDADE (*in disbelief*). Jeeesus Christ!!! I don't believe it ...

Holds it up. Kisses it. Weeps.

FATHER MANNION (*greatly alarmed*). You rest there, Francis.
I'll throw the leg over the bike and fetch an ambulance. Don't
go away now ...

Exits hurriedly.
McDADE *tears open packet to reveal charred school cap and note.*

McDADE (*reads*). 'We found this in the grounds after the fire.
we think it must belong to you. Dominus vobiscum. Father
M.' Suffering God!!! (*Sinks back on bed.*)

Pause.

Enter DOUBLE-DAVIS *with holdall.*

DOUBLE-DAVIS (*loudly*). Wotcher, Frank!

McDADE. Christ!

DOUBLE-DAVIS. Wrong again, Frankie boy! Double-Davis is
the name. Just blew down from the Windy City ... on my
way to the Kelvin Hall, exhibition of lino. Boss sent me down
to catch the floor show. Had a couple of hours to kill, thought
I'd look up a few old pals. You were the first on the list,
Frankie ...

McDADE. Let's have a gander at you. Godalmighty, I don't
think you've changed since Wick ...

DOUBLE-DAVIS. Just the blazer, Frank ... Some weekend
that, eh? They're still talking about it in Thurso ... ha,
ha ...

McDADE. How's Fiona? And the kids ... they must be getting
big, eh? Eleven, the last I heard ...

DOUBLE-DAVIS. Twelve now, old cock. Fi was terribly
pleased ... always wanted a boy. Spiers Bluemel Grimes
Double-Davis. (*Pause.*) How's Pam?

McDADE. She left me ... in 1955. Didn't Beano ...?

DOUBLE-DAVIS. Bugger, Frankie, so he did! Sorry ... about
bringing it up, I mean. If you ask me you're better off. The
way Beano described her ... well ...

McDADE. What do you mean, the way Beano described her? Why, he hardly knew Pamela . . .

DOUBLE-DAVIS. That's how he told it, Frank . . .

McDADE. The bastard!

DOUBLE-DAVIS. Live locally, does she?

McDADE. No . . . Cairo . . . with her disgustingly rich girlfriend, Coco. Coco, I ask you!

DOUBLE-DAVIS. No, thanks, Frankie, don't want to nod off on the motorway . . .

McDADE. How's Fiona coping with the young 'un? 'Spect it stops her from wearying. The girls must be flying the coop . . .

DOUBLE-DAVIS. I'll say . . . Fluvia was the first to go . . . been a steady stream since then. (*Pulls out snapshot.*) Then Barbarella got itchy feet. That's her with the peep-toe sandals. And, Doris . . . ginger Afro, freckles . . . she's a roustabout on the oil-rigs . . .

McDADE. Big girl, Doris . . .

DOUBLE-DAVIS. Then Concepta . . . that's her poking the stick up the leg of Grimes's Bermuda shorts . . . she went out to Ceylon . . . got hitched to a rubber planter out there . . . don't think we'll see her again . . .

McDADE. I don't know, I expect she'll bounce back . . .

DOUBLE-DAVIS. She is worth a packet!

McDADE. Talking of packets, DD . . . talking of packets . . . you don't happen to have brought one with you?

DOUBLE-DAVIS. Bugger, Frankie, completely slipped my mind. Too busy gassing. (*Opens holdall.*) Here, you don't think you could shift some of this merchandise for me? It's all high-class gear . . . microwave ovens, cheese presses, hearing aids . . .

McDADE. What?

DOUBLE-DAVIS (*loudly*). Hearing aids.

McDADE. No, I thought you were in lino, DD?

DOUBLE-DAVIS. That's just a cover, Frank . . . this is where the big pennies are. You want to give it a try? Transistors, quartz egg-timers, Jubilee jock-straps . . . kids have been up all night painting in the corgis ... what d'you say? There's ten per cent commission on all sales ... Get rid of this lot and we'll forget about that business with the pump, Frankie boy. (*Pause.*) Aw, forget it. Here. (*Pulls out packet and chucks it onto bed.*) Better zip off, anyway. Got the Robin double-parked. See you around, Frankie. If you're ever up in Nairn let us know so we can be out. Give my love to ...

McDADE. Cairo.

DOUBLE-DAVIS. Bugger! Sorry ...

McDADE (*holding up packet*). I'm ever so grateful, DD. You don't know what this means to me ...

DOUBLE-DAVIS. It's nothing, Frankie ... really ... nothing. Well, Bonsoir, old thing ...

McDADE. Cheerio, chin, chin ...

DOUBLE-DAVIS. Napoo ...

McDADE. Toodleoo ...

DOUBLE-DAVIS. Goodbye.

Exits.

McDADE *rips open packet to reveal two squashed toilet rolls. Allows one to unroll and reads.*

McDADE. Cell 14, D Block ... I am at the bottom of the abyss. The walls are closing in and the inky blackness is swallowing me ... up. I am at my lowest ... ebb ...

Falls back upon bed and sobs.
Enter CHICK BRAZIL.

CHIC. Daders!

McDADE. Chickers ... (*Sits bolt upright.*) Chickers! What the hell are you doing here?

CHIC. On my way to Luchres. Spot of the old shooters. Anners' pater's got a thousand acres up there. Didn't y'know? Anners and me got splicers. Dickers splitters, left Anners in the shitters ... ran off with a brace of scrubbers from Brummers. Anners was always mooners over me ... don't y'recall me givin' it a mensh at Oxford ...?

McDADE (*wearily*). When are you pushing off, Chickers? It'll be getting dark, soon, and unless you're after luminous hares you'll not get much shooters in.

CHIC. Ain't seen yer kisser in the glossies of late, old sport. Made quite a name for yourself few years back. Caused quite a brouhaha . . . yes . . . (*Pause.*) How's Pammers? Ain't see hide nor hair of her since that 'how's-yer-father' with the rowin' Blues . . . back in thirty-eight, wasn't it? Hauled her stark naked up Tom Tower . . . after the Bumps Party . . . yes . . . God knows what they got up to then . . . hmmmmm . . . (*Pause.*) Well, better chunter along, old fruit . . . can't have Anners baggin' all the bally game, eh? Tell the nipper Uncle Bentwood left him a shillin' on the drainin' board. How is the little chap? Solly, ain't it?

McDADE (*very wearily*). Polly . . . Last I heard he was in Hollywood peddling dope . . .

CHIC. They shoot up, don't they . . . Well, best be on me way . . . (*Heads for door.*)

McDADE. Close the door quietly, Chickers. Wasn't expecting so many visitors. I told Brendan just to give . . .

CHIC (*stops*). Brendan! Good lor', forgot to give it a mensh. In the Daimler . . . met the duffer off the puffer . . . had a couple of pinkers together . . . said y'were in sickers . . . gave me this. (*Pulls package from pocket.*) Asked me to do the honours. (*Hands it to McDADE.*)

McDADE (*accepts it disbelievingly*). Good God . . .

CHIC. Not one of yer bally books, is it?

McDADE. No . . . no . . . something infinitely more precious. (*Sobs.*) Gosh, thanks, Chickers . . . you're a real brick.

CHIC. Don't give it a mensh, old bean. (*Moves towards door.*)

McDADE (*tears of joy*). Chickers!

CHIC (*turns*). Daders . . .

McDADE *holds up package.*

Stiff uppers.

CHIC. Toodlepip. (*Exits.*)

McDADE *rips open package to reveal great wad of tenners.*

READER. Chickers, Double-Davis,
Brother Brendan, Priest . . .
The zoo . . . at the end of his life.

McDADE *expires.*

John Clifford was born in North Staffordshire in 1950 but has lived in Scotland since 1968. He began his playwriting career by translating two plays by Calderon, *The House with Two Doors* and *The Doctor of Honour*. His first original plays were written for radio: *Desert Places* (BBC Radio Scotland, 1983) and *Ending Time* (BBC Radio 3, 1984). *Losing Venice* was the first of three plays written for Jenny Killick at the Traverse Theatre, Edinburgh; first staged in 1985, it was subsequently seen at the Almeida Theatre, London, at the Perth Festival, Australia, at the Hong Kong Festival, on tour throughout Sweden, and in Los Angeles. It was followed by *Lucy's Play* (1986; also seen in Aspen, Colorado, and Los Angeles) and by *Playing with Fire* (1986). For TAG Theatre Company, Glasgow, he adapted *Romeo and Juliet* in 1984 and *Great Expectations* in 1988 (revived in 1989 to tour Iraq, Egypt, India, Sri Lanka and Bangladesh).

Clifford has translated Lorca's *The House of Bernarda Alba* (Royal Lyceum Theatre, Edinburgh 1989), and Calderon's *Schism in England* (National Theatre & Edinburgh Festival 1989). He has also both adapted and translated Tirso de Molina's *Heaven Bent, Hell Bound* (Actors' Touring Company 1987) and *Celestina* by Fernando de Rojas (scheduled for the National Theatre in autumn 1990).

He has just completed *Santiago*, a drama-documentary for Channel 4. His latest play for the Traverse, *Inés de Castro* (published by Nick Hern Books in *First Run 2*) was set in medieval Portugal; his next will be set in the Third World.

Losing Venice was first performed in the Traverse Theatre, Edinburgh, on 2 August 1985 with the following cast:

MUSICIAN	Duncan Bell
QUEVEDO	Bernard Doherty
PABLO	Simon Donald
MARIA	Carol Ann Crawford
DUKE	Simon Dormandy
DUCHESS	Kate Duchene
SECRETARY	Duncan Bell
KING	Ralph Riach
PIRATE ·	Duncan Bell
PRIEST	Kate Duchene
SISTER	Irene Macdougall
MR DOGE	Ralph Riach
MRS DOGE	Carol Ann Crawford
CONSPIRATORS:	
ONE	Duncan Bell
TWO	Ralph Riach
THREE	Carol Ann Crawford
FOUR	Irene Macdougall
WOMAN WITH BABY	Irene Macdougall

Directed by Jenny Killick
Designed by Dermot Hayes
Lighting and Sound by George Tarbuck

ACT ONE

Two benches on the stage. The audience enter to find QUEVEDO *writing and a* MUSICIAN *playing a guitar.* PABLO *and* MARIA *run on with a basket of food which they put down in front of* QUEVEDO.

QUEVEDO. What's this?

PABLO. Food.

MARIA. A picnic.

PABLO. For you.

QUEVEDO. I'm not hungry.

PABLO. Liar.

MARIA. You haven't eaten for days.

PABLO. Weeks.

MARIA. Months.

QUEVEDO. It is true I hunger but not for food.

MARIA. There. (*Exits with* PABLO.)

QUEVEDO. Bread and wine. The sacraments. The holy
sacraments.
We suffer hunger in a filthy world,
Slaves to physical necessity. And yet . . .
I break the bread. I drink the wine.
Communion. Hunger is sanctified.
I rise above the needs of the body,
And I enter the kingdom of the soul.

MARIA *rushes across the stage chased by* PABLO. PABLO *is caught.* MARIA *exits.*

QUEVEDO. Pablo!

PABLO. What?

QUEVEDO. Stop it.

PABLO. What?

QUEVEDO. That.

PABLO. Why?

QUEVEDO. Because I have forbidden it.

PABLO. How?

QUEVEDO. I said I forbid it.

PABLO. You can't.

QUEVEDO. I most certainly can.

PABLO. It's my day off.

QUEVEDO. I don't care.

PABLO. Look. When I'm working I'm yours. Your beck and your call. But not now. No disrespect. (*Exits.*)

QUEVEDO. Well . . .
This urge to procreation I could never
understand. Two lumps of flesh.
Rubbing together. Frotting. Frot,
frot. And what, I ask, what is the
outcome? We are. What a way to start.
What a grotesque beginning. Imagine.
The slimy contact.

Enter MARIA.

MARIA. Do you mind?

QUEVEDO. Yes I do. Very much. And to do it here in public.

MARIA. Well, we can't do it in private.

QUEVEDO. You could try.

MARIA. The roof's fallen in.

QUEVEDO. The mansion of poetry is in some little disrepair.

MARIA. Have a grape.

QUEVEDO. I don't like grapes.

MARIA. Oh you do.

QUEVEDO. Not today.

MARIA. It's this wedding. Got you all upset.

QUEVEDO. I hate weddings.

MARIA. You should have been asked. That Duke. What a cheek. Should have invited you. And you wrote his speech for him, too. It's a shame.

QUEVEDO *takes grapes.*

MARIA. There.

QUEVEDO. But these are grapes.

MARIA. True.

QUEVEDO. Pablo! (*Enter* PABLO.) These are grapes.

PABLO. Very perceptive.

QUEVEDO. You stole them.

PABLO. No, we didn't. They just happened to be there.

QUEVEDO. And the wine.

PABLO. It was hanging about.

QUEVEDO. And the knives and forks. The ducal crest.

PABLO. They just came with the wine.

QUEVEDO. If the Duke finds this we're finished. No more money.

PABLO. That's serious.

QUEVEDO. Yes. We can't go on like this.
  On the edge of things.
  We have got to get jobs, but if the
  Duke catches us stealing, that's it.
  The end of opportunity.
  The door closed against us forever.

PABLO. But he won't catch us, will he?

MARIA. No.

PABLO. He's busy. He's getting married.

MUSICIAN *starts to play a wedding tune. He gives a malicious look to* QUEVEDO, PABLO *and* MARIA *who rush to clear the food and the paper off the stage.*

Enter the DUKE *and* DUCHESS, *leading the wedding procession. The* DUKE *looks pleased; the* DUCHESS *looks distracted. She wears spectacles,* QUEVEDO, PABLO *and* MARIA *rush back on to join the procession which has lined up centre stage. A great occasion. The* DUKE, *in sudden panic, searches for his speech.*

DUKE. Quevedo, my speech.

QUEVEDO. In your pocket.

DUKE. Thank you. My subjects. My people.
  My friends. I bid you welcome.
  Welcome to this hallowed place,
  This seat of learning, this sacred spot,
  To celebrate the joy of peace.
  The consummate the power of love.
  Thank you. Thank you.

Applause.

The DUKE *kisses* DUCHESS. *She looks about for a way to wipe her mouth.* MARIA *gives a hanky to the* DUCHESS.

DUKE. A touching gesture.
  Quevedo. A splendid speech.

QUEVEDO. Not too long, I hope?

DUKE. Not at all, my dear fellow, not at all. But let me present you.

  My bride. My poet.

QUEVEDO. Your hand is white as winter snow
    but your cheeks proclaim the spring.
    Your beauty makes these flowers grow
    and in your hair young birds do sing.

Enthusiastic applause.

DUKE. Bravo. Bravo. But come, a feast awaits.

QUEVEDO. Honoured.

PABLO. Delighted.

MARIA. Dead chuffed.

DUKE. Your pleasure's mine. My dearest.
  All leave. The DUKE *makes* DUCHESS *stay behind.*

DUCHESS. Are you drunk?

DUKE (*on his knees*). Drunk with beauty.

DUCHESS. I was afraid so.

DUKE. Your lips like . . .

DUCHESS. Apples.

DUKE. Apples?

DUCHESS. Pippins.

DUKE. Is that right?

DUCHESS. Apples are red.

DUKE. Some. Not all. And your lips are red all over.
And your eyes.

DUCHESS. Like razors.

DUKE. No. Not razors. Not right. I need a poet. Quevedo!

QUEVEDO (*enters*). You called?

DUKE. I need a poem.

QUEVEDO. Did you have anything in mind?

DUKE. The beauty of women.

QUEVEDO. In general?

DUKE. The beauty of this woman.
The joys of marriage.

QUEVEDO. Do you want something long?

DUCHESS. Make it short.

DUKE. Yes. Nothing too long.

DUCHESS. Make it a sonnet.

DUKE. Of course. A sonnet, Quevedo.

QUEVEDO. A sonnet. On the joys of marriage.

DUKE. By tomorrow morning.

QUEVEDO. Tomorrow morning.

DUKE. If you'd be so good.
And now I must ... we must, my wife and I, retire.

Exit DUKE *and* DUCHESS.

QUEVEDO. The marriage bed's a trough of shit.
Fit for pigs to lie in it.

That won't do.
A sonnet.
On the joys of marriage.
Imagine.

Enter PABLO *and* MARIA *with a bag and rolls of bedding. Exit*
QUEVEDO, *disgusted.* PABLO *and* MARIA *survey their*
bench.

MARIA. Is this it?

PABLO. It?

MARIA. Yes.

PABLO. Said so on the door.

MARIA. It's tiny.

PABLO. It is compact.

MARIA. Couldn't swing a cat in it.

PABLO. I don't want to swing a cat in it.

MARIA. Didn't know you were fond of animals.

PABLO. I'm not fond of animals. I had other things in mind.

MARIA. Like what, for instance?

PABLO. Bed for instance.

MARIA. You call that a bed?

PABLO. What do you call it?

MARIA. A snot rag.

PABLO. Well I've got a cold.
    Look, it's better than nothing.

MARIA. It smells.

PABLO. It's got an aroma. Who cares?

MARIA. I do. Call this a castle.

PABLO. It's a palace.

MARIA. It's a pigsty.

PABLO. Look we got what we wanted. Didn't we? Well didn't
    we. We all got jobs. We're all in the palace.

MARIA. And look at it.

PABLO. It is a bit run down. For a palace.

MARIA. I worked to get here.

PABLO. You didn't.

MARIA. I was nice to the Duchess.

PABLO. I thought you liked her.

MARIA. That's not the point. She owns things. And now she
  owns me.

PABLO. She doesn't.

MARIA. She does. Oh it's alright for you.
  You don't try for anything.
  You don't care. But I try.
  I make an effort.
  I try to get things right.
  And where do I end up? Here.
  It's not encouraging.

PABLO. It's a room.

MARIA. It's a hole. A dark dank hole. I want to cry.

PABLO. Don't.

MARIA. Why not?

PABLO. We could be on the street.

MARIA. You're a great comfort.

PABLO. And we're together.

MARIA. Yes. We're together.

PABLO. And all we got to do is cuddle up and forget all about
  it.

MARIA. We deserve better.

PABLO. We all deserve better. Everyone does. Everyone in the
  whole wide world. But it's alright. It doesn't matter.

MARIA. Doesn't it?

PABLO. No, not a duchess. Not a mushroom. Not a mousehole.
  Not a louse. Sssshhh.

  They cuddle down. QUEVEDO *comes on with papers, which he starts
  to lay down on the other bench.*

QUEVEDO. What rhymes with cock? Hock. Drunken.
  Shock. Stimulating. Clock. Moralistic.
  It's the new dawn, you see.
  Not what you think. Marriage as a new
  morning. Mourning. A new death.

Funeral baked meats. Marriage tables.
Not that. No. The crowing of the cock.
Lock. Padlock. Wedlock. Hate it.
It won't do. It's not worth it.
Not even for a roof. Not even for ten
roofs.

Enter DUKE *and* DUCHESS. QUEVEDO *hastily clears up his papers.*

QUEVEDO. Oh it's you. My lady. My lord. Well, the joys of marriage. They're coming. We progress.

Exit QUEVEDO. *The* DUCHESS *sits and starts to read.*

DUKE. Well.

DUCHESS. Yes.

DUKE. Here we are.

DUCHESS. So it seems.

DUKE. The time has come, so to speak.

DUCHESS. Apparently.

DUKE. Shall we . . . shall we begin?

DUCHESS. If you like.

The DUCHESS *carefully marks her place and closes her book.*

DUKE. You could help.

DUCHESS. Could I?

DUKE. Well, yes.

DUCHESS. How?

You're frightened.

DUKE. Me? Of course not. A slight tremor. An old wound.

DUCHESS. But you've fought battles. I could never do that.

DUKE. You're a woman.

DUCHESS. Not even if I were a man.

DUKE. But then you're not.

DUCHESS. Not even if I were.

DUKE. Can we get on with this?

DUCHESS. Can't we do it tomorrow? It's been a long day.

DUKE. No.

DUCHESS. But it has.

DUKE. Yes. No we can't do it tomorrow. We must do it today.

DUCHESS. Must we?

DUKE. We are married.

DUCHESS. Yes. I don't see the connection.

DUKE. You don't?

DUCHESS. I was brought up by nuns.

DUKE. Nuns?

DUCHESS. Poor Clares.
  Enlighten me.

DUKE. Certain things are expected of us.

DUCHESS. I see.

DUKE. Yes. Yes, you see the family. There is a ceremony . . .
  they are waiting for issue.

DUCHESS. Where from?

DUKE. They will look at the sheet.

DUCHESS. What for?

DUKE. Blood.

DUCHESS. But it's not my time.

DUKE. No no no. Not that sort of blood.

DUCHESS. I don't understand.

DUKE. And that damn poet's in bed!

DUCHESS. Shall I ring for him?

DUKE. No!

DUCHESS. A servant?

DUKE. No. We have to do this ourselves.

DUCHESS. But you are a Duke.

DUKE. It makes no difference.

DUCHESS. Your palace is huge.

DUKE. Yes. Yes it is big.

DUCHESS. Miles of corridors.

DUKE. Forty-four miles. We had them measured.

DUCHESS. Astonishing.

DUKE. Yes. Longer than the other duke's. Longer than anyone's. Except the king, of course.

DUCHESS. Empty.

DUKE. Sorry?

DUCHESS. Your house. Very empty.

DUKE. But not in the old days. It was full of people then. Horses and servants and relations. Fodder and saddles and spurs. And soldiers of course. A whole regiment on foot.

Those were the great days.

DUCHESS. Where did they all go?

DUKE. To the war, of course. Great days.
Look can we get on with this? We are married.

DUCHESS. What of it?

DUKE. Well, love.

DUCHESS. Love?

DUKE. I thought it was expected.

DUCHESS. Is there anything in your life that's unexpected?

DUKE. I should hope not. I try to be correct. Straightforward in all things but strategy.

DUCHESS. Strategy?

DUKE. In battle. The secret of success is to take the enemy by surprise. If he expects you in front, attack him in the rear. If he expects a retreat, attack. If he expects an attack, retreat. Or else attack. So, were you a city under siege . . .

DUCHESS. But I'm not.

DUKE. No. More's the pity. It would be easier.

I'm sorry. I'm boring you.

DUCHESS. Not at all.

DUKE. We have a little in common.

DUCHESS. A contract

DUKE. I was hoping some day it would be more. A little one.

DUCHESS. A little contract?

DUKE. Look if we did it now it would be over.

DUCHESS. There is that to be said for it.

DUKE. Yes.

DUCHESS. But if you did it now you might want to do it again.

DUKE. No. Never again. I promise. On my honour. As a soldier. We must think of it as a duty. (*Points to the DUCHESS'S spectacles.*) Please take these off.

DUCHESS. I can't see without them.

DUKE. That's how I like you.

DUCHESS. I've changed my mind.

The DUCHESS evades DUKE, rings a bell. PABLO and MARIA sit up abruptly. The DUKE and DUCHESS freeze.

PABLO. Oh fuck.

MARIA. We can't.

PABLO. Why not?

MARIA. That bell.

PABLO. What do we do?

MARIA. Answer it I suppose.

PABLO. You go.

MARIA. No you.

PABLO. Won't be for me.

MARIA. How do you know?

PABLO. Men don't ask for things.

MARIA. Oh don't they?

PABLO. Not at night. Anyway I don't know the way.

MARIA. Oh alright.

Why's it always me?

MARIA *crosses over to the* DUKE *and* DUCHESS.

MARIA. You rang?

DUCHESS. Yes.

DUKE. Well you've got her. Tell her what you want.

DUCHESS. I need . . .

DUKE. Yes?

DUCHESS. A hairpin.

DUKE and MARIA. A hairpin?

DUCHESS. It's a custom. A well known custom. In the south.

MARIA. I'm sorry. I come from the North.

DUCHESS. Of course you wouldn't know. The bride must always lie beside a hairpin. The touch of steel. Wards off the evil eye.

MARIA (*holding out hairpins*). A small one or a large one?

DUCHESS. I wonder.

DUKE. What are you talking about?

MARIA. I'd say large.

DUCHESS. Would you?

MARIA. I remember now. In the mountains they always say large. And very sharp in case the devil comes.

DUCHESS. These superstitions. So quaint. One should always keep up with them don't you think? I think that one. It looks sharper. There. Now we're well protected. Thank you Maria. You may go.

Exit MARIA.

DUKE. Thank God for that. At last.

DUCHESS. I feel safer now.

DUKE. Dammit it's gone.

DUCHESS. Where?

DUKE. So much for courtesy. So much for consideration. I should never have waited.

DUCHESS. Something wrong?

DUKE. My sword rusts in my sheath.

DUCHESS. So sorry.

DUKE. My flank has been subdued.

DUCHESS. Then we must retire.

DUKE. A tactical retreat, I do assure you.

DUCHESS. Of course.

DUKE. I shall prepare a new assault.

DUCHESS. I await your battery with interest. Good-night.

DUKE. Good-night.

Exit DUKE and DUCHESS.

QUEVEDO *and* MARIA *come on and meet each other.*

QUEVEDO. Yurrchh.

MARIA. Sorry?

QUEVEDO. Petrarch. He's got a lot to answer for, inventing the sonnet. Hope he's in hell. Reading them all.

MARIA. Are you alright?

QUEVEDO. No. I'm lost. (*Shows* MARIA *half-completed poem.*) Just before the final couplet. The darkness before the dawn.

Exit QUEVEDO.

MARIA. (*Moves over to* PABLO, *who has meanwhile been masturbating*). I'm off. Pablo!

PABLO. (*Embarrassed*). Yes.

MARIA. Your hand's wet.

PABLO. Yes.

MARIA. And sticky.

PABLO. Yes.

MARIA. Couldn't you wait?

PABLO. I was lonely.

MARIA (*pushing him off the bench*). You idiot. You stupid selfish idiot.

PABLO. I couldn't help it.

MARIA (*picking up luggage, ready to go*). You could so.

PABLO. What did she want anyway?

MARIA. A hairpin. (*Exits.*)

PABLO. A hairpin? (*Exits.*)

The DUKE *cries out in pain from off-stage. Enter* QUEVEDO *and then the* DUKE, *limping. He carries a dispatch case.*

QUEVEDO. It's finished. Fourteen lines, six rhymes, three puns and an extended image. And on time. Your grace. Your poem.

DUKE. The joys of marriage? Later, Quevedo. They've been postponed.

QUEVEDO. I'm sorry.

DUKE. Sorry? Ha. Quevedo, sit. Are you my friend? Even a Duke must have a friend. Sit, sit.
Women, Quevedo. Women. What are they for? What use are they? What function do they serve?

QUEVEDO. The ancients found uses for them.

DUKE. And have we progressed no further?
Must we continue to be enslaved?
Why did I get married?
To get a son, Quevedo. A son.
It is most unfortunate.
Why is there no other way?

QUEVEDO. Plato believed –

DUKE. Plato. That upstart. My line, Quevedo, stretches back to the Goths. The glorious Goths. Is it to die? Can it not stretch forward to the . . . the . . .

QUEVEDO. The future.

DUKE. Yes. Thank you. The future. But not even there can she be trusted. God knows, she might even spawn a daughter.

QUEVEDO. It is possible.

DUKE. Possible? Quevedo if only she were a man. She would understand the necessity. We would talk it over, like sensible people, agree on what had to be done. And then we would do

it. Whatever was necessary. And then it would be over. All
over. We could have a drink and be friends. But with her.
Tears. Recriminations. Contradictions. A painful scene.

QUEVEDO. You're limping.

DUKE. It's nothing. Nothing. An old wound. Gained in war. A
source of pride.

Oh it is peace Quevedo, peace that
underlies our ills. Peace. A woman's
invention. Peace rots the soul.
Spain was not made for peace.
Spain's greatness was forged in war.
Our empire built on the blade of a sword.
Several swords. A hundred.
Several hundred thousand swords.

QUEVEDO. That now rust.

DUKE. Precisely. Rust. Rot with disuse.
You see the people? Look at them.
Decaying in idleness.
They lead such hopeless, senseless lives.
No aspiration beyond riches. No direction.
They need a purpose Quevedo. To take
them outside their lives.
And where will they find it? In war.
Ask any man still old enough to remember.
Ask them of the times they felt alive.
They will tell you: it was in the war.
That was when they had purpose.
That was when they lived. Our duty is
plain. To bring an end to peace.

QUEVEDO. I had not known you were at peace.

DUKE. Precisely. Enemies surround me.
Leeches tug at my heels.

QUEVEDO. Dogs.

DUKE. I beg your pardon?

QUEVEDO. At your heels. Dogs.

DUKE. Yes dogs. They suck me dry.
The usurers are at my back and I am
helpless. Helpless. My hands are tied.

It takes a bold stroke, Quevedo, to turn
upon the snivelling rats and drive them
backwards. Will you join me?

QUEVEDO. Me?

DUKE. Are you content to scribble poems, indulge in your
fantastic theories?

QUEVEDO. My fantastic theories?

DUKE. Isn't that what you do, you poets?

QUEVEDO. We write poems.

DUKE. And who reads them? Forgive me if I talk frankly. No
doubt your work is much admired. So people tell me, people
who know such things. But this country. This country we so
dearly love, is she admired? She used to be. She used to be
great, used to be respected, used to be feared. But now what
part do we play in the world?

We apologise. It is not worthy of us. I sense in you a great
impatience. Will you join me? Are you with me?

QUEVEDO. I have always been with you. In spirit.
I watched you, striding through the fields
of Flanders
Dealing out death on the Italian mountains.
I was with the vultures, glorying in the
downfall of our enemies.
But what became of your victories?
They slipped away like grains of sand.

DUKE. A tragedy. Lost opportunities.
Peace undoes all that war achieves.
Fudge and mudge, Quevedo.
Disgraceful compromise.
Where is the scope for resolution?
We belong to a nation of pygmies.
Men of straw totter across the public
stage, posturing and mouthing
Dummies.

QUEVEDO. Spain is sick. I watch her agony on the
sidelines. Words. Words.
I am tired of words.

DUKE. Do not underestimate the power of words.
We have great men on our side, Quevedo,
men of the greatest courage and resolution,
but we have problems.
The problem of communication.
People do not understand.
Once in Italy we came upon a house.
It stood right in the enemy's line of fire.
A sitting target for their cannons.
And so of course we burnt it.
What else could we do?

There was a lull in the fighting.
Women, old men crawled about in the wreckage.
Don't weep, I told them, we did it for you.
Your house is safe. We have saved it.
But they would not believe.
You see, I speak so badly.
But had you been there, you with your
gift for words . . .

But enough talk. Time for action.
We must act swiftly. We cannot wait for
agreement, we must act from conviction.
But there is danger. Ignoble as it is
I too, have learnt to conspire.
And now I have the ears of the King.
Here. In this dispatch case.

QUEVEDO. Are you sure?

DUKE. One can never be sure. I think, I suspect, I surmise. I can say no more. For now we are surrounded by spies. But I can tell you this: I am setting in train a foreign adventure. The king is sick, but I have access to his secretary. I go to seek him now. Farewell.

QUEVEDO. Farewell?

DUKE. Trust me Quevedo. Together we shall change the world.

QUEVEDO. But my poem . . .

DUKE. You still care about your poem? Then write me another. The treachery of women, the futility of love. For this evening. Read it to my wife. We will surprise her. Farewell. (*Exit* DUKE.)

QUEVEDO. He's mad. What of it? Power is madness.
The world is corrupt. Action is futile.
Love is a farce. Happiness, impossible.
Poetry the only meagre consolation.
To work, Quevedo. Destroy happiness. (*Exit* QUEVEDO.)

Enter DUCHESS *and* MARIA *with a basket.*

DUCHESS. Is this the place? We'll just say it is, shall we? And
if anyone complains, we'll just tell them we didn't know. We'll
say we weren't told.

MARIA. It's nice here, anyway.

DUCHESS. Must be the one pleasant spot in the whole place.
Must be a mistake. Oh Maria what shall I do?

You know what we're supposed to do?
We're supposed to take the sheet and hang it up where
everyone can see it. They say it makes the ground fertile. And
it has to happen at noon. And why does it have to happen at
noon? Because it's always happened at noon. And why does it
have to be this basket? Because it's always been this basket.
That's all this basket's for. The basket of the virgin's blood.

It's like everything else. It's there because it always has been.
They do it because they always have. That's why it's such a
great house, Maria, that's why it's stood so long. That's why
it's so dark that's why it's so full of dust. That's why it's so
damp that's why it's so cold. That's why I can't breathe in it.

Oh Maria what shall I do? I shouldn't have married him. I
knew it was a mistake. Have you got a hanky? Men, Maria.
What's the use of them? What possible function do they serve?
What conceivable benefit are they to any part of the world?
Well? Can you think of any?

MARIA. Don't we need them?

DUCHESS. Whatever for?

MARIA. Children?

DUCHESS. I wonder. My father had precious little to do with
me. He just did the one thing, the one thing he couldn't get
out of, and then he died. And all his money went into trust.
Every penny of it. He gave it all to some lawyer so I wouldn't
get it until I married. And now I am married who gets it? My
husband. The Duke. It isn't right and it isn't fair and I can't
do a thing about it.

MARIA. There must be something.

DUCHESS. Well I can't think what. Are they all like him? Men? I haven't met that many. Thank God. He's so boring. Not what I expected at all. Not what I dreamed of. You know Maria when I was a girl you know what I did? I ran away. I crept out one night when no one was looking. I'd read all these books about knights in armour and I wanted . . . I wanted an adventure. I think I wanted to meet St. George. I never did. They brought me home on a mule. And here I am. And what'll I do?

MARIA. I wish I knew.

DUCHESS. We'll think of something. Shall we? Anyway. Is your room nice?

MARIA. No.

DUCHESS. And mine's horrid too. We'll have to do something. We'll just have to get rid of him, that's all. You know anything about poison? Neither do I. I don't think I could use it anyway. I'd be too nervous. Put it in the wrong glass. Why can't he go to war? He's very good at war. Are there any?

MARIA. I don't know.

DUCHESS. Where could he go? Somewhere distant. Somewhere impossibly remote. London, for instance.

MARIA. Where?

DUCHESS. You're right. Who'd ever want to go there. Anyway how could we send him?

MARIA. Couldn't someone else?

DUCHESS. Maria you're brilliant. I know someone who could do it. Writes letters for the king. Someone terribly important. I'll ask him. I'll go this minute.

MARIA. But you can't.

DUCHESS. Oh the sheet. I was forgetting.

MARIA. There's people coming.

DUCHESS. But what'll we do?

MARIA. You take one end.

DUCHESS. Yes.

MARIA. And I take the other.

DUCHESS. You're right. Oh Maria. Shh. Here they come.

> *MUSIC. Enter all the cast, in procession, the* DUKE *leading. They pass ceremonially under the sheet, turn round, applaud it. Confetti.* MARIA *and the* DUCHESS *fold up the sheet and join them as they process off-stage.* QUEVEDO *stays behind and prepares to write.*

QUEVEDO. Pablo!

PABLO (*enters*). Yes.

QUEVEDO. I want paper.

PABLO. Paper?

QUEVEDO. Reams of it. Mountains of it.

PABLO. Coming.

QUEVEDO. Cut down the forests and bring them to my desk.

PABLO. This enough?

QUEVEDO. And lakes of ink.

PABLO. Lakes?

QUEVEDO. No oceans. The wide storm tossed seas.

PABLO. Give us a minute.

QUEVEDO. And a flock of pens, Pablo, a cloud of whitened wings.

PABLO. You want pens.

QUEVEDO. Goose pens, Pablo.

PABLO. Goose pens.

QUEVEDO. Flying over the inky waters
and burying their heads in the depths
for food.
Then let them vomit on the paper to
their hearts content.

PABLO. Yes.

QUEVEDO. I'm thinking of ducks. No matter.

PABLO (*hassled*). No.

> QUEVEDO *settles down to write.* PABLO *about to strangle* QUEVEDO. *Enter* MARIA.

MARIA. How's it going?

PABLO. Terrible!

MARIA. Oh.

PABLO. People keep shouting at me.

MARIA. Oh. Poor thing.

PABLO. I can't get a minute's peace.

MARIA. Things are fine for me.

PABLO. Are they?

MARIA. The duchess is really nice.

PABLO. You watch her. She'll be up to something.

MARIA. She's not like that.

PABLO. They're all the same.

MARIA. I think I'm going to like it here.

PABLO. I know I'm going to hate it.

MARIA. Oh Pablo. It won't be for long.

PABLO. Oh won't it.

MARIA. She'll set me up. She said she would. Well, she almost
did. Just think. A place of our own. A little shop. What'll we sell?

PABLO. Fish.

MARIA. Ugh. Not fish. Something nice. Bread. I love the smell
of bread. And those sticky cakes.

PABLO. Lot of work.

MARIA. I'd stay up all night, baking. And when I got tired I'd
just look up at the stars. And when dawn came I'd give
children the pieces of hot crust and the loose ends of fresh pies.
I'd spend the morning handing out this lovely food.

We'd make love all afternoon and in the evening I'd go to sleep.

PABLO. You'd put chalk in the flour.
You'd paint the crusts brown.
You'd buy the flour cheap and you'd sell
the bread dear.
You'd drive beggars from your door with
dogs.

MARIA. Am I that cruel?

PABLO. It's not you, love. It's the world. No one's honest in the world.

MARIA. But you are.

PABLO. Me? I steal things.

MARIA. That doesn't stop you being honest.

PABLO. Doesn't stop me being poor.

MARIA. Everyone's poor.

PABLO. Except the rich.

MARIA. Everyone who matters. And (*Makes a rude noise.*) the rich.

PABLO. (*Makes a rude noise*). The rich? Na. (*Makes a ruder noise.*) them.

Both make ruder and ruder noises. QUEVEDO interrupts. He's finished his poem.

QUEVEDO. That's it. The end. It's all over.
  Human happiness? Denied.
  Marital bliss? Ridiculed.
  The joys of love? Negated.
  And in blank verse.

Rude noises from PABLO and MARIA.

QUEVEDO. Oh go away.

Exit PABLO and MARIA. QUEVEDO calls out after them.

  No more marriages. An end to fornication.
  No more births. No more squealing
  monsters.

A huge fart off-stage. Enter the DUKE.

DUKE. Quevedo! The King will see us.

QUEVEDO. But my poem.

DUKE. Your poem?

QUEVEDO. Yes my poem!

QUEVEDO. Later Quevedo.

QUEVEDO. Later?

DUKE. Don't fret. Write another. For the King.

QUEVEDO. The majesty of state?

DUKE. Yes.

QUEVEDO. The generosity of ministers?

DUKE. Of course.

QUEVEDO. The glory of the garden!

DUKE. Yes! An ode, Quevedo. An ode. As long as you like.
But don't be late.

He scatters QUEVEDO's *papers, and leaves.*

QUEVEDO (*furious*). Pablo!

Enter PABLO. QUEVEDO *bashes him with a roll of paper.*

PABLO. More paper?

QUEVEDO. I've got too much. Take it away.

PABLO (*clearing up scattered paper*). Only trying to help.

QUEVEDO. Then help me.

PABLO. What with?

QUEVEDO. I've got to praise a King.

PABLO. That's your job.

QUEVEDO. Praising marriage was bad enough. This is worse.

I don't want to do it. I'm tired.

PABLO. Then go to bed.

QUEVEDO. I can't. All I know is words. They paper over
hollow spaces.

PABLO. Then let them.

QUEVEDO, *furious is about to attack* PABLO. *Enter the* DUKE.

DUKE. The king will see us now.

They line up. Enter SECRETARY, *with papers.*

DUKE. Let me present you. The ears of the King. His
secretary. My poet.

QUEVEDO. Honoured.

SECRETARY. At your service. And this?

QUEVEDO. My squire.

SECRETARY. I see. As the King approaches you will kneel. You are not to die. Be grateful. You will remove these.

QUEVEDO (*takes off spectacles*). But I can't see without them.

SECRETARY. So much the better. The king is not to be seen. He is to be feared. You will see nothing. Hear nothing. Say nothing. You will approach in silence. You will not wish his Majesty health: that is no longer desirable. The King bears his cross with joy. He slept beside the corpse of the blessed Catherine. You will see the benefit. His stench, coming from a mortal, would be unbearable. From him it is incense. You will take pleasure in it. He comes. Withdraw.

Enter the KING. *He smells. The* DUKE *takes pleasure in it.* QUEVEDO *and* PABLO *are disgusted. They retreat and await the* SECRETARY's *orders.*

SECRETARY. Your majesty.

KING. Who are you?

SECRETARY. Your secretary.

KING. My under-secretary.

SECRETARY. Under the shadow of your majesty's might.

KING. Naturally. You have business with me?

SECRETARY. Indeed, your Majesty. The ... (*Begins to point out the* DUKE. *The* KING *forestalls him.*)

KING. The Fourth Regiment of foot?

SECRETARY (*hastily searching through his papers*). The Fifth, your Majesty means the Fifth.

KING. And what do they want?

SECRETARY. Boots sire.

KING. How dare they.

SECRETARY. They beg you. Humbly your Highness.

KING. I can hardly walk. Why should they?

SECRETARY. They are infantry.

KING. My legs rot.

SECRETARY. Your legs mature.

KING. Maggots crawl between my toes.

SECRETARY. Magnificent beasts.

KING. My confessor says I must love them.

SECRETARY. Nothing is beyond your highness's power.

KING. I tell him I try. I try, but there is so little time. The affairs of the state, leave little space for love.

SECRETARY. Indeed your Majesty. And now –

KING. Our loyal dwarfs?

SECRETARY (*looking for the document*). They beg permission to marry.

KING. Have we not dwarfs enough?

SECRETARY. The figures are not currently available.

KING. Collect them. Remit the matter to council. I trust you are not well?

SECRETARY. Indeed not, your Majesty. My chest is stuffed with phlegm.

KING. I hate to see a man in health.

SECRETARY. Your Majesty, the matter of the Duke.

KING. Which duke?

SECRETARY. Osuna.

KING. We have too many Dukes.

SECRETARY. He wants to be sent away.

KING. Oh does he?

SECRETARY. I received representations only yesterday.

KING. Did you? Hmmm. Is he fat?

SECRETARY. Quite thin.

KING. Dangerous.

SECRETARY. A man of determination and resolve.

KING. The worst of all. A menace to the state. You know my view: people are the bane of government. They continually get in the way. But since they must be tolerated let them at least be docile. Activity and independence I simply cannot stand.

SECRETARY. The world trembles at your Majesty's wrath.

KING. Good. And so. This Duke. What of him?

SECRETARY. He asks to be sent away. With his poet.

KING. There are too many poets.

SECRETARY. I was thinking of Venice.

KING. Venice ... The best assassins in Europe. The deepest dungeons. Threatened by invasion and riddled with plague. Excellent, excellent. Are the papers ready?

SECRETARY. Naturally. And the subjects await your pleasure.

KING. I have no pleasure. I have only pain.

SECRETARY *gestures to the* DUKE. *The* DUKE, QUEVEDO *and* PABLO *move toward the* KING *on their knees.*

KING. News of the dwarfs?

SECRETARY. It is the Duke, your highness.

KING. The Duke?

DUKE. At your service.

KING. The worms are getting fat.

DUKE. Indeed.

KING. What think you of Venice?

DUKE. Venice, your Majesty? Er ... the centre of Europe ... strategically vital ... menaced by the Turk ...

My poet ...

QUEVEDO. Venice. City of dreams. City of the sea ...
    A city of music and secret harmonies,
    Which glorifies in the arts of life
    And has forgotten all the arts of war.
    Where swords rust in their sheaths
    And cannons moulder in dark corners.
    Seabirds sing in the streets.
    Wine flows from the fountains.
    The prisons are empty.
    Every door is open,
    And the people have thrown away the keys.

KING. I can't find it on the map.

SECRETARY. We had it removed.

KING. Of course. It displeased us.

SECRETARY. You appreciate the position.

DUKE. Of course.

KING. Good. We appoint you governor.
Viceroy of Venice. Here are the papers.

DUKE. But it is not in our dominions.

KING. Precisely. A test for your valour. Your zeal for our
cause. We appreciate initiative.

DUKE. A chance for glory.

KING. Oh yes. Great glory.

DUKE. I accept.

KING. I will pray for your victory. (*To* SECRETARY.) To the
chapel. Conduct me. A Te Deum.

Exit KING *and* SECRETARY.

DUKE. Venice! Italy! The world! Our troubles are over. Our
glories begin.

PABLO. Was that the King?

DUKE. Of course.

PABLO. Should be different.

DUKE. What an audience! What magnificent presence! (*To*
QUEVEDO.) You seem sad.

QUEVEDO. Is this wise?

DUKE. Wisdom has nothing to do with it! This calls for
resolution. And we have it. If we are together, who can stand
against us?

Come. Together we will change the world.

Exit DUKE. QUEVEDO *follows.* PABLO *hides under a bench.*
Enter MARIA.

MARIA. What's happened?

PABLO. I've got to go.

MARIA. Where?

PABLO. I don't know. I don't want to.

MARIA. Then don't go.

PABLO. I must. I've been ordered.

Enter DUCHESS.

DUCHESS. It's worked, Maria. He's going! What's wrong?

MARIA. They're sending him away too.

DUCHESS. Oh.

Enter DUKE *and* QUEVEDO. QUEVEDO *with arms and conquistador's helmet.*

DUKE. Congratulate me.

DUCHESS. Of course.

DUKE. Now you're sad too. What's the matter with everybody?

DUCHESS. We're sad at your going.

DUKE. Yes. I know. The women stay behind.
The fate of war. Be strong.
We move to higher things.
A greater challenge. A higher glory.
Pablo!

PABLO *reluctantly crawls out from the bench, kisses* MARIA, *and falls in beside the* DUKE.

DUKE. Quevedo. We have our orders.

QUEVEDO. I want to write a poem.

DUKE. It's too late. Poetry is finished.
Words are useless. We count on action
alone. Follow me. To Venice!

They march off. DUCHESS *and* MARIA *wave goodbye.*

ACT TWO

Sea noises. QUEVEDO, PABLO *and the* DUKE *sit on one bench. A* SAILOR *stands on the other. They all rock together in the gentle swell.*

Enter PIRATES *behind a door. They push it across the front of the stage, take up position, and burst through the door with a flash and a bang. Shrieks and yells. A fierce fight.* PABLO *hides in the audience.* QUEVEDO *and the* DUKE *are captured.*

QUEVEDO. Curious failure of the intellect, this.

PIRATE. You sound rich.

QUEVEDO. I am.

PIRATE. Good.

QUEVEDO. Rich in distinction.

PIRATE. I want gold.

QUEVEDO. Why didn't you ask?

DUKE. Don't listen to him. He's a poet.

PIRATE. And who are you?

DUKE. A Duke.

PIRATE. Are you rich?

DUKE. In honour.

PIRATE. Overboard.

DUKE. Wait. You can't.

PIRATE. Want to bet?

DUKE. But I'm a Duke. You hear me? A Duke!

The DUKE *is forced to exit through the door.*

PIRATE. Search him.

QUEVEDO. You won't find anything. I'm a poet.
I have a finer gold. In here (*Points to head.*) Locked and bolted.
And you don' t have the key.

PIRATE. What's this? (*Takes off* QUEVEDO's *glasses.*)

QUEVEDO. Glasses. Give them back.

PIRATE. What are they for?

QUEVEDO. Seeing. Please.

PIRATE. Can't see a thing. Useless. (*He throws them away.*)

QUEVEDO. I can't see.

PIRATE. You don't need to.

QUEVEDO. Wait. Remember Arion.

PIRATE. Why?

QUEVEDO. He was a poet, captured by pirates off
the coast of Tyre.
They stole all he had and threw him
into the sea.
But, before they did, they granted him
one last request.
They let him play his flute.
A dolphin, who happened to be passing,
found the notes so sweet it rescued the
poet from his watery grave and carried
him home to Tyre.
He thanked the dolphin, and then, as he
walked up the beach one day, playing
his flute, suddenly at his feet he saw a heap of gold.
He looked up and there was the dolphin.
It had swum back to the ship, stove in
its planks with one lash of its furious
tail, sunk the ship, stole the gold,
and brought it back to the poet.
The music-loving beast.
And all the wicked pirates drowned.

The PIRATES *confer.*

PIRATE. You got a flute?

QUEVEDO. No.

PIRATE. No problem. Overboard.

QUEVEDO. You can't. You need me. I'm a poet!

QUEVEDO *is forced to exit through the door. The* PIRATES *find*
PABLO.

PABLO. Heard the one about the sad sea-captain?
  He always went out whaling. Wait.
  I once knew a mate of yours.
  Retired from the trade.
  Went on shore, turned respectable.
  Bought a bakery. But after two weeks
  he burnt it down. You know why?
  He wasn't happy with the pie rate.
  Do you ever laugh?

(*About to exit, changes his mind.*)

There was once a dolphin, swimming sadly
in the sea. You know what made him so
unhappy? He couldn't see a porpoise
in it.

Exit PABLO. *The pirates get the joke. They collect their weapons and
exit through the door.* QUEVEDO *and* PABLO *crawl on, gasping.*

PABLO. Lucky about the plank. Pity about the Duke.

QUEVEDO. Where are we?

PABLO. How should I know?

QUEVEDO. It smells like Venice.

PABLO. Smells like rotting fish.

QUEVEDO. Nonsense Pablo. We're there.
  Smell it. The dreaming towers.
  The golden domes.
  And what a journey!
  I must write an epic.

PABLO. Must you?

QUEVEDO. Boréas blew our battered bark . . .

PABLO. Who?

QUEVEDO. Boréas. The North Wind. Wait a minute. Boréas?
  Boréas?

  Isn't it Bóreas?

PABLO. How should I know?

QUEVEDO. When Bóreas blew our battered bark . . . This is
  serious.

PABLO. It's blowing from the south. (*Holds up finger.*) Look.

QUEVEDO. That's irrelevant. It was fierce,
it was ferocious. It blew us off course.

PABLO. But it was pirates.

QUEVEDO. Look are you the poet or am I?

PABLO. Sorry.

QUEVEDO. Now I'll have to start again.

PABLO. You can't.

QUEVEDO. And why ever not?

PABLO. No paper. No pens. No ink. No Duke.

QUEVEDO. You're right. We're stuck. What'll we do?

Enter PRIEST, *a strange and sinister figure.*

PABLO. There's someone. I'll ask.

Excuse me ...

QUEVEDO. Pablo!

PABLO. What's wrong?

QUEVEDO. We're Spaniards.

PABLO. We need help.

QUEVEDO. Aren't we supposed to be secret?

PABLO. Don't worry. I'll be secret.

QUEVEDO. At least inconspicuous.

PABLO. Excuse me is this Venice?
Venice? Venice. Venice.
V-e-n-i-s. Are you deaf?
Blind? Deaf and blind?
Do you speak Spanish?

QUEVEDO. Pablo!

PABLO. Don't worry. Go and write your poem. Leave it to me.

QUEVEDO. Alright. I will. (*Goes and sits down.*)

PABLO. Oy. You. Listen. I need help.
Help. No speak Spanish?
Italian. Italiano. Help.
I needa help. Helpa.
Helpo.

PRIEST *approaches,* PABLO *Panics.*

PABLO. Help. Help! *Help! Help!!*

PABLO *faints on the bench. Music.* PRIEST *goes over to* PABLO, *checks he's asleep, then listens to* QUEVEDO.

QUEVEDO. (*in a reverie: unaware of PRIEST*).
Peace. Peace. Nothing happens.
The secret rhythms of the sea.
The sun sinks. And then it rises.
Always knows just what to do.
Always knows. Always.
The hidden harmonies.
Always under all this nonsense of politics.

PRIEST. Quevedo. Come.

QUEVEDO. Who are you?

PRIEST. I am a watcher by the shore.

QUEVEDO. How do you know my name?

PRIEST. I seek lost travellers.

QUEVEDO. You don't know me. No one knows me.

PRIEST. Your fame has preceded you.

QUEVEDO. I'm not famous.

PRIEST. Not famous? Quevedo the poet? Quevedo the satirist?
Quevedo whose wit is a lash under which the mighty tremble?
Quevedo the man of action? Quevedo the saviour of Venice?

QUEVEDO. It's not possible.

PRIEST. It is very possible. This is Venice.

QUEVEDO. It *is* Venice. But where is my servant?

PRIEST. Taken to a place of rest.

QUEVEDO. Have I been betrayed?

PRIEST. How could you be? This is Venice. Nothing is hidden here. All is known.

QUEVEDO. Then all is lost.

PRIEST. Nothing is lost. Now come.

QUEVEDO. Don't want to go. I want to stay here. In the sun.

PRIEST. I am offering you help.

QUEVEDO. I don't need help. Everything is normal.

PRIEST. You appear to be in trouble.

QUEVEDO. A little local difficulty perhaps. But I'll manage.

PRIEST. You will sleep.

> PRIEST *looks at* QUEVEDO. *Music.* QUEVEDO *yawns, sleeps.*
> PRIEST *moves across to* PABLO.
>
> *Enter* SISTER, *with towel and basin. They quietly greet each other.*
> *The* PRIEST *moves back to beside* QUEVEDO. SISTER *begins to*
> *wash* PABLO's *feet. He wakes with a start.*

PABLO. What are you doing?

SISTER. Washing your feet.

PABLO. Don't. They're dirty.

SISTER. All the more reason to wash them.

PABLO. No one's ever washed my feet.

SISTER. Time someone did.

PABLO. You're tickling.

SISTER. There. What a fuss. Now your hands. That one first.
Now this one. Your hair needs brushing.

PABLO. Am I dreaming?

SISTER. What do you think?

PABLO. I was. I dreamt I was safe. I was taken in. I was
washed and dressed and laid to sleep.

SISTER. And so you were.

PABLO. And nothing was asked in return.

SISTER. This is Venice. Brush your hair.

PABLO. Why do you do this?

SISTER. This is what I do.

PABLO. All the time?

SISTER. Some of the time.

PABLO. Then who are you? May I ask?

SISTER. A sister.

PABLO. A nun? I know all about nuns. They're big and they're black and they beat you.

SISTER. Is that right?

PABLO. You're not like that.

SISTER. I hope not.

PABLO. But are you ... are you ..?

SISTER. Chaste? Oh yes. Very chaste.

PABLO. Not the other kind.

SISTER. Is there another kind?

PABLO. At home, yes. Nunneries are just a joke. Perhaps I shouldn't say such things.

SISTER. No, Pablo. Not ever. Not here.

PABLO. Don't go. But ... what else do you do?

SISTER. We pray. We study. We sing in the choir.

PABLO. Doesn't sound very interesting.

SISTER. Should it be?

PABLO. But don't you like it?

SISTER. It's hard. I don't sing well, and the services are very long.

PABLO. Then why did you come?

SISTER. I had nowhere else. Someone brought me.

PABLO. How can such things happen? It's wrong.

SISTER. It happens.

PABLO. Is there nowhere else?

SISTER. Nowhere.

PABLO. A lovely person like you. It's a waste. It's such a waste. And you are lovely. In every way. You are. Maybe I shouldn't say it, but you are.

SISTER. Where do you want to take me?

PABLO. I never said that.

SISTER. There's no harm in wanting.

PABLO. I can't. I'd like to, but I can't.

SISTER. No harm. It may not happen, but there's no harm.

PABLO. You're right. I want to take you out. Out of here. Out to the world.

SISTER. You know all about the world?

PABLO. I get by. But you mustn't rot in here. You mustn't. You must belong somewhere. Can't I take you?

SISTER. I lived not far from here. In a village.

PABLO. Is it nice?

SISTER. It was. I had a lover there. His name was Pablo.

PABLO. Like mine.

SISTER. He was a good man. We were going to have a child. We were happy. Then he went away.

PABLO. Why? How could he?

SISTER. He was taken. Someone had started a war. Then soldiers came. Spaniards.

PABLO. Like me.

SISTER. You burnt my village.

PABLO. I'm sorry.

SISTER. I hid, and they never found me. They were too busy killing. But they found my friend. Marcella. She was pregnant. They split open her belly and took out the baby in front of her eyes. They called it pacification. I saw it. She was still alive. She called for water, but I couldn't give her any. Then she died. After dark I ran away. They were drunk. I hid in the graveyard. I went underground, I gave birth to my baby. I bit my lip so I wouldn't scream. I cut the cord with my teeth. I had watched the midwives. He was a boy. His eyes were blue. He looked up and laughed. The soldiers moved on. They had emptied the granaries. I found some potatoes. My child no longer smiled, he was potbellied and sickly. I went to the city, they told me we'd be safe. We found somewhere, not much, off an alley. I thought things were better. The third week, the child died. Why should I have any use for the world?

Exit SISTER. PRIEST *follows.* QUEVEDO *wakes up. He sees*
PABLO *and rushes across to embrace him.*

QUEVEDO. Pablo my friend. My dear dear friend.

PABLO. I want to go home.

QUEVEDO. Listen. I've got it.

PABLO. I'm sick of this place.

QUEVEDO. The spirit of wit. The soul of poetry.

PABLO. Where have you been?

QUEVEDO. Talking with the mother.

PABLO. I never saw her.

QUEVEDO. No. No you wouldn't ...
  It's all graded you see.
  Everything has its level. You have
  yours, I have mine. Not lower, not
  higher, but ordered. Perfectly
  ordered. The old astronomy was right.
  I know what you're going to say.
  Galileo.

PABLO. Not exactly.

QUEVEDO. But he only saw. With his eyes.
  And what use are eyes? And through
  a telescope. And what's a telescope?
  A lens. A distorting lens.
  A piece of glass. Look at me. Look.
  Look. You see the change?
  I have thrown away my glasses.

PABLO. It wasn't you, it was the pirates!

QUEVEDO. Precisely. The pirates. We're so lazy,
  we have to be pushed. That's what
  pirates are for. Don't you see?
  I see better than ever! Imagine.
  Looking at the world through discs of
  glass. Ridiculous. And I never needed
  them. Never needed them at all.

PABLO. You were blind.

QUEVEDO. Precisely. Blind to the harmonies.
The inner harmonies. And deaf, yes,
you're right. Deaf too. I never saw
the web. Never saw it. And it was
left to a woman, to a woman to show me.

PABLO. You've gone mad.

QUEVEDO. No it's the world, Pablo. The world is
mad. Madness incarnate. Total chaos.
Or so it seems. But underneath is the web.
Pablo, I've seen the light.
The light of the world.
The web, the wondrous web.
Everything, Pablo. Everything is inter-
connected. Everything.
Even the most disparate of objects,
the most hopelessly contrasting events
. . . all connect. They all connect.
A puddle, Pablo, a puddle connects with
the stars.

PABLO. How?

QUEVEDO. Exactly. How? That, Pablo, that is
the point of poetry. The object of wit.
To make the connections apparent.
And the greater the disparity, the greater
the wit. Then understanding brings the
homage of laughter.

PABLO. I don't understand.

QUEVEDO. You don't understand? Pablo listen. I call you a
pen.

PABLO. A what?

QUEVEDO. A pen, Pablo. A pen. I know.
The intellect objects. You are not a pen.
You have no feathers. You have no nib.
You are not sharp, you are blunt.
Very blunt. And you do not write.
But Pablo, but: you speak. You record
events. You tell me your day has been
good. Or perhaps bad. Who cares?
You ate spaghetti. You pen. You
speaking pen. I know. The intellect

objects. Pens do not speak. Pens have
no tongues. But on paper, on paper,
Pablo, a pen can be more eloquent than
silver-tongued Cicero himself.

PABLO. Stop.

QUEVEDO. Yes. The intellect objects. A silver
tongue could not speak. But think, Pablo,
think of the worth of the spoken. And so
we speak of a ruby tongue.

PABLO. Do we.

QUEVEDO. Yes. Of course. Yours for instance.
I take it it is red. Or a golden tongue.
A tongue of diamonds.

PABLO. Shite.

QUEVEDO. Yes. 'Shite' too. We are surrounded
by metaphors. Hordes of them. They
overcrowd our wardrobes, they overflow
from drawers. They drop from the ceiling
in golden showers, and then they run
towards us wagging their dear little tails.
Oh Pablo, Pablo my dear friend, we live in
a labyrinth of connections, trapped like
flies in a web. And yet we do not
struggle, for the web upholds us, the
intellect travels free within its
boundaries, and wanders amazed in awe and
in wonder.

PABLO. But what do we do?

QUEVEDO. Do, Pablo do?

PABLO. Yes.

QUEVEDO. We lose ourselves in contemplation.

> QUEVEDO *loses himself in contemplation. Music.* PABLO *fidgets.*

PABLO. But shouldn't we be doing something? Even if it's
wrong? Things need doing.

Shouldn't we at least be conspiring?

QUEVEDO. But my dear man whatever for?

PABLO. I thought that was why we came. To save Venice.
From the Turk.

QUEVEDO. Oh, the Turk. I was forgetting. Yes, yes that was
what we said. But tomorrow. We'll do it tomorrow.

PABLO. But this is today. And we've been here for months.
And I want to go home.

QUEVEDO. You can't. You don't know the way. Don't worry.
Listen. Listen to the harmonies.

PABLO. There's a world out there.

QUEVEDO. Where?

PABLO. And what about the Duke?

QUEVEDO. The Duke?

PABLO. Yes the Duke. What if he comes? What'll he say?

Enter the DUKE. PABLO *and* QUEVEDO *fall into line.*

DUKE. What indeed, dear Pablo, what indeed? You seem
surprised.

PABLO. We are.

DUKE. And what have you been doing?

PABLO. Us?

DUKE. Of course.

PABLO. This and that.

QUEVEDO. Hearing the harmonies.

PABLO. Testing out the ground.

DUKE. I have heard nothing.

PABLO. These days you can never trust the post.

DUKE. You think I have been testing?

PABLO. Oh no.

DUKE. I have been acting.

PABLO. I'm sure.

DUKE. Shall I tell you? Sit.
I was carried by the current to a city
by the sea. A sad city.

Factions fight in the streets.
Blood spurts from the fountains.
Thieves ransack the mansions.
Law and order have both completely
disappeared. So what do I do?
I assemble an army.
It is greeted with bullets.
I return the compliment with cannons.
Having crushed criminality, I turn to the
slums. Verminous warrens where vices
breed like rabbits. I erase them.
The prisons overflow with human dregs.
I take up lead, I carry steel, and I
cleanse them. I scour the streets for
catamites and I burn them. Their fat
sizzles and spits in the gutters.
I meet like minds. I meet a man who
has killed four adulterous wives.
I make him Chief of Police.
Together we investigate.
We carry through reforms.
We find methods of interrogation both
slow and inefficient. We improve them.
Soon criminals are hanging with the ink
still wet on their confessions.
People are children. Strictness develops
them. The idle are set to work.
Beggars are banished. I find priests
preaching sedition from the pulpits.
They have forgotten the Gospel.
I cut out their tongues.
I issue a proclamation.
'Citizens of Venice', I tell them.
They tell me I am in Crete. I hang them.
My work is done. Order has been restored:
the streets are silent.
I leave Crete for Venice.
Citizens bewail my absence.
I harden my heart, I commandeer a
frigate, and hoist up every sail.
We are shipwrecked at the Lido.
A priest conducts me, I hurry here
towards you, and what do I find?
What do I find?

PABLO. Don't tell me. Let me guess.

DUKE. I find you sunk in idleness.
Submerged in sloth.
Venice totters on its axis,
With baited breath the world awaits,
And you do nothing. Nothing at all.

PABLO. Appearances are deceptive.

DUKE. They had better be.

PABLO. We've been terribly busy.

DUKE. Have you?

QUEVEDO. I have laid the foundations of a new aesthetic.

DUKE. Is that all?

QUEVEDO. Isn't it enough?

PABLO. Don't take any notice. He's joking.

DUKE. Joking?

PABLO. No I mean he's not joking. Not exactly. He knows we
cannot talk freely. There are spies everywhere.

Be patient. All will be revealed. He'll take you up to his room.

QUEVEDO. What?

PABLO. You will show his highness your room. He will be
interested.

QUEVEDO. Will he?

PABLO. Yes. Fascinated. The strategic situation.

DUKE. Very well.

PABLO. I'll join you later.

QUEVEDO. The view is splendid. The dreaming spires. The
bustle on the canal. The human comedy.

Exit QUEVEDO *and* DUKE.

PABLO. Dukes. Conspirators. Poets. What a nightmare. Who's
in charge?

Enter PRIEST.

PRIEST. May I help?

PABLO. Yes.

PRIEST. You seem concerned.

PABLO. I am. You see, there's this duke –

PRIEST. I sympathise.

PABLO. He wants a conspiracy. We don't have one. He's angry.

PRIEST. Naturally.

PABLO. And the poet's gone mad.

PRIEST. Had a vision of the truth.

PABLO. I don't see the difference.

PRIEST. Perhaps there is none. Don't worry. All will be well.

PABLO. Will it?

PRIEST. I know your needs. You want a conspiracy? You shall have one. This very night.

PABLO. You're awfully kind.

PRIEST. Think of it as Venetian hospitality. And before the conspiracy, a visit. A special one. In secret.

PABLO. He'll go for that.

PRIEST. Tonight then.

PABLO. Ay tonight.

PRIEST. By the canal. As the moon rises, the owl will hoot.

PRIEST *snaps his fingers. The lights dim. Exit* PRIEST. PABLO *is impressed. He snaps his fingers. Nothing happens. Enter* QUEVEDO *and the* DUKE.

DUKE. Are you sure this is the right canal.

QUEVEDO. Of course it's the right canal.

QUEVEDO *stays in his corner.* DUKE *goes over to* PABLO.

DUKE. Pablo. What's happened to him?

PABLO. Maybe the water.

DUKE. All he can talk about is Vitruvius. What does that mean?

PABLO. It's a bad sign.

DUKE. And spheres. Some kind of singing spheres. I told him it was just the canal. He said it was subsumed into a greater harmony. I think it's the air. Unhealthy. Of course we'll have it removed.

QUEVEDO. Pablo. What's he saying?

PABLO. He's glad to see you.

QUEVEDO. Poor man. I showed him my window. The most beautiful view in Europe. All he saw were gun emplacements.

DUKE. Pablo. He's talking about me.

PABLO. He's just admiring the view.

DUKE. There isn't a view.

PABLO. Well you know how he is.

DUKE. We used to talk so well together. The science of war. The lives of the generals. Alexander. Julius Caesar. Scipio Africanus. Me.

QUEVEDO. Pablo.

PABLO. Yes.

QUEVEDO. Look at the moon.

PABLO. Which one?

QUEVEDO. There. Look. Just there. The secret of the universe.

PABLO. You sure?

DUKE. Pablo.

PABLO. Coming.

DUKE. Where is that priest?

PRIEST. Behind you. Did I startle you?

DUKE. Not in the least.

PRIEST. Allow me to apologise.

DUKE. Certainly not. Where are the conspirators?

PRIEST. Assembling in their place and time. First we must make a journey. Through danger and darkness to the heart of power.

PRIEST *snaps his fingers. Lights go out completely.*

PABLO. We'll need some candles.

PRIEST. Of course. Allow me.

Enter SISTER, *who distributes lighted candles.*

QUEVEDO. The flickering lights of faith.

PRIEST. Naturally. Follow me.

PRIEST *takes them on a conducted tour of the stage. They crawl, skirt invisible obstacles etc. As appropriate.*

PRIEST. Take care. The doorway is low.

DUKE. The walls seem thick.

PRIEST. We are in the cellars of the palace.

DUKE. Are there any dungeons?

QUEVEDO. The prisons of the intellect.

DUKE. Your prisons are famous. I would be honoured to visit them.

PRIEST. Take care. The oubliette.

DUKE. Is it deep? (*Echo from well*: . . . eep . . . eep.)

QUEVEDO. Deep as ignorance.

PRIEST. Thirty feet.

DUKE. A bagatelle. In Madrid they are deeper.

PRIEST. The poisoned spike.

QUEVEDO. The barb of malice.

DUKE. Will it kill?

PRIEST. In fifteen seconds.

DUKE. In Madrid they are slower.

PRIEST. The strangling lasso.

DUKE. Where?

PRIEST. Under your feet. One step, there, on that stone, a rope falls and (*Strangling sound.*)

DUKE. Most interesting.

PRIEST. You don't have it in Madrid?

QUEVEDO. The stranglehold of lies?

DUKE. Not in Madrid.

PRIEST. Take care. The Ducal sewer.

DUKE (*treads on something*). Yurrccchhh. How dare it?

QUEVEDO. Outside is beauty. Filth and darkness lie within.

PRIEST. We are under the privy.

QUEVEDO. The privy council. The stench of power.

PRIEST. Almost at our destination. Ssshh. We have travelled through the perils of the path to power. And now we are there. Hide in the shadows. Don't breathe a word. Behold the Doge.

Enter MR *and* MRS DOGE, *with elaborate robes, carrying candle lanterns.*

MR DOGE. Are we almost there?

MRS DOGE. I hope so. I think I can see the bed.

MR DOGE. Why can't we have a small bedroom?

MRS DOGE. It wouldn't be right, dear, you know it wouldn't. I tell you what. We'll stop for a minute and have a little rest. Here let me loosen your buckles. There. Isn't that better?

MR DOGE. Oh what a relief. Turn round and I'll do yours. These damn fasteners. So stiff. There.

MRS DOGE. Oh that's better.

MR DOGE. My feet are sore.

MRS DOGE. Sit down and I'll give them a rub. There.

MR DOGE. Oooh. What a day.

MRS DOGE. Was it the arsenal again? You've never taken to that place.

MR DOGE. I never have and I never will and there's an end to it. But it makes no difference. I have to go. It's my duty.

MRS DOGE. You've always done your duty. There's not many as can say that.

MR DOGE. Always have and always will. Doesn't stop you wishing, though.

I've to wed the sea tomorrow.

MRS DOGE. Tomorrow is it?

MR DOGE. Same every year. Out I go, in the blazing heat, in that barge. Nothing but a painted bath tub, that's all it is. One day it's going to go straight down to the bottom with me and all the council in it. Maybe not such a bad thing, far as the Council is concerned, but I don't want it to happen to me.

MRS DOGE. Quite right dear.

MR DOGE. But no one takes a blind bit of notice.

MRS DOGE. Still you must admit it's a nice ceremony. I always like the music. They do manage them very well.

MR DOGE. That's as may be love but it's not my cup of tea. I mean I just drop a gold ring into the sea and it's meant to be my wife. Doesn't make sense. It's meant to do my bidding. Never does.

MRS DOGE. You've a point there of course.

MR DOGE. I tell them every year. And I told them today. I said look that ship is rotting on her moorings, rotting away, and that cannon is so rusty you'd think it was underwater and I promised last year to do something and what have they done? Nothing. They ignored me. So I said, can I go to my garden? But oh no. It was back to the office. Reports from the secret police. This month's victory. This time it's Crete. Plans for the celebration. Receipts for the fireworks. Year in year out. If this is greatness they can keep it.

MRS DOGE. Well all we can do is our best.

MR DOGE. If it weren't for you, I don't know how I'd manage.

MRS DOGE. No matter what, we've still got each other.

MR DOGE. Things were better in the old days.

Remember those bean stews?

MRS DOGE. Fresh from the garden.

MR DOGE. You don't get beans like that any more. They look nice and green, but they don't have the taste. If I could just have a decent patch of ground, and a couple of years to work on it.

MRS DOGE. It's no use hankering after what you can't get. We're Doges for life and we'll just have to lump it.

MR DOGE. If we could only get some sleep.

MRS DOGE. Come on, let's have a go. We've had our rest, and it can't be far to that bed now. Come on. We can take our time. Easy does it. Hold tight. That's the way . . .

Exeunt DOGES. DUKE *leaps forward.*

DUKE. This is an outrage!

PABLO. I thought it was very sad.

PRIEST. You see? He's seen it. The pathos.

DUKE. Pathos be damned. It's pathetic.

QUEVEDO. The pathetic emptiness of power.

DUKE. You and your damned cynicism.

PABLO. No, I think he's right.

DUKE. Perverting the lower orders! It's shameful. The Doge. Ruler of one of the great states of Europe! An old man. An ordinary dull old man.

PRIEST. Will you not also get old?

DUKE. I doubt it. But I might: I'll concede that, I might. But think of our king. His unquenchable dignity. His courageous defiance of disease. And that is the measure of greatness: the extent to which we overcome. Overcome our human weakness. Of course.

PRIEST, PABLO *and* QUEVEDO *blow out candles and exit.*

DUKE. And that confirms me in my purpose. To overthrow the decrepit state of Venice and replace it with the throne of Spain. The old empire will be reborn.

Where are you?

PRIEST (*a long way off-stage*). The conspirators await.

Take care. The lasso.

DUKE. The lasso? Yurchh. The sewer. One false step . . . Ah. Safe. Now what? The poisoned spike. Fifteen seconds. There. But what next? I've forgotten. The oubliette!

The candle goes out. The sound of a falling DUKE. *The* CONSPIRATORS *and the* PRIEST *rush on in darkness.*

CONSPIRATOR 3. The state is a rotten door.

DUKE. Who's that?

CONS. 4. If you don't kick it, it won't fall.

CONS. 1. It's the same with sweeping the floor.

CONS. 2. Where the broom does not reach ...

CONS. 4. The dust will not go away by itself.

CONS. 3. Are we gathered?

Light goes up on a huddle of CONSPIRATORS, *cloaked and masked, raising their daggers in a spotlight. The* PRIEST *stands apart.*

CONSPIRATORS. We are gathered.

The CONSPIRATORS *crouch down in a huddle.*

DUKE (*sees* PRIEST). What's this?

PRIEST (*motioning him back*). A conspiracy.

DUKE *withdraws.*

CONS. 3. The agenda.

CONS. 1 and 2 (*raising bottles*). Have some wine.

CONS. 3. When you have quite finished ...

CONS. 4. The agenda.

CONS. 1. A toast. Death to the Doge.

ALL. Death to the Doge.

CONS. 3. As I was saying. The condition of the people.

CONS. 2. Very grave.

CONS. 3. As the comrade says, it is very grave.

CONS. 4. The people have lost all direction. Bombarded with an incessant barrage of lies, conditioned for work –

CONS. 3. Which is denied them.

CONS. 2. Yes.

CONS. 4. Without direction or hope they drift into prostitution and crime.

CONS. 1. Yes. Into crime.

CONS. 4. What then, in this grave situation, is the next step?

CONS. 2. What is it?

CONS. 4. The answer is clear. Re-education.

CONS. 3. I disagree.

CONS. 4. What?

CONS. 3. The priority must lie with the provision of work.

CONS. 4. I say education!

CONS. 3. You used to say work!

CONS. 4. Yes, but I meant *work!*

CONS. 1. But comrades who wants to work?

CONS. 2. Absolutely.

The CONSPIRATORS *confer together. The* DUKE, *dissatisfied, addresses* PRIEST.

DUKE. This is meant to be a conspiracy.

PRIEST. It is.

DUKE. It's a tea party. A talking shop. Isn't it time for action?

PRIEST *taps* CONSPIRATOR 3 *on the shoulder.*

CONS. 3 (*to* DUKE). The situation is complex. It has to be correctly analysed.

The DUKE *still dissatisfied, takes* CONSPIRATOR 3 *confidentially off to one side.*

DUKE. Analysed? This is no time for analysis. We must *do* something. What do you propose?

CONS. 3 (*returns to others, raises dagger*). Death to the Doge!

CONS. 1. An end to oppression!

CONS. 2. A true republic!

CONS. 4. Peace and justice!

CONSPIRATORS *drop back into a huddle.*

DUKE (*to* PRIEST). You fool! Took me to the wrong conspiracy. I don't want peace. I don't want justice. I want the rule of law.

The CONSPIRATORS *look up.*

CONS. 3. A Spaniard!

DUKE. Yes, a Spaniard. And proud.

CONS. 4. The ageing empire.

CONS. 3. The most backward state in Europe.

DUKE. The most advanced. The leader of the world.

CONS. 2. Yeah?

DUKE. Yes. We are not backward. We invented the stirrup.

CONSPIRATORS *laugh derisively.*

DUKE. The aqueduct. The cathedral.

CONS. 4. The inquisition and the stake.

DUKE. We are Christian, yes.

CONS. 3. (*to* PRIEST). I think we should kill him.

CONS. 4. Re-educate him.

DUKE. I'd rather die.

You talkers. You dabblers in shopworn theories. You cowards. You think life is just a matter of debate. Some kind of sick joke.

CONS. 3. I take life very seriously indeed. And I will take great pleasure in ending yours.

DUKE. That's all you're good for. But I tell you I have changed the world.

PRIEST. And do you like it any better?

DUKE. That's not the point. I have stamped my mark on the world. I have won victories. I have conquered cities.

CONS. 1 (*to* PRIEST). He killed my son.

CONS. 2. He burnt my crops.

CONS. 3. He poisoned my wells.

CONS. 4. He tortured my friend.

DUKE. I did what I had to. It was nothing personal. I did my duty and now I defy you.

CONSPIRATORS *advance on the* DUKE. PRIEST *holds them back.*

PRIEST. Wait.

DUKE. What for?

PRIEST. Wait for you to change.

DUKE. You want repentance? Reformation? You're too late. I will never change. I will hold firm to the very end. Firm and resolute.

CONS. 1. Stupid. (*Exit.*)

CONS. 2. Predictable. (*Exit.*)

CONS. 3. Tedious. (*Exit.*)

CONS. 4. Cruel. (*Exit.*)

DUKE *advances on* PRIEST.

PRIEST. Go away.

PRIEST *looks at* DUKE. DUKE *slowly retreats. As he does, enter* PABLO *and* QUEVEDO, *as if pulled on by invisible thread.*

DUKE. (*to* QUEVEDO). I blame you for this.
I shouldn't have listened to you.
Should never have set foot in Venice.
Why didn't I stay where I was?
Taking decisions.
Implementing clear cut policies.
In the daylight.
Under the harsh sun.
And then I left it all,
And entered your damn world of shadows.
Why did I do it? Why did I need you?
But I won't die. You'll see.
You can't kill me.
I won't die. I won't die.

Exit DUKE.

PRIEST. Did you see? Aren't you glad. Well? You wanted rid of him, didn't you? And now he's gone. Celebrate. What's the matter with you?

PABLO. But you can't get rid of him that easily.

PRIEST. But I have.

PABLO. He'll come back.

PRIEST. Then let him.

QUEVEDO. My man is right. We should not rejoice. Nothing has been won.

PRIEST. Nothing has been lost.

QUEVEDO. But he will come back. He will.

PRIEST. If he must then let him. For now he's gone. Celebrate.

QUEVEDO. Celebrate?

Music and laughter off-stage.

PRIEST. Yes.

PABLO. You're joking.

Enter MUSICIAN *and ex-*CONSPIRATORS, *without their masks.*

PRIEST. Don't begrudge us our little celebration.
You must allow us our little festivals.
You remember the story our teacher told.
Of the wise man who built his house upon
the rock and the foolish one who built
his on the sand? We built ours on the mud.
We compromised.
And now we are sinking.
Year by year the cracks widen in our
foundations
Year by year the tide water rises.
Already it has flooded our cellars;
Soon it will beat against our doors.
Then the waves will come and wash us
from the face of the earth.
The clouds gather. The storm is rising.
And it will come. Nothing can stop it.
We know. We laugh when we can;
we live, as we must.
Fear eats away our hearts. Will it spare us,
We wonder, will it spare our children?
Yet what can we do? Tear down our city?
Label the stones and move them, stone by stone,
Rebuild them on the higher ground?
All our energy is taken up with living.
Besides, is there any mountain high enough
to hide us,
Is there depth enough in any cave?
I doubt it. Crying is easy, Quevedo,
Laughter requires a little more strength.

The MUSICIAN *starts to play, quietly at first. He and the others move across the stage.* PABLO *hesitates, then goes to join them. They greet him. Music and laughter as they leave. We continue to hear them off-stage. The* PRIEST *waits for* QUEVEDO.

PRIEST. Come. Or it will all be over.

QUEVEDO. Is theology a kind of dancing?

PRIEST. A very special kind.

QUEVEDO. I don't know how. Teach me.

PRIEST *and* QUEVEDO *exit together. Light drains from the stage. Off-stage a door slams, and the party is over. The light turns bright and harsh.*

QUEVEDO *and* PABLO *are coming back on stage.* PABLO *with cases. They are wearing each other's hats. They squint a bit blearily at the light. They exchange hats.* QUEVEDO *takes out his glasses and tries them on. Then he holds them up and puts them away again. He doesn't need them.* PABLO *takes a swig from a bottle and has a good look round.*

PABLO. Well, we're back. Madrid hasn't changed.

A WOMAN *comes on with a parcel.*

WOMAN. Are you Pablo?

PABLO. Yes.

WOMAN. Something for you.

PABLO. For me? What is it?

WOMAN. You'd better sign for it.

PABLO (*signing*). Right. But what is it?

The WOMAN *goes.* PABLO *unwraps the parcel.*

PABLO (*dismayed*). It's a baby! Someone's given me a baby!

MARIA (*enters*). Pablo!

PABLO *tries to hide the baby. Then he understands.*

PABLO. Maria! Is this –

MARIA. Ours.

They have a big hug. QUEVEDO *smiles benevolently.*

PABLO. He's lovely.

MARIA. She is, isn't she?

PABLO. Oh it's a girl. She's beautiful. She's got your eyes.

MARIA. Poor thing. She's got your nose.

They have another cuddle. Enter DUCHESS.

DUCHESS (*to* QUEVEDO). You're back. You've changed.

QUEVEDO. So have you.

MARIA. What's it like in Venice?

PABLO (*with baby*). Amazing. They have great parties.

QUEVEDO. I've got presents.

He opens first case, which is full of scarfs and silks.

It all comes from China. Across the desert. By camel.

Great excitement. Opens second case.

And there's perfume. And. Best of all.

He opens the third case.

Books. From the new presses. And.

He takes out parcels.

(*To* MARIA.) That's for you. And that's for the baby.

MARIA. But how did you know?

QUEVEDO. I guessed. Poetic intuition.

He carefully hands a third parcel to the DUCHESS.

And that's for you.

DUCHESS. Is it fragile?

Enter the DUKE.

DUKE. I'm back!

DUCHESS *drops her parcel. A sound of breaking glass. A deathly hush.*

DUKE. Aren't you pleased to see me?

PABLO. We'd better be going.

They start to pack up all the presents.

DUKE. But I saved Venice.

QUEVEDO (*politely*). Did you?

DUKE. Yes. I fought a horde of pirates. I defied the Doge. I masterminded a conspiracy. I conquered Crete. Where are you going?

The others are beginning to drift off-stage.

DUCHESS. Home. It's time to go home.

DUKE. But we must celebrate. A banquet.

DUCHESS. I'm sorry. We had to sell the gold plate. (*Exits.*)

DUKE. Can't we have some music?

MARIA. We sent the orchestra home. (*Exit with* PABLO.)

DUKE. But we must have something. Quevedo this calls for an epic. In rhyming couplets.

QUEVEDO. I'm sorry. I've got another commission. (*Exits.*)

PABLO *briefly re-enters, still cuddling the baby.*

DUKE. Pablo!

PABLO. Ssssshhh. You'll wake the baby. (*Exits.*)

DUKE. But I saved Venice! We must celebrate. I saved Venice! Doesn't that mean something? Doesn't it?

The light fades.

The play ends.

ANN MARIE DI MAMBRO was born in 1950 and went to
Glasgow University, Girton College, Cambridge and Bolton
College of Education, before becoming a teacher. Her stage plays
include *Hocus Pocus* (Annexe Theatre Company, 1986), *Dixon's
Has Blasted*, (a community play, Glasgow Mayfest, 1987), *Joe* (a
one-woman play produced by Annexe Theatre at the Traverse,
Edinburgh 1987), *Visible Differences* (toured to schools by
TAG – Theatre Around Glasgow – in 1988), *Sheila*, (Traverse,
1988; toured, 1989; radio, 1989) and *The Letter-Box*, which
formed part of *Long Story Short*, (toured by 7:84 Scottish People's
Theatre in 1989). For Scottish Television she has written two
plays for *Dramarama*, many episodes for the twice-weekly drama
series, *Take the High Road,* and two of the three parts of *Winners
and Losers*.

From February 1989-1990 she was Writer-in Residence at the
Traverse under Thames TV's Writer's Bursary Scheme. At the
time of going to press, she has commissions from both the
Traverse and Cumbernauld Theatres; *Tally's Blood,*
commissioned by the Traverse Theatre, toured Scotland in
February 1990 and Hamilton District Council have
commissioned her to do a large-scale community project.

The Letter-Box was commissioned by 7:84 Scottish Peoples'
Theatre as part of *Long Story Short: Voices of Today's Scotland*, and
first performed at Isle of Skye on 28 February 1989 at Sabhal
Mor Ostaig, with the following cast:

MARTHA   Anne Marie Timoney
JACK   Vincent Friell
JILL   Patricia Ross

Directed by Finlay Welsh
Designed by Colin MacNeil
Lighting by Alastair McArthur

A door, with a letter box in the centre.
Spotlight follows a pair of lovers (JACK and JILL, say) – smoochy,
giggly, on way to JILL's flat.

JACK. How many more flights?

JILL. Why? Can't you wait?

They stop as when they see her there, slouched against the door, head
drooping, semi-conscious.

JACK puts his arm protectively round JILL's shoulder and turns her
away from the sight.

JACK. Come on, don't look.

They turn their backs and walk away, more subdued, but their high
spirits return before they disappear completely.

Spotlight stays on MARTHA.

She moves uncomfortably as if in pain: she looks round about,
disoriented, as if trying to locate a sound: she comes to slowly:

MARTHA. What? . . . Who's that?

Pulls herself up, with difficulty, against the door, directing her voice to
the letter box, as she does throughout.

Is that you, Wendy? . . . Yes, I'm still here . . . I'm alright,
love, you're not to worry . . . No, I'm alright I said. So get
back to bed, eh? It's the middle of the night . . . You what?
. . . Oh don't worry about it. Just take off the wet sheet and
I'll see to it in the morning . . . I know. I know, angel. Go get
yourself a wee shawl or something. Keep yourself warm. It's a
cold cold night . . . No I'm alright, I don't feel it . . . No on
you go. You know where to find one?

Pause as she goes: MARTHA shifts position, wincing. Spits in her
hanky, moves her jaw around, feels inside her mouth, moves closer to the
letter box: she reaches up and opens it: whispers urgently into it:

Wendy, Wendy, try not and make a noise hen, whatever you
do – there's a good girl . . . The bottom shelf. Ssshhh. Is that
you? Sssh . . . Good. Where is he anyway? . . . Oh thank God
. . . No, no, don't wake him. Just leave him . . . I said leave

him. Let him sleep. Please hen . . . No I'm fine here. Honest.
I know you can't reach, doll. Don't worry. He'll let me back
in in the morning. He always does. Anyway, I'm alright here
. . . Oh don't cry, Wendy, please, it'll be alright.

Listen hen – you've not to let all this bother you. Me and your
dad – well, we were just having a bit of fun. It just got a wee
bit out of hand . . . Yes, darling, like the last time . . . No,
love, he wasn't hitting Mummy. I don't want you to think he
was hitting Mummy . . . He wasn't really mad at me, not
really. He was just . . . just tickling me – that's right, tickling
me – for fun. Then he got a wee bit too rough . . . Yes I
suppose he did hurt me a wee bit . . . A wee bit sore, yes. But
he didn't mean it . . . Please don't cry, don't cry, Wendy. It's
not your fault. It was Mummy he was mad at not you.

Now get to bed, eh? You've got school tomorrow . . . Don't
worry about it. I'll clear it all up in the morning . . . He didn't
did he? . . . Yes, I liked that vase too. But it was an accident,
hen. Mummy bumped into it when she fell . . . What's your
Grannie Baillie got to do with it? . . . Oh yes, I forgot, she gave
you it, didn't she? . . . Well, tell her it was an accident . . .
(*Rising panic*.) No, don't tell Grannie Baillie about Dad. Do you
hear? You can't. She'll only worry. She's too old for all that
worry. Or she might even get on to your dad and that will just
make him mad again. Please, hen, please. You don't tell people
these things. It'll be our secret, OK. I'll get you another one.

You not frozen, Wendy? Let me tell you something. Your
daddy loves us. I know sometimes maybe it's hard to
believe – but he does love us . . . Well these things happen. It's
just the way men are. They expect a lot of you, angel . . .
You'll understand it when you're older . . . I don't know why
he does it. It's not as if he was drunk this time. I think maybe
he just has bad days. He's got a lot on his mind. Maybe when
he was out tonight something made him mad, then when
Mum burnt the toast it just set him off.

What – what is it? . . . What is it? . . . Blood? Where? . . .
Ssshhh, keep your voice down. Don't worry, Wendy, don't
worry. I'm alright . . . I'm alright I said . . . Yes, it must be
Mummy's. But I'm not bleeding much. It's not as bad as it
looks. It's just a big scratch that's all. It must have been when
that vase got broken. I'll clean it up tomorrow hen . . . No, just
you leave it. Leave it for now . . . I just don't want you making a
noise in case you wake him . . . Because he needs his sleep.

How can you help me, Wendy, you'll be at
She's nice your teacher, I know. Miss Graha
remember your mum used to be pretty too ..
always crying. I'm not ... Well Miss Graham
It's easy for her to be pretty ... what do you n
newsbook? ... You've got to write what? ... O
No, hen, no. Don't write about this – please hen.
know what you'd be doing. You're meant to put n......ngs in
that ... Oh I don't know. What you had for your dinner –
What you watched on TV – stuff like that ... I'm not crying.
I'm not. If you tell your teacher hen – do you know what she'll
do. She'll tell the other teachers and they'll all think your
mother's a terrible woman ... I don't care what the
policeman told your class – or what anybody asks you – you tell
them nothing. You got that? Or they'll come and take you
away. Give you to strangers. You want that, do you? You'd
never see your mum and dad again and then your mum would
be crying every single day for the rest of her life. You want
that? ... OK hen, stop crying, I didn't mean to make you
cry. I just love you so much – I love you so much and I'm so
so frightened ... Right I'll stop. I promise I'll stop. I'll not
cry any more if you promise not to tell your teacher ... You
promise? ... You promise? There's a good girl. There's my
good, good girl.

You're your mum's wee pal, aren't you? You're all I've got.
Somehow, someday, Wendy, I'll make this up to you. I
promise you. I know you've seen things – you've seen
things – (*Breaks off, shivers.*) are you not frozen, angel?

What's that? ... Yes, I know it would be nice, but where
could we go, eh? This is our house. Anyway, he would just
come after Mummy and it would make him so mad. No
matter where we went, he'd find us. He's told me that. And if
he ever did – well – it won't come to that.

No, Wendy, we'll be alright. So long as I've got you and
you're OK then I'm happy. I'll try not to let it happen again.
We'll put this behind us, eh? Tomorrow I'll clear up the
mess – and try to be nicer to your dad. Maybe when he sees
your mum's face – he'll be sorry and he'll change. And I'll try
harder too. And so can you. We'll try together eh, me and
you.

You're alright now, love, eh? What about going to bed, get
some sleep ... What are you frightened of? ... Did you get

shawl? ... Well alright then, come on, wrap up
ight – give me your hand – there we go. We'll be like two
tumshies. There ... What wee song is that? ... What now?
... Right, right, OK if you promise to go to sleep. It's a long
time since I sang you that wee song.

Alright.

> Jesus bids us shine with a pure clear light,
> Like a little candle burning in the night,
> In a world of darkness see how we shine,
> You in your small corner and me in mine.

Now, go to sleep, Wendy, go to sleep.

Hand through the letter box, head against the door, she drops off.

JACK rushes past on his way out, hurriedly pulling on his jacket, he stops at the sight of her and shakes his head in disgust.

JACK. Pissed!

He walks away.

The End

CHRIS HANNAN was born in Glasgow in 1958. Apart from *Elizabeth Gordon Quinn* (1985), his plays include *Klimkov: Life of a Tsarist Agent* (1984) and *The Orphans' Comedy* (1986). All of these were first produced at the Traverse Theatre, Edinburgh. At the time of going to press, he is working on a play for the Bush Theatre, London called *The Dark Hope*, and one for the Tron, Glasgow, called *The Wailers*.

A SERIOUS MELODRAMA

Author's Note

The play is set in Glasgow, 1915.

The Quinn household is squalid. The floor is laid with newspapers. Instead of lifting the newspapers when they get damp and dirty, fresh newspapers are simply laid over the old ones. The most important thing in their small house is a piano which, however, has become a part of the squalor. On top of it are sheet music, unwashed dishes, a Sacred Heart statue, books etc.

The Quinns are of course exotics – their language and their selves are fantastic and extreme. But the orotundity of their language is about the energy and imagination required to divert from the actual poverty. This tension is also true of their characters – an element in the grandiose manner of Elizabeth is her personal filth. (I see her as being filthy but presentable!)

In spite of the Quinns' pretensions it is their neighbours who are the more respectable. Clean, hardworking, employed as shipyard-workers at a time of high demand and with a tradition of good union organisation – they are nevertheless people who are not far from poverty. That is, they are well off now but can't afford to take this for granted.

It's important that the Quinns' accents aren't markedly different from those around them. This is to do with how we look at them: perspective. We shouldn't for example take Mrs Quinn more or less seriously than Mrs Black: they are of the same class and are in analogous situations, and it's because they have so much in common that Mrs Black is a perpetual point of embarrassment to Elizabeth. Or again – when the shipyard workers come with the piano the additional irritation for Elizabeth is that Brogan and McCorquindale are more cultured than she is, not less so. I'm talking here of course not about the accents themselves but what should inform the accents.

Elizabeth Gordon Quinn was first performed at the Traverse Theatre, Edinburgh on 29 June 1985, with the following cast: –

A SPECIAL BRANCH OFFICER	Bernard Doherty
ELIZABETH GORDON QUINN	Eileen Nicholas
WILLIAM QUINN, her husband	Ralph Riach
AIDAN QUINN, her son	Duncan Bell
MAURA QUINN, her daughter	Frances Lonergan
MRS BLACK	Carol Ann Crawford
MRS SHAW	Irene MacDougall
SHERRIFF'S OFFICER	Duncan Bell
DOLAN	Simon Donald
DOOLAN	Bernard Doherty
BROGAN	Bernard Doherty
McCORQUINDALE	Simon Donald
SERGEANT	Bernard Doherty
PRIVATE	Simon Donald

Directed by Stephen Unwin
Designed by Dermot Hayes
Lighting and sound by George Tarbuck

PART ONE

Scene One

WILLIAM *and* ELIZABETH *are doing nothing. Then – out of boredom – * ELIZABETH *goes to the piano and tries to get a tune out of it.* WILLIAM *is very aware of all this. There is a knock at the door and* WILLIAM *answers it.*

OFFICER. Special Branch.

ELIZABETH *stops playing the piano.*

ELIZABETH. Please come in, officer. This is indeed an honour! If we can be of any assistance to the country in this time of war we will be only too glad. I apologise for the floor. We've been terribly preoccupied or else we'd have laid *fresh* newspapers.

OFFICER. Don't apologise. These are my working shoes. I had heard some reports of Glasgow and expected to find filth of this kind, at least in the streets.

ELIZABETH. This is my husband.

WILLIAM. William. William Quinn.

ELIZABETH. Mr Quinn is a civil servant.

WILLIAM. Yes. That is, was. Formerly. I was a civil servant. May I have your coat?

OFFICER. No!

WILLIAM. We do of course have a coatstand. Naturally!

OFFICER. I would not deny it, Mr Quinn. However, I am here under protest as it is and the circumstances of my visit are so squalid that I frankly don't wish to give you my coat, even briefly.

Pause.

You have a son. Aidan Quinn. He volunteered for service with the 6th Royal Munsters, currently seeing action in the Dardanelles.

ELIZABETH. Yes.

OFFICER. He's deserted. It's something of a joke. He deserted in Dublin when his regiment was still some distance from the front. Indeed it had yet to embark. Since then he has disappeared. Normally deserters turn up after a week or less – when they get hungry in fact. Yet your son has – miraculously! – disappeared. The least ridiculous hypothesis is that he's dead.

ELIZABETH. No!

OFFICER. Unless of course he doesn't eat.

WILLIAM. I'm sure our son will turn up, officer.

Pause.

The OFFICER *takes a look at the piano on top of which amongst other things is a Sacred Heart statue.*

OFFICER. I see you are Catholics.

WILLIAM. Yes.

OFFICER. What Irish connections do you have Mr Quinn?

WILLIAM. None.

OFFICER. You're not of Irish origin?

WILLIAM. No doubt we Quinns were Irish once but we are much intermingled by this day and age. I'm far from being an immigrant.

OFFICER. Mrs Quinn?

WILLIAM. My wife's maiden name is Gordon, you understand. Elizabeth Gordon Quinn.

ELIZABETH. Not all Catholics in Scotland are of Irish origin, officer. The Gordons are Scots Catholics, as are some of our finest and oldest families. You will have heard of the Crichton-Stuarts, personal and, I might add, very dear friends of mine. That is how far I am from being Irish. Naturally I despise the Irish as filthy progenitors of filthy offspring in filthy circumstances.

OFFICER. Yet of all the regiments in the British army your son joined the Royal Munsters. An Irish regiment. Why? He must have known of your unusual antipathy.

ELIZABETH. Yes.

OFFICER. So he despised your feelings. He joined an Irish regiment to spite his mother and for no other reason? (*Slight pause.*) He might have been marching away to his death!

ELIZABETH. In any case I no longer want to discuss the matter. I simply refuse to accept that my son is a deserter.

OFFICER. How very patriotic of you.

ELIZABETH. And I resent the way in which you have come into my house and questioned me! I am a loyal British subject and, I may say, in this part of the city I am almost alone in that!

Slight pause.

OFFICER. In this tenement you are of course very adjacent to the notorious shipyards.

ELIZABETH. And we hear criticism of the government which is unmusical in the extreme.

WILLIAM. Yes! Strikingly discordant.

ELIZABETH. Take prices, for example. In my experience the working-class is only capable of perceiving a *rise* in prices.

WILLIAM. Though prices have not in fact fallen. Naturally! This is of course due to excessive shipping costs.

ELIZABETH. The most important thing is that they are our prices. British prices!

OFFICER. Stop – this is all nonsense. That is, it may or may not be true that the working-class here is particularly rabid, but I have no desire to stay in Glasgow longer than it takes me to make up my mind about you, and your son. As I remarked earlier, the least ridiculous hypothesis is that your son is dead. The next least ridiculous is that he is being harboured – either by family connections, or Fenian ones. No? – In that case I'll leave you with your dirt. Except to say, harbouring deserters is a crime. Some of us no longer have sons to harbour . . . except in our hearts.

The officer goes.

ELIZABETH (*to* WILLIAM). Please don't say anything! And don't ask me where I'm going. I'm going for a walk! (*She goes out.*)

Scene Two

WILLIAM *is holding a letter informing him of the forthcoming increases in rent. He is very anxious.* ELIZABETH *comes in with flowers.*

ELIZABETH. Hot – it's breathless! I've never known a summer extend itself to this extent.

WILLIAM. Elizabeth.

ELIZABETH. I bought some flowers. So refreshing – you could wash your face in them. They're like eager hearts.

WILLIAM. We got a letter.

ELIZABETH. Received. 'Got' is not a word. At least not in English. Aren't these lovely?

WILLIAM. Rent increases.

ELIZABETH. Where will I put them? On top of the piano? Yes. They'll make the whole room resound.

WILLIAM. We're in arrears as it is. We're in arrears as it is!

ELIZABETH. Don't be dramatical, William. You're such an amateur.

WILLIAM. No. We're not in arrears. I imagined we were but we're not. I was only being dramatical.

ELIZABETH. Your voice, William – you are not being strangled.

WILLIAM. I simply want to understand why it has all become so unmanageable. I agree I no longer have a position. I no longer have a position I agree. But that is no reason for us to continue living as if I did! (*Pause. Tentatively.*) Elizabeth.

ELIZABETH. Please do not adopt that tone. You adopt that tone of appeasement when you're about to raise something unpleasant.

WILLIAM. If I adopt a tone, it's because you make it impossible to discuss anything.

ELIZABETH. What, for example?

WILLIAM. You know what! The piano – the unmentionable.

ELIZABETH. We have discussed the piano interminably.

WILLIAM. Discussed, yes.

ELIZABETH. Yet you roundly asserted almost in your last sentence that it was impossible for us to discuss anything.

WILLIAM. Look at it! It's still here – the animal. Look at the size of it. I don't know how we got it in here.

ELIZABETH. Manoeuvred.

WILLIAM. Manoeuvred. I can't describe the panic I feel when I look at it. I look at it and I – completely! – panic.

ELIZABETH. Don't look at it then.

WILLIAM. Then I think about it even more. I keep expecting it to back into me and stamp on my foot.

ELIZABETH. You're a clown, William. Anyone would think you were trying to say something, yet tomorrow you won't remember a thing you've said. If you're saying anything at all you are simply agreeing with me that the house is too small. I don't have room to take a deep breath! In my opinion, what makes everything so unmanageable is that we can't escape from it, with the result we are completely overcrowded!

MRS BLACK *comes in.*

MRS BLACK. Oh Mrs Quinn – did I interrupt you? I'm in a terrible state, I don't know where I am.

WILLIAM. Mrs Black. Has anything happened?

MRS BLACK. Has something got to happen before a woman can visit her neighbours?

WILLIAM. No – of course.

MRS BLACK. I'm after forgetting what I came for now! How's your son, Mrs Quinn – no news? It's the silence that's dreadful, the way the papers go quiet whenever there's a major new offensive. Only a mother can know what it feels like to be separated from her son.

WILLIAM. Your son's still missing then?

MRS BLACK. What a tragedy! First we get word he's been wounded in France and he's being sent to hospital in England. Then nothing. I don't understand it – how can you lose a soldier? He was a stretcher-case, it's not as if he could walk off.

WILLIAM. I'm sure your son isn't missing as such, Mrs Black. That is, it's his papers which are missing. As a former civil

servant I can assure you that he has most likely been
mislaid – administratively.

MRS BLACK. They can't find him! And Mr Black blames me,
says I can't put a thing in the right place. As if it's my fault!
No wonder I'm going daft, with the things going on around
me I wouldn't want to be in my right mind, would I?

MRS SHAW *has come on. She is carrying Union Jacks and a round-
robin letter. She's wearing her Sunday best, and looks impressive,
Presbyterian.*

MRS SHAW. That depends on whether or not you're already
beaten Mrs Black.

WILLIAM. Mrs Shaw!

MRS BLACK. That's what I came to tell you – that Mrs Shaw
was going round everyone in the tenement asking them to sign
a protest.

MRS SHAW. The door was open, Mrs Quinn.

ELIZABETH. Please come in, Mrs Shaw. This is a tenement
after all. We have no alternative but to enter into the spirit of
it.

MRS SHAW. You'll have received a letter regarding the rent
increases.

MRS BLACK. Will I go? I don't want to intrude on the privacy
of others.

MRS SHAW. You will both have received the same letter, Mrs
Black. The rents aren't worked out on an individual basis. The
increase is ten per cent for everyone.

MRS BLACK. Excuse me!

ELIZABETH. I believe we have 'received' a letter, as you put
it. However, I think more of myself than to discuss my affairs
in public. And after all, Mrs Shaw, prices are apt to go up
from time to time as well as down. This is to do with the
economic climate.

MRS SHAW. I haven't come to discuss the weather, Mrs
Quinn. The Tenants' Defence Committee is asking all those
affected by the increases to withhold rent. So far over a
hundred women have signed this letter which the Committee
will send on to the factor, indicating that the proposed

increases are not mutually agreed to. All those who intend withholding rent will be asked to post Union Jacks in their windows beside a 'WE ARE NOT REMOVING' bill.

Pause.

WILLIAM. You want to abolish rent? I don't say it's not appealing, Mrs Shaw ... but supply and demand, supply and demand. There's a shortage of housing.

MRS SHAW. Yes. And now that they've packed us in like shells in cases they think they can ask for whatever rent suits them.

WILLIAM. We cannot simply stop paying rent. There are laws. We could not hope. That is, 'we' plural. 'We', all of us. Could not hope!

MRS SHAW. Mrs Black. Will you sign?

MRS BLACK. I don't know Mrs Shaw. With all this talk about prices I'm splitting in two down the middle. I'm a loyalist!

MRS SHAW. Of course, Mrs Black, I understand that, I would never ask anyone to be disloyal. As I see it, there's two wars going on, that's all. And in this war it's the landlords who are the Huns.

MRS BLACK. And is one war not enough for you you have to be starting another? I'm very sorry, Mrs Shaw, but I don't want to get myself all back to front – my son went away to fight for that flag!

MRS SHAW. The landlords have evicted the wives and mothers of servicemen too, Mrs Black.

MRS BLACK. That is neither here nor there! And as a loyalist I am not going to stand here believing this that and the next thing. So – let that be the end of it.

MRS SHAW. Mrs Quinn?

ELIZABETH. In my opinion your scheme somehow contrives to be both grandiose and squalid at the same time. Furthermore I have no arrears currently and I have no intentions of incurring any. Does that indicate my position adequately? I have a right as an individual and a free British subject to pay rent if I so choose. And I do not expect to be intimidated on the subject!

There is a loud knocking at the door.

MRS BLACK. Oh Mrs Quinn! Who can that be? It must be the police. It can't be. But who else would knock like that?

More knocking at the door.

MRS BLACK. The police knock like that – like it's three o'clock in the morning and they've got to get you up.

The SHERIFF'S OFFICER *comes on, with two workmen in brown khaki overcoats –* DOLAN *and* DOOLAN.

SHERIFF'S OFFICER. Mr Quinn?

WILLIAM. Yes?

SHERIFF'S OFFICER. I'm the Sheriff's Officer. The court has granted the factor of the property a warrant of sequestration which I have been appointed to execute. This warrant of sequestration gives me the authority, if you would be so good, to seize any and all belongings, in this case *all*, belongings appertaining to the household.

DOLAN. Hereinafter known as the *invecta et illata*. The belongings, that is.

SHERIFF'S OFFICER. Which will then be held as security in respect of rent owing, interest on rent owing and current rent.

DOLAN. Plus, of course, expenses occurred by the actual sequestration. I simply want to inform you of the facts.

SHERIFF'S OFFICER. Dolan.

DOLAN. Yes?

SHERIFF'S OFFICER. Enough.

DOLAN *and* DOOLAN *begin to remove whatever there is to remove – stacks of plates, cutlery, whatever.*

MRS SHAW. I'll be going now then, Mrs Quinn. I've seen enough of these. And anyway, you'll be shocked right now.

MRS SHAW *goes.*

WILLIAM. I question the whole legality of this. We're in arrears, I admit. I don't know by how much – the exact sum is immaterial. It can't entitle you to walk in here as if you would open every drawer in the house.

The SHERIFF'S OFFICER *is more or less oblivious to all this. He is by now considering a photograph of* ELIZABETH *with her original family.*

SHERIFF'S OFFICER. So – this is very impressive.

WILLIAM. I forbid you to take something as personal as a photograph.

DOLAN. If I may say so, mister, the factor's rights of hypothec can be attached to anything in the house other than, in point of fact, personal clothing.

MRS BLACK (*shocked*). I beg your pardon!

WILLIAM. There are items which are more personal than clothing.

DOLAN. I'm simply informing you of the law, Mr Quinn. I study law at night-school. I want to better myself.

SHERIFF'S OFFICER. Dolan. What colour is your overcoat?

DOLAN. Khaki.

SHERIFF'S OFFICER. And why pray is it a dirty colour like khaki?

DOLAN. Because moving furniture is a dirty job.

SHERIFF'S OFFICER. Which you do in order that I can look good and do the big words. Agreed?

DOLAN (*to Quinn*). Just because I know more law than he does! In this case for example I'd surmise that the court will have declared you *vergens ad inopiam* and will have granted a warrant on presentation of the factor's *ex parte* statement. I go to night-school!

SHERIFF'S OFFICER. Dolan. Get dirty?

Pause.

So – this is your wife's own family?

WILLIAM. Yes.

SHERIFF'S OFFICER. It's a fine-looking family. You must have opened your mouth slightly as the photograph was taken, Mrs Quinn. It has blurred.

ELIZABETH. Give that to me.

SHERIFF'S OFFICER. The effect is bewitching.

WILLIAM. I fell in love with the photograph almost as much as with the real thing.

SHERIFF'S OFFICER. Your father is a striking man, Mrs Quinn.

WILLIAM. We always say you might take him for a hussar, almost.

SHERIFF'S OFFICER. No 'almost', Mr Quinn. No 'almost'. And what in fact was he?

WILLIAM. He was employed by the Corporation.

ELIZABETH. Yes! He was a manure-carter employed by the Corporation. He shovelled shite! This photograph was taken in a studio of course. What an illusion! What a grand illusion! Perhaps you would like to keep it as an aide-mémoire? You must meet so many 'types' like us. 'Characters'!

SHERIFF'S OFFICER. I was only attempting to make some civilised conversation, Mrs Quinn.

WILLIAM. Take it. Take everything.

SHERIFF'S OFFICER. That won't be necessary. Dolan – the piano! Move it – let's get out of here.

WILLIAM (*furious, humiliated*). Can I help at all? Please direct me. Simply say what it is you want me to do and I'll do it. You want help with the piano? Let me. I insist!

DOLAN *and* DOOLAN *helped by* WILLIAM *push the piano off complete with books, dishes, Sacred Heart etc.*

SHERIFF'S OFFICER. The piano will be sufficient, Mrs Quinn. Here's your photograph.

ELIZABETH. It was only a cheap upright piano. No doubt we will obtain a better one.

The SHERIFF'S OFFICER *goes out.*

MRS BLACK. Oh Mrs Quinn. What a tragedy! God forgive me for seeing what I've seen today. Those men walked into your house off the street – as if there was no such thing as privacy. You're a woman! Your house might not be as clean or as well-kept as most, but you're still a woman.

DOLAN *and* DOOLAN *return to clear the room.* WILLIAM *returns with them.* MRS BLACK *goes out.*

WILLIAM. Elizabeth. I'm sorry. I admit there were moments I may have wished the piano away. But now it's gone, I feel responsible. I'm frightened you won't forgive me.

ELIZABETH *goes out.*

Scene Three

WILLIAM *on his own.* ELIZABETH *comes in.*

ELIZABETH. Please stop walking up and down! It's giving me
a headache. Once I played the 'Ave Maria'. Schubert's. Now
I listen to you walking up and down the room. The cacophony
is unpleasant to say the least.

Pause.

WILLIAM *has stopped walking up and down, uneasily obedient.*

ELIZABETH. Oh walk up and down if you want!

MAURA *comes in, home from work. She places her wage-packet on the
floor or on a chair perhaps – if there is a chair.* WILLIAM *and*
ELIZABETH *are both very aware of where the wage-packet is.*

WILLIAM. Maura!

MAURA. There's my wages. By the time I got away from work
it was too late to go shopping.

WILLIAM. So we've no food.

Pause.

ELIZABETH. Without the piano this is an empty house. The
piano was a living presence.

WILLIAM. I agree.

ELIZABETH. So you agree that the house is now empty.

WILLIAM. Yes.

ELIZABETH. Good! At least we are agreed on that.

Pause.

MAURA. The pots aren't washed.

WILLIAM. No.

MAURA. She's had all day to wash the pots.

ELIZABETH. What's the point in washing pots when there is
no food? If anything I would have thought that would make us
more hungry.

MAURA. It's not my fault there's no food! As a female post-
office clerk I do not earn a fortune. However, the money
might last out the whole week if you didn't insist on paying the

increased rent. You enjoy it! You dress up for it! It's a treat now to pay the rent.

WILLIAM. This is not producing food, Maura.

MAURA. A treat! Like the trout she buys us.

WILLIAM. A trout would be better than nothing. We can't eat wages.

ELIZABETH. Wages! We seem destined to earn nothing but wages in this household. It was always a grave disappointment to me that William's particular grade of the Civil Service did not receive a salary. Your father has done the best he can, Maura. However I had higher hopes of my children. (*While saying this she has picked up Maura's wage-packet.*) Your father has set his wife up in an empty house!

WILLIAM. There is of course a slight possibility of the piano's being restored. The factor has to store our belongings for a certain length of time, before he can sell them. You see? – I've been thinking about this. Obviously! I have thought of nothing else.

ELIZABETH. And do you have a suggestion?

WILLIAM. Mrs Shaw. She's the only possibility. You saw what happened to the factor's man when he came to deliver their notices to quit – the women threw everything at him. Flour, soot even.

ELIZABETH. How resourceful!

WILLIAM. They're Amazons. Natives.

MAURA. Mrs Shaw has certainly got them organised. She knows what she's doing.

ELIZABETH. Whereas I can't wash pots!

WILLIAM. Their personal standards are irrelevant. The point is – the piano. The factor is about as popular with them as the Kaiser, or the government. It's possible that – if they were encouraged – they might go on the offensive – invade the factor's office! Elizabeth? (*Pause.*) You must ask her now. Yes. Immediately! Maura, go and tell Mrs Shaw your mother would like to see her please.

ELIZABETH. Not 'please'.

WILLIAM. No. No 'please'. Just – your mother would like to see her.

MAURA *goes.*

ELIZABETH. My piano is no more ridiculous than this rent-strike. Those women threw flour and soot from their windows.

WILLIAM. Wild Indians. Ha!

ELIZABETH. It is *their* behaviour which is ridiculous.

WILLIAM. Yes. So – I'll go for a walk. You'll want to speak to Mrs Shaw alone.

WILLIAM *leaves.* ELIZABETH *stands, ready to receive* MRS SHAW. MRS SHAW *when she comes is still wearing the khaki overalls of a munitions worker.*

ELIZABETH (*too pleasant*). It's odd. Munitionettes are things I read about in the newspapers. Yet here you are – a munitionette! One of those gay girl workers who, they say, are not happy unless they're making something that explodes. (*Pause.*) What is it you do, exactly?

MRS SHAW. I'm a turner. I turn shells.

ELIZABETH. Oh! I've a lovely mental picture of you turning a shell. I can see the shavings curl off like hot bacon fat. (MRS SHAW*'s hand goes involuntarily to her stomach.*) Mrs Shaw! Was it something I said?

MRS SHAW. Nausea.

ELIZABETH. I only meant to suggest that you are in all probability the kind of woman who can make any environment, no matter how foreign, seem like your kitchen.

MRS SHAW. Thank you.

ELIZABETH. You have the gift of making everything seem – manageable. Yes – that's the word exactly.

MRS SHAW. Almost all the girls suffer from nausea. The TNT is also bad for the complexion.

ELIZABETH. So I see. It's unnatural, of course. Young women in particular should not be doing work of that kind. In my opinion, to be producing both shells and children confuses the issue. Please don't misunderstand me. You're doing vital work and you are obviously exhausted. On the other hand you are also well paid for it. I confess to a wish that labour, like service in the trenches, had been given voluntarily and without intrinsic bribes.

MRS SHAW. They are usually referred to as wages. Soldiers also receive wages.

ELIZABETH. They are not however paid overtime. (*Pause.*) I want my piano back. I'm asking you for your assistance. As you know the piano is being stored by the factor at his office. I presume it would be possible for the piano to be restored to us.

MRS SHAW. I imagine it's possible.

ELIZABETH. It's ridiculous, of course – a piano! A piano can only be taken seriously in certain circumstances – and we don't have a drawing-room. Yet why should the beautiful only be beautiful in certain circumstances? (*Pause. None of this is impressing* MRS SHAW.) I will of course give you my full support. That is, I will personally make my views known to the factor.

MRS SHAW (*amused*). Since that won't materially affect the position in respect of the rent-dispute, Mrs Quinn, I'm afraid I can't help you.

ELIZABETH. In that case please note that I did not actually ask for assistance. That at least is gratifying. You, Mrs Shaw, are a materialist! Therefore you cannot understand anything. We are not for one moment discussing a piece of furniture. A piano is not a piece of furniture.

Slight pause.

MRS SHAW. There are five hundred of us on strike now, Mrs Quinn. I have come from a meeting at Parkhead Forge. That's where I work. The Ordnance Department there passed a motion saying they would regard any eviction of rent-strikers as an attack on the working class as a whole, and one which would call for the most vigorous and extreme reply. Do you understand? It's illegal for them to go on strike. It's illegal for them to say they might consider going on strike. Yet they are prepared to lose wages and go to jail because they believe that the rent-increases affect the working-class as a whole.

ELIZABETH (*ferocious*). I am not the working class! I am Elizabeth Gordon Quinn. I'm an individual – although that is becoming increasingly difficult to believe. It seems there's no room for the individual in this world.

MRS SHAW. The pathos of this family reminds me sometimes of the reactionary elements amongst the drinking-classes.

ELIZABETH (*inflated*). I still have my pride – I will not beg!

MRS SHAW. I'm not asking you to beg.

ELIZABETH. Yes. I will beg. Why not? What have I got to lose? My pride? (*In a desperate, grand gesture, she goes down on her knees.*) Please!! I beg you!!

MRS SHAW. You won't embarrass me, Mrs Quinn. If you want the piano restored you would have to agree to withold rent. It's as simple as that.

ELIZABETH. I agree. I agree to withhold rent.

MRS SHAW. In that case I'll see what can be arranged.

MRS SHAW *stops – surprised by the intensity of the climax and the sudden resolution. She smiles, then goes.*

Scene Four

MAURA *comes in.*

MAURA. They're coming. They've got the piano. You should see it. The whole street's hanging out of their windows.

ELIZABETH. This has got – or grown – ridiculously out of proportion. It is only a piano. I simply wanted my piano rightfully restored to me, I did not expect to become a public spectacle.

MAURA. You should see it.

ELIZABETH. Come away from the window. And please stop running in and out.

MAURA. I've only been out once!

ELIZABETH. Then stay in!

MAURA. You'd think the children had never seen a piano before. They're all around it, they all want to help the men deliver it. And because it's appeared in their street they think like it's their piano.

ELIZABETH. Children don't think. They get in the way.

MRS BLACK *comes in.*

MRS BLACK. Oh Mrs Quinn! I don't believe it. I heard a lot of noise and looked out the window and there was Mr Quinn entertaining the whole street, raving away like a speaker at the shipyard gates. And he was supervising men moving your piano.

MAURA. The woman must have persuaded the factor one way or another.

MRS BLACK. The piano! I don't know – this comes and that goes, this appears and that disappears, you'd think we were living in a shipyard so you would.

ELIZABETH. You exaggerate all the time of course, Mrs Black. Nothing is greatly changed.

MRS BLACK. That's what I said to Mr Black. I said, I don't care if Mrs Quinn has joined the rent-strikers, if she's still the same Mrs Quinn she won't have changed a bit. How will you manage the piano? You must have been just getting used to having room to breathe and now you have to squeeze up to let the piano in again.

ELIZABETH. There is very little adjustment to be made. I never imagined for a moment my piano had ever gone as such.

MRS BLACK. I'm glad nothing has changed. Don't get me wrong, Mrs Quinn – we can all change. So long as nothing's different. You can join their strike without being a part of it!

The piano enters in triumph. It is draped in a Union Jack.
WILLIAM *sits on the piano lid – elated – as* BROGAN *and*
McCORQUINDALE *push him to the middle of the room.*
Handclapping to a Scottish jig.

WILLIAM. We did it. We're here.

MRS BLACK. Oh look Mrs Quinn. I don't believe it.

WILLIAM. We simply walked into the factor's office and asked for it.

MRS BLACK. The three of you?

WILLIAM. Yes. Though there were fifty women there too.

BROGAN. We let them go in front. After all, it's a women's fight.

WILLIAM. We simply walked in there. It was like walking through walls. The factor was afraid of us.

BROGAN. You should have seen the looks on the women's faces. I was frightened and I was on their side.

WILLIAM. Mrs Shaw explained she could only guarantee the continued goodwill of those present on condition our piano was re-instated!!

BROGAN. Hoo! 'Goodwill'! I wouldn't have liked to have seen what fifty women would have done to that place.

ELIZABETH. I trust their actions remained within the law.

Pause. There is no answer to this.

WILLIAM. Please let me introduce you. This is my wife, Mrs Quinn.

BROGAN. I'm Brogan. This big boy is McCorquindale.

MRS BLACK. McCorquindale! And what's your first name.

McCORQUINDALE. Ebenezer.

MRS BLACK. Oh! That's quite unusual.

BROGAN. My name's John. John Brogan.

WILLIAM. These are the men who brought the piano home. She was an awkward big beast but these men handled her like natives.

MRS BLACK. You must be delighted, Mrs Quinn.

BROGAN. She'd better be. It's not going back.

ELIZABETH. I had hoped you would draw less attention to yourselves.

Pause. BROGAN *and* McCORQUINDALE *are being as courteous and good-humoured as possible even though they have clearly seen the 'type' they are dealing with.*

WILLIAM. Ha! That is a joke. Obviously! So – (*He produces a small bottle of whisky.*) Let's have a celebration. As for myself I am intoxicated already – with elation. I am almost frightened with it. When I'm elated like this I always go too far. I end up making a fool of myself. My wife on the other hand is unforthcoming in company – so please have no worries on her account. She watches happily enough. She expects everyone else to entertain her as I have done all my married life.

WILLIAM *is trying to mollify everyone though primarily* ELIZABETH *and he somehow feels obliged to arrange the group as if its purpose was to entertain an enthroned* ELIZABETH.

WILLIAM. A song. A song from you, me fine boy.

McCORQUINDALE. Me?

BROGAN. He's too shy. Naturally enough – with a name like that. If I had a name like that you'd have to dig me out.

WILLIAM. He needs a whisky – is that it? Maura, get some glasses, please. We are going to enjoy ourselves. (*He opens his arms to apostrophise.*) Joy!

BROGAN (*sings*). Joy, thou fairest child of Eden,
Joy, thou spark of life divine,
Drunk with holy fire we hasten,
Heavenly Maiden to thy shrine.

WILLIAM. Marvellous! You hear that, Elizabeth?

BROGAN. I learned it at the Socialist Choir.

WILLIAM. Beethoven! That is, the tune is by Beethoven. The words are by someone else. A German.

McCORQUINDALE. Schiller. Johann Christoph Friedrich. 1759 – 1805. Beethoven was German too, of course. He was born in Bonn.

BROGAN (*in case* McCORQUINDALE *is in danger of getting too much attention*). Ebenezer knows a lot of facts. I take him to the Socialist Choir with me. I like to try and get him into company as much as possible. Look at that. Shy? When he smiles you'd think he'd been scalded. The choir's good for him, though no one knows if he sings or just mimes the words. Maybe your daughter would like to join the choir – she looks the deep type too.

WILLIAM. She certainly seems 'struck' with something. I would be grateful, Maura, if you poured the men a whisky.

MAURA. We don't have any glasses.

WILLIAM. We need five glasses.

MAURA. You know we've none.

WILLIAM. I know nothing of the kind. We have a superfluity of glasses. We have glasses of all descriptions. So please do not contradict me. And don't stand looking at me either. Dumb insolence I will not tolerate.

MAURA *doesn't move.*

BROGAN. I'll take mine in a cup.

McCORQUINDALE. So will I.

WILLIAM (*fiercely, to* MAURA). Cups then! Use your imagination!

MAURA *goes to pour out the whiskies.*

ELIZABETH (*who has been getting restless*). I agree that there was a time, Mr Brogan, Mr McCorquindale, when I did find my husband entertaining. However now I am of the opinion that a pantomime is all well and good once a year.

WILLIAM. Ha! (*Whether anyone has a glass of whisky or not* WILLIAM *proceeds to propose a toast.*) May I now propose a toast? I'm not used to public speaking. As a civil servant I did not have much to do with the public. I was in fact a minor clerk. So let me simply propose as the toast – our piano!

BROGAN. Our piano!

McCORQUINDALE. Our piano!

ELIZABETH (*viciously*). 'Our' piano! 'Our' piano! Though, I agree, it is an expression of unusual accuracy. The piano which has traversed a city! The piano whose banal comings and goings are the talk of the street! And now – the working-class's piano! Or, should I say, 'joanna'.

WILLIAM. When I said 'our piano' I was of course simply using a form of expression.

ELIZABETH. What a performance! You bring those men in off the street and then proceed to give a performance like that.

WILLIAM. I was anxious. I didn't know how you would react.

ELIZABETH. Clown! How should I react?

WILLIAM. You could have joined in.

ELIZABETH. I didn't want to 'join in', as you put it. And I refuse to show my feelings – nakedly – in front of complete strangers *in working boots*! You won't understand that of course – you have as little sense of privacy as an incorrigible drunkard. But this is what I must expect living in a tenement where even my toilet is not private, where everything is overheard!

WILLIAM. When I said 'our piano', what I meant is that my wife and I wish to extend our thanks, and what more after all can we give?

ELIZABETH. I don't want that thing in my house.

WILLIAM. Elizabeth!

ELIZABETH. Get it out. It's not mine.

Long pause.

WILLIAM *has come to the end of his humble tether. He puts down his cup of whisky.*

WILLIAM. I've tried to please you, Elizabeth, but since you won't forgive me that's impossible. I love you so much it seems that every year I get smaller and smaller. So perhaps I ought to leave now before I completely disappear. I cannot be both your clown and your husband! (*He goes out.*)

BROGAN. Where will we put our cups?

MAURA. I'll take them.

BROGAN. We've our work to go to now. We're on a backshift.

MRS BLACK. I'll show them out, Mrs Quinn.

MRS BLACK *takes* BROGAN *and* McCORQUINDALE *off.* ELIZABETH, *alone with* MAURA, *is consumed by the piano.*

ELIZABETH. Look at it. It has been – literally – dragged through the gutter. Oh I feel nauseous. I want to cut off my hair or something. You won't understand that. I have been violated!

PART TWO

Scene Five

ELIZABETH *is sitting on the piano stool, beside the piano. The piano is set at the back of the room, from where* ELIZABETH *will now see enacted the drama of her own creations – her children. She has a coat on because it is now moving towards winter and they have no fire. Everyone who comes wears coats too and generally acts as if they were outside.* MRS BLACK *comes on, more circumspectly than usual.*

MRS BLACK. Oh Mrs Quinn! Now the family downstairs has disappeared. Gone! Yesterday a family of twelve lived there – now it's empty. They must have gone in the night, though I never heard a thing and I wake up if Mr Black turns on his side. It's unnatural – the silence! They must have used a lorry – some form of transport. That was a good family too. When she had them washed and dressed for Mass on a Sunday they were so clean they were like little Protestants, so they were. (*She has intended this as a compliment and can't work out why it hasn't turned out like one.*) No offence, Mrs Quinn. I only meant they had lovely little Protestant faces. I'm frightened, Mrs Quinn. That family hadn't joined the rent-strike either, what's going to happen to me? I'm not wanted in this tenement. I'm not welcome. There's fifteen thousand of them on strike and I'm only myself! Everything's different now – even you! Now when I come here it's so quiet 'quiet' isn't the word. It's like you've moved out. (*Pause.*) If it wasn't for the slops on the floor I wouldn't know where I was.

MAURA *comes in.*

MAURA. Mrs Black.

MRS BLACK. Maura.

MAURA. I'm surprised to see you here.

MRS BLACK. I like to look in and see how your mother is.

MAURA. Oh you're very welcome. I can't stop you seeing my mother. And it's nice to see you making some kind of contribution to the life of the tenement, even if it's not financial.

Almost from when she comes in MAURA *has gone to a drawer to find a jotter and a tea-caddy, which contains the tenement's rent-money.*

MAURA. So – what's your opinion, Mrs Black? Why has my mother decided to stop eating? In my opinion she's doing it to frighten us. And of course because she wants attention.

MRS BLACK. I've never seen anyone who was as fidgety with her hands as she is – that's what frightens *me*.

ELIZABETH. I can't eat. It's as simple as that.

MAURA. Can't or won't?

ELIZABETH. Does it matter? I have no appetite. Although the truth is, the less I eat the stronger I become.

MAURA. You see, Mrs Black, why I can't take my own mother seriously. If I could take my own mother seriously I could maybe start to take myself seriously.

MRS BLACK. Everybody has to eat, Mrs Quinn.

MAURA. She would rather be an angel.

ELIZABETH. Stop giving me advice! As far as I can see there is no problem. Therefore why you are giving me advice is a mystery. You are the one with problems. (*This is to* MAURA *who is now doing the accounts, with papers and money spread out round her.*) I hear the family downstairs has actually moved out. No doubt you and the rest of the Committee regard that as socialism.

MAURA. I couldn't say: I'm not a socialist.

ELIZABETH. It is yet another instance of their intolerance of the individual stance. They hate the individual because they themselves are not individuals!

MAURA. The woman downstairs was paying rent to the landlord.

MRS BLACK. She wasn't wanted. Like me.

MAURA. That's right. She wasn't wanted.

MRS BLACK. This is the kind of treatment that can drive a woman insane. Don't get me wrong, Mr Black's a good man but there are times when a woman needs company. You can't live without company!

MAURA. Mrs Black, you can't refuse to join in with your neighbours and then be surprised when you're lonely. (*Pause.*) We're going to picket the empty property as from tonight. We want to stop the factor moving anyone else into it.

Pause.

MAURA *has passed this off as ordinary business, head down, doing the accounts.*

MRS BLACK. You're happy, Maura Quinn! You would *rather* have downstairs empty.

MAURA. Yes. It's another twenty-five shillings out of the factor's pocket.

MRS BLACK. That was a home! That was a part of this tenement!

ELIZABETH. A home! She doesn't care about homes any more than the factor does. Since she became the tenement's treasurer, she's only interested in her rent money. Look at the devotion she gives to those accounts. And she counts and re-counts the money so often the coins are sweaty. Look – she's embarrassed!

MAURA. I'm the tenement's treasurer. I can't afford to be out a penny.

ELIZABETH. Isn't she the image of the factor's man? That's what happens to you when you merely collect the rent for the tenement and put it in the bank.

MAURA. It's a big responsibility. We're withholding rent – we are not defaulters. And we have the rent here to prove it.

ELIZABETH. What is it that's so ridiculous about her? 'We are not defaulters!' says she. As if anyone's in a sweat about it. And she has the tenement's rent neatly arranged in front of her as if it was hers. Hers!

MAURA. It is mine!

ELIZABETH. It is hers!

MAURA. I'm responsible for it.

ELIZABETH. You see, Mrs Black. Maura has always been ridiculous where money was concerned. I like to think that I on the other hand kept a certain distance from it.

MAURA (*fierce, humiliated*). Yes – so *I* had to go to the shops as a
girl when you'd no money. *I* learned to make my eyes look
like big wide pennies. *I* learned to tell lies. Lies? When I talked
I stumbled but when I lied the lies ran away with me. (*Slight
pause.*) Yes I'm ridiculous: I've no money. So I work. I make
money. The more money I have the less ridiculous I'll look.

MRS SHAW *comes in, or is already there.*

MAURA. Mrs Shaw. I'm almost ready.

MRS BLACK. You haven't even had time to eat.

MAURA. I'm not hungry. I'll eat later.

ELIZABETH. Please, Maura – don't be in such a rush. I always
think that speed, particularly in a woman, suggests someone
who thinks too little of herself. It's almost Irish.

MRS SHAW. There's news, Maura. The factor's taking
eighteen of us to the Small Debts Court. He's hoping to
persuade the Court that payment of rent due should be re-
directed as debt. That way the Court would have powers to
arrest our wages.

MAURA. Our wages!

MRS SHAW. It's clever. Now that there's fifteen thousand
women on strike they're beginning to get clever. So far they
haven't been able to enforce a single eviction – so this is the
new approach. The employers will deduct money from our
wages and pass it straight to the factor. It's legal of
course – and you can't picket the movement of money.

MAURA. That's – like opening our private mail.

ELIZABETH. See! And you imagined you could shift the law on
and off like a piano.

MRS SHAW. We have a few days before the case comes up in
court in which to talk to 'our friends' about it. Are you ready?

MAURA. Yes.

ELIZABETH. When will you be back? Do you know?

MAURA. Late. After the Committee meeting we'll be outside
picketing the tenement.

MAURA *and* MRS SHAW *go out.*

MRS BLACK. I'd better go too.

ELIZABETH. Yes.

MRS BLACK. I wish you'd eat. I worry about you. I wouldn't be human if I didn't worry. If I didn't worry I'd go mad – I'd have nothing to think about. I worry about my son too. (*Slight pause.*) I want everything to be back in its right place again – that's all.

ELIZABETH. I'm so detached. I want to touch everything – I touch everything – but I'm so detached.

MRS BLACK. I better go.

MRS BLACK *goes out.*

ELIZABETH. Yet I keep repeating the same things. The same things! Again and again. Again and again and again and again! (*She is playing with the words. She is amused at herself, briefly.*) It's a compulsion.

Scene Six

ELIZABETH *is on her own, very restless. Then* MAURA *comes in.*

MAURA. So – you're still up. It's three in the morning.

ELIZABETH. I can't sleep.

MAURA. You do nothing all day then you wonder why you're not tired.

ELIZABETH. I'm exhausted. I'm too restless to sleep.

Pause.

MAURA. That fog's not going to move.

ELIZABETH. No.

MAURA. They've cancelled all shipping in the Clyde. Nothing can shift.

ELIZABETH. It will sit there for a week, that fog.

MAURA (*slight pause*). Oh – it's cold! I wish I could hibernate. Maybe when I woke up everything would be better. See? I would like to be a little girl too. *I* would like to pretend.

ELIZABETH. It's three in the morning, Maura. You should have stopped thinking by this time of night. But no – you keep turning things over.

MAURA. I agree – I think too much. That's because I have to do everyone else's thinking for them. (*Slight pause.*) Oh – I'm fed up! Look – this is what I come home to every night. This is why I'm standing out there round a brazier till all hours in the morning. For this! I don't know why I bother. The most that can be said for it is that it gets me out of here!

ELIZABETH. I would give quite a lot to get out of here. (*Slight pause.*) You must enjoy their company.

MAURA. Sometimes. Sometimes I hate them. They've all got things. I think, you've all got reasons to do this, you've got homes.

ELIZABETH. You're still only a girl, Maura. You've plenty of time.

MAURA. I want my own home.

ELIZABETH. Yes – you look at me and what I have made of my home and you want to emulate my success.

This comes out – unintentionally – sounding quite harsh.

That was a joke. I don't know why I said that. I suppose I'm afraid for you, that's all.

There is a loud or at least insistent knocking at the door.

MAURA. I'll answer it.

ELIZABETH. Don't – and they might go away.

There is louder, more insistent knocking so MAURA *moves to answer it at which point* AIDAN *bursts in.*

MAURA. Aidan!

AIDAN. So – I've come home. I'm a deserter! You can throw me out if you like – I'm disgusting. I smell like rancid butter. And I'm a coward.

ELIZABETH. Where have you appeared from?

AIDAN. I was outside in the fog. Don't worry – unless someone recognised my cough, I'm safe. So – what a welcome! We are – all three of us – overwhelmed. You don't know which question to ask first!

MAURA. No.

AIDAN. Maybe you don't want to ask me anything, it might touch you. Will I tell you how I contrived my total disappearance? Easy! Dublin is dirty and densely populated. And in the slums it's even worse. In some rooms there are five families – one in each corner of the room and one in the middle – so one more body was hardly even noticed.
But – finally – I decided to come home. I was frightened, that's why! I thought I was going to disappear altogether.

Pause.

AIDAN. PLEASE SAY SOMETHING.

MAURA. You must be hungry. I'll get you some food and a blanket.

AIDAN. You don't want me here. Is that it? You despise me because I couldn't go to war and make 'the supreme sacrifice'. How could I? I don't even know who I am yet.

ELIZABETH. You're a coward! My only hope is that you give yourself up to the authorities and ask their permission to re-join your regiment.

AIDAN. No!

MAURA. You can't stay here, Aidan.

AIDAN. Why not?

MAURA. We have only two rooms, where are we going to hide you?

AIDAN. People with only a corner of a room turned on their sides to make room for me.

MAURA. Everyone in the tenement knows you. It's too dangerous.

AIDAN. Of course, this is what I expected. I expected you to throw me out. I'm even glad. After all, it's what I expected. You don't want people to know your brother is this ridiculous thing.

MAURA. Please keep your voice down, Aidan.

AIDAN. No! I've got nothing to hide. Why should I keep my voice down? It's you who's got something to hide.

Slight pause.

ELIZABETH. He can stay here for the time being, Maura. He can get a decent sleep and recover his senses.

AIDAN. Yes! I can find my bearings again – here in my natural surroundings. The filth was different over there. There the filth didn't have to share a room with a standing joke like your piano. It was simple ankle deep filth.

Slight pause.

MAURA. If you're not going to go, I'll get you some blankets.

MAURA *goes to get the blankets.*

ELIZABETH. Aidan. Your father's gone.

AIDAN. Gone? What? – just – gone?

ELIZABETH. He left four weeks or so ago. He just disappeared.

AIDAN. 'Disappeared'! Nobody can disappear even if they want to. He has to eat. He has to sleep somewhere. If you want to find someone all it takes is the will and hard work.

ELIZABETH. He knows where we are.

AIDAN. At least if you had contacted the police it would have shown you were mildly interested in the duffer.

ELIZABETH. Please do not describe your father as a duffer.

AIDAN. How would you describe him? A clown? At least *I* had a liking for the duffer. He was my father. *You* haven't even tried to find out where he is.

ELIZABETH. You always were a little hysterical, Aidan, but now you're vindictive with it, which is very unattractive. I think I even preferred you when you collected wild flowers.

MAURA. There's the blankets. I'm going to bed.

AIDAN. Yes. I've changed. What did you expect? I've seen terrible things! Of course I've changed.

ELIZABETH. We'll see you in the morning.

AIDAN. No – don't go. I'm afraid.

MAURA. We're all afraid. Goodnight.

MAURA *and* ELIZABETH *go.*

AIDAN. The door doesn't even close. What if someone walked in? Anyone could walk in! (*Slight pause.*) I've seen terrible things, all right. There were nights you would think there was

a war being fought in the streets of Dublin. There were so
many casualties lying around – unconscious, so drunk they
couldn't roll over. 'Unattractive' she said! Of course, I'm
unattractive. I'm frightened. I've woken up in the same room
as someone who has died of cold.

Scene Seven

AIDAN *wakes, gets up. He realises he's alone in the house and finds this
strange, eerie but beautiful – the space. Then he becomes frightened. When
he folds up his blankets they aren't even approximately folded.* MRS
BLACK *comes in.*

MRS BLACK. Aidan! Aidan Quinn! But you're with the 6th
  Royal Munsters.

AIDAN. How did you get in?

MRS BLACK. The door was open. The door's always open.

AIDAN (*aggressively*). I've just folded up my blankets – I've just
  got up! Where's my mother? I woke up and there was no one
  here.

MRS BLACK. I don't know, it's not like your mother to be out.
  Especially in a fog like that.

AIDAN. So she *wants* to frighten me. She either wants me to
  think she has gone to the authorities or she has gone to the
  authorities.

MRS BLACK. Why should she want to do that?

AIDAN. Because I'm a deserter!

MRS BLACK. I don't believe it, Aidan Quinn. That's an
  unholy lie.

AIDAN. I see. You're one of those people who for the duration
  of the war will refuse to see what's in front of their eyes.
  Deserters, for example, Or the unusual number of soldiers who
  return from the front missing an index-finger. Have you
  noticed that? Our 'lads' are chopping off their own fingers.

MRS BLACK. Oh Aidan – now I *know* you're making things up.

AIDAN. So that they can't fire their rifles! Of course I never
  went to the front but I have an imagination. That is the whole

problem with us Quinns. We have an imagination which we can ill afford.

ELIZABETH *comes in.*

Pause.

MRS BLACK *decides to carry on as if she has not seen* AIDAN.

MRS BLACK. Oh Mrs Quinn. I got a letter! The War Office has found my son! What a thing it is for a mother to have her son restored to her after so long. I'm so happy I don't know myself.

ELIZABETH. I'm very pleased for you, Mrs Black. So where is he?

MRS BLACK. Oh I forget the name of the place. The letter said the hospital was nicely situated.

ELIZABETH. So – you'll soon have your wounded hero back in your arms. Like me.

AIDAN. I've already told Mrs Black I'm a deserter. What else was she to think – she walked in and saw me like this! (*Slight pause.*) Oh? You don't care? You don't care I made it public because you have just gone and betrayed me to the authorities! See! She doesn't deny it.

ELIZABETH. Yes I've been to the authorities. I informed them that since my son is a deserter I am no longer entitled to my nine shillings a week Separation Allowance. I handed in my book.

AIDAN. You went to the authorities today?

ELIZABETH. Yes. I opened a drawer this morning and the first thing I saw was my Allowance book. I didn't want it in my house any more.

AIDAN. My own mother. What else did you say? Nothing probably – you wouldn't want any fuss, you'd rather I quietly disappeared. You've always wanted rid of me. That's why I joined the army in the first place.

ELIZABETH. No one listening to your tone of voice, Aidan, would imagine you joined the 6th Royal Munsters of your own free will and volition.

AIDAN. Yes – I volunteered. Ha! On the other hand I was aware you would rather have me dead than a post-office clerk.

ELIZABETH. I agree you had limited ability. I thought you might make an officer.

ELIZABETH *sits on her stool.*

AIDAN. I was a perfectly good post-office clerk! That was too ridiculous for words of course. It carried connotations of petty cash, as well as the ignominy of being a minor public servant. Your enthusiasm for the war on the other hand was fanatic. You talked of nothing else. You knew exactly how many of those awarded the VC were Catholics. You knew the official number of casualties in every major engagement. We were up to our waists in offal. Finally I volunteered. This was how I could stop being ridiculous.

ELIZABETH. You always were too sensitive. We loved you, Aidan.

AIDAN. Who's 'we'? Don't say 'we' like that! It makes me feel like I'm being dressed. Also – I would have preferred it if you had simply hated me. If you had simply hated me all the time that would at least have been consistent.

MRS BLACK. That's not your son, Mrs Quinn. Your son wouldn't have come home and announced – announced – he was a deserter. And the language he's used – 'love'! In front of his own mother. That woman's not well. She's stopped eating. She can do without abuse from you.

AIDAN (*forceful, pleading, desperate*). Have you noticed how often things disappear from round about you? I don't mean only material things though I notice there is less and less here all the time. But now people are disappearing too. Why? What is it you do? Why for example did your husband simply vanish.

AIDAN *finishes up on his knees in front of her, appealing to her as a son. We see her wanting to respond – a mother.*

ELIZABETH. You could ask him.

AIDAN. I can't ask him. He's vanished!

ELIZABETH. We had an argument.

AIDAN. About what? Something petty?

ELIZABETH (*points to the piano*). That thing.

AIDAN. You argued about that all my life.

ELIZABETH. We argued all your life because I was too good
for him! (*Pause.*) Or rather, he was too good for me. I was a
liar.

She clasps AIDAN*'s head and takes it to her lap.*

The piano was his wedding-present to me. He couldn't afford
it and I couldn't play it. Though we led each other to believe
the opposite. When I married I imagined I would never be
poor again.

MAURA *comes in.*

MRS BLACK. Tell him nothing! He's polluted.

Pause. They register MAURA*'s presence.*

MAURA. I'm going straight out again. I've come to get a
bucket – we're collecting money for our relief fund at the
shipyard gates. (*She goes to find a bucket.*)

MRS BLACK. He has to go! I thought this was a good
house – now I wouldn't be surprised if I came in here and
found you were keeping a pig. Not only has that animal
deserted but he has to come back to pollute his home. If he
was your son he would go of his own accord.

AIDAN. Go! Ha! Go where?

MRS BLACK. He's incriminating you, Mrs Quinn. If you get
caught harbouring him you'll go to jail.

ELIZABETH. I will take the consequences, Mrs Black.

MAURA. You don't know what the consequences are! The
consequences are six month's jail.

MAURA *has found a bucket and is on her predetermined way out when
she is stopped by* ELIZABETH*'s bombast.*

ELIZABETH. Six months is not an eternity. I carried him
inside me for longer and that's a prison too, of a kind.

MAURA. And what would we do when we got out of prison?

ELIZABETH. Please, Maura.

MAURA. Once we were released, then what?

ELIZABETH. You have obviously thought this out.

MAURA. Yes!

ELIZABETH. That was wrong, do you understand?

MAURA. We would have no house. We would have no means of support. We would be defiled. What would we do then? Say it! Say what we would do!

ELIZABETH. There are times when it is wrong to think things through. There are times when the consequences are so overwhelming they make any actual decision look small.

Pause.

MAURA. I'm sorry. I can't stop thinking. It's a bad habit I have. And what are you going to do about the door? Of course we may not be the most popular people in the tenement but even so you could start thinking about how to stop people simply walking in.

MAURA *goes.*

MRS BLACK. I won't say anything – it's nothing to do with me. None of this is any of my business! (*She goes out.*)

AIDAN. I'm safe. Why should anyone find me? The authorities only find someone if they receive co-operation from the people. This is what I discovered in Dublin. If the people don't want to supply the authorities with information the authorities don't know where to look.

ELIZABETH *touches him. The gesture is motherly but too much about her own sadness to be reassuring. She goes out.*

Scene Eight

AIDAN *is looking out of the window.* ELIZABETH *is sitting at the piano stool.*

ELIZABETH. Aidan, please come away from there. How can you see anything in that fog?

AIDAN. They're carrying candles. Look! There are so many lights and they're all moving, it's like a drunk man looking at gas lamps.

ELIZABETH. Aidan – hanging out of windows is vulgar. Someone might see you!

AIDAN. They're jumping up and down on top of one another. Ha! You can't tell where one person ends and the next one begins.

MRS BLACK *comes in.*

MRS BLACK. We've won! The case at the Small Debts Court was dropped. I went out to meet them coming back from the court. The streets are pandemonium. Everyone's happy and yet it's as if everyone's keeping it to themselves a bit. And what with the fog – it might all be happening in secret!

ELIZABETH. Secret? Glasgow never did anything in secret.

MRS BLACK. Oh Mrs Quinn – they say there's five shipyards out on strike. (*She whispers the word 'strike'.*) I was shocked! But there – it just shows you. The law has taken their side. The government has decided they're in the right – so they were supporting the government all along. I don't know – you're only just ready to accept things when suddenly everything's different again.

AIDAN. Speed, Mrs Black! If you go forward, you stay up.

MRS BLACK. Oh?

AIDAN. Like a bicycle. A bicycle keeps its balance – balance! understand? – by forwards propulsion.

MRS BLACK. By that logic if you stand still you will fall.

AIDAN. Yes! Yes!

Slight pause.

MRS BLACK. I'll never understand you, Aidan Quinn.

MRS SHAW *comes on.*

MRS SHAW. I'm looking for . . .

ELIZABETH. She's not back yet, Mrs Shaw.

MRS SHAW. I lost her outside the court. I thought she might have got home before me. (*Pause.*) She never mentioned that Aidan was home.

ELIZABETH. So what exactly happened, Mrs Shaw?

MRS SHAW. The prosecution was persuaded to drop the case. The papers are saying there's twenty five thousand of us on strike now, and there was a big demonstration outside the court. As well as that the Sheriff heard shop stewards from different munition works who said the whole city would go on strike if the Court went against us. So the Sheriff had a few quiet words with the prosecution and that was it. The prosecution was persuaded.

ELIZABETH. What about the law?

MRS SHAW. There is no law which says that the law must always on every occasion be upheld. There were seventy five thousand workers on strike illegally today. The law knows it can either say 'It's against the law to go on strike,' and jail the lot of us; or it can say 'But then there will be no one left to build ships,' and leave us alone. What decision the law takes depends on how much the country needs what you've got.

MAURA comes in. She has a big Union Jack wrapped round her shoulders. MRS SHAW immediately goes to her.

MRS SHAW. Maura – I was looking for you.

MAURA. Don't touch me! Stay where you are!

Pause.

MRS SHAW. Have you been assaulted?

Pause.

MAURA. The military police are in the street. They're doing a house-to-house search.

ELIZABETH. Aidan – hide!

AIDAN. Where?

ELIZABETH. Where?

AIDAN. Yes. Have they got dogs?

MAURA. They've got dogs in the van.

ELIZABETH. Go!

AIDAN. No. I refuse to be thrown to the dogs. There is nowhere to run to! I would be running for the sake of it. Also, I refuse to go on hiding.

Pause.

ELIZABETH. It wasn't me, Aidan. I'm not responsible for this.

MAURA. Of course not. You couldn't be held responsible for anything! You're a child.

MRS SHAW. Maura!

MAURA. I did it. I informed the authorities. It was only a matter of time before the whole street knew. This is a tenement! We can't hide our feelings here, never mind anything else.

MRS SHAW. You hid your feelings from me well enough.

MAURA. When we won today I thought, now I have a house I can afford to stay in. I couldn't face having it taken away from me. I couldn't face having nothing at all.

AIDAN. So – I am to be sacrificed after all. That if I may say so is a satisfactory conclusion to an unpalatable drama. Unpalatable! Ha – as in food. Food! In Dublin I attended many funerals – in order to eat! And I noticed how reluctant people are to eat after a funeral. That is why everyone must eat together – so that no one thinks too much to be sickened off their unholy food. And because it would be more ridiculous not to eat. We are mortal flesh. Yes. That's it. It would be more ridiculous not to eat. So – please!

This last 'So – please!' is an invitation to dine. At this point the military police burst in. There is a Regimental Sergeant-Major and a Sergeant, and they have assumed that the deserter is armed.

SERGEANT. DON'T MOVE.

RSM. And don't speak except to answer questions.

SERGEANT. Nobody makes any clever remarks.

RSM. We're not too clever. We might not understand them.

SERGEANT. And then we'll get annoyed.

RSM. Private Aidan Gordon Quinn.

AIDAN *comes to attention, salutes.*

AIDAN. Sir!

RSM. I'm warning you, son.

SERGEANT. We're under a lot of pressure.

RSM. Don't move too quickly.

SERGEANT. Nice and easy does it.

RSM. Are you Private Aidan Gordon Quinn serving in His Majesty's 6th Royal Munster Regiment.

AIDAN. Yes, sir.

SERGEANT. You're under arrest, son.

When the RSM produces handcuffs AIDAN puts his hands out with alarming alacrity. He is anxious to show how co-operative he is.

AIDAN. Thank you, sir. I'm relieved, almost.

RSM. Don't tell me what your feelings are, son. I don't want to know what your feelings are.

SERGEANT. I'm going to have you, son. I'm going to eat you!

RSM. Enough, sergeant. Remember you're in someone's home.

SERGEANT. That was a bloody liberty, son. Don't you ever do that again. Understand! Don't you ever say what your feelings are.

AIDAN. Yes, sir.

RSM. Right, Quinn. I take it this is your family.

AIDAN. Sir.

SERGEANT. SAY GOODBYE.

Pause.

AIDAN. I could have disappeared in Dublin. But I came home. I was frightened, that's why!

He looks at the MP*'s anxiously. He's finished – that is, he doesn't know what to say, and they motion him out. Once* AIDAN *is gone – as the* MP *closes the door behind them –*

ELIZABETH. Aidan!

Pause.

Tell me it's all my fault! It's my fault! Tell me! Tell me it's all my fault! Don't you think I know? Of course I know. I wanted to be rich, that's all. So I lied. I pretended. I became detached. I dreamed my children's dreams – while they lay awake thinking. I made *monsters* of them!

She picks up a chair and attacks the piano with it.

It's my fault! It's my fault!

MRS SHAW *goes over and holds her as if to hold her in,* ELIZABETH *struggles then holds onto her.*

MRS SHAW. Mrs Quinn. I'm not saying I haven't judged you in the past. Of course I have. I judged you all the time – that's why I tried to be in your company as little as possible. I'm sorry I judged you so much. I have pretensions too. I have a lot of pretentions. And *I* have an imagination too. *I* can imagine what it would be like to have more space. More privacy.

ELIZABETH. I refused to learn how to be poor. That's my whole story. And I still refuse!

MAURA *is left to look on. She still has the Union Jack around her. She's conscious of it – it's grandiose, bombastic and liable to draw attention. She takes it off.*

The End.

JOHN McKAY started writing and performing professionally with the radical Scots comedy group The Merry Mac Fun Show in 1985, contributing topical revue material to such shows as *Macattack, Psychoshanter,* and *The Claimant Kid* as well as writing *I Love You Baby But I Gotta Run,* an all-action soul thriller, for the parent Fun Co theatre company.

In 1988 *Dead Dad Dog* was premiered at the Edinburgh Traverse Scottish Accents New Writing season; it was revived for the Edinburgh Festival and transferred to the Royal Court Upstairs in London. A new production toured Scotland in 1989.

Other work includes *Hellbent on Christmas* (Traverse, 1988), *Stubborn Kinda Fellow* (Channel Four Television, 1989), *Onan* (written and performed with Robert Llewellyn, Edinburgh Festival, 1989) and *Up with Bob and Jessie* (Traverse, 1990).

John McKay is currently adapting *Dead Dad Dog* as a situation comedy for Channel Four TV.

Characters

ECK, young, twenty-four in fact. An aspiring Scottish media
type, currently unemployed.

WILLIE, old, late fifties at least. A dead hoover salesman,
dressed in a horrid, loud, flared seventies suit, with one of
those tacky wide seventies haircuts, including big sideburns.
Cheery and dour.

Setting

As little as possible. The play is designed to be *performed* in all
respects – so most of the objects mentioned, sound effects, etc
should be mimed and mouthed by the performers themselves.

In the original production, the set was entirely composed of a
marked-out floorspace and four chairs, which the actors swung,
re-arranged and played with to suit each particular scene.

Importantly however, this same production made effective use of
onstage costume-changes during the action, which prevented
sparseness being visually dull.

Dead Dad Dog was first staged at the Traverse Theatre,
Edinburgh on 17 May 1988 and subsequently at the Royal Court
Theatre Upstairs, London, on 20 October 1988 with the
following cast:

DAD   Ralph Riach
ECK   Sam Graham

Directed by Steve Unwin
Designed by Emma Fowler
Lighting by George Tarbuck

Scene One

Breakfast surprise.

Music: 'Nothin' But Blue Skies' – Jackie Wilson

ECK *walks into his kitchen, yawning. Opens shutters.*

ECK. Today.

Hm. A wee bit dull.

No matter. Hello birds. Hello back green. Hello pink tee-shirt on somebody's line.

Today.

Today's gonna be a good one. An I'll tell you why.

Number one. I've got up. Thank you, God.

Number two. After watchin most of my friends scurry south to weather the long winter of recession and repression, my efforts to hang on in the country where the action's at but the cash is not have finally been rewarded. That is, this morning I've landed an interview for a halfway decent job. At 10.30 a.m. BBC Scotland will be exposed to the irresistible charm and dynamic ideas of hotshot Alexander Dundee. By 10.45 I'll have ma own series.

(Confidential.)

Yesterday I got a card from ma pal Donald. Just started workin for a trendy newspaper in London. Says they're lookin for another writer. Says I should apply. Well I say ha ha no sell out.

Number three. M-hm, number three, tonight I'm meeting Roseanne. So if you hear a sound like a pneumatic drill, it's no Embra Corporation digging up the roads again – it's my heart saying to my brain, wise up greystuff, this girl makes me wanna play the bongos. Wah!

(Watch.)

9.15. Time enough to have some breakfast. But on a day like this, it's no just breakfast. It's hello cornflakes in yer bright

square box, what a nice free gift you gave me last week, out
you come, dinnae mind ma hand, and then hello milk chock
full of calcium yum yum sploosh.

He bends over and listens to the bowl.

ECK. No sound. Wrong brand. No matter. You're fresh and
you're crunchy and today you are mine, you are indeed
my . . .

Willie has appeared.

WILLIE. Hello son.

ECK *drops the bowl of cornflakes. Smash!*

ECK. Dad.

WILLIE. Aye. Son.

ECK. Dad.

Pause.

ECK (*extended amazement*). You . . . you . . . em . . . you're . . .
deid.

WILLIE. Oh aye. Right enough. But A wouldnae mind a cup of
tea.

ECK *double-takes and slaps himself. But* WILLIE *is still there.*

ECK. Em, Dad, I mean you are deid aren't you? I mean you've
no just been hiding out in East Kilbride or somewhere, done a
bunk, like?

WILLIE. Oh no. A've been deid . . . oh . . . twelve year now.
You should ken that. A saw yez at the funeral.

ECK. You saw me at the funeral.

WILLIE. Oh aye. (*Winks.*) A wis watchin.

ECK. Like how? From in the coffin or what?

WILLIE. Well sort of in and out. A hadnae gone upstairs yet,
you see.

ECK. To em Heaven?

WILLIE. Oh aye. Heaven. Aye.

Pause.

ECK. Well.

WILLIE. Well what?

ECK. Well what's it like?

WILLIE. What's what like?

ECK. Heaven.

WILLIE. Oh. Fine. Fine. Rains a lot. Bit like Rothesay, really.

Pause.

ECK. So ... why? I mean why?

WILLIE. Am A here? Oh A don't know really. A'm a bit scunnered maself. I didn't put in for it or anythin.

ECK. I see.

He turns forward.

Breakfast time and ma father's ghost is sitting in my kitchen and he says Heaven is a bit like Rothesay and he's scunnered as to why he's here seeing as how he didn't put in for it.

Get a grip, Alec. Wash yer face. Aye just go and wash yer face, eh?

ECK gets up and walks to the 'door'.

ECK. I must be a wee bit nervy this morning. Seein ghosts. Make that a lot nervy.

But suddenly, as he gets to the threshold, both he and WILLIE are wracked with terrible stomach pain ...

BOTH. Oooyah!

ECK. Aw ma guts ...

ECK looks at WILLIE, puzzled, then he takes a step forward. The pain gets worse. He steps back. At a certain distance from WILLIE the pain stops.

ECK. Aw ... oh.

ECK steps forward and backward a few times, then rounds on WILLIE.

ECK. Ma God. You're real.

WILLIE. Of course A'm real.

ECK. So what is this? What is this? Are you doing this?

WILLIE. Sit down. A'm daein nothin.

ECK. You are. You bloody well are. You're doing some kind of spell aren't you, you're doing voodoo so I cannae get away from you . . .

WILLIE. Look A'm a ghost, A'm just a ghost, son, A'm no Ali Bongo. An' ma stomach went wild too. Anyway, what's it matter? We've got a lot of catching up tae do. We want tae stick the gether. An' we've got aw day . . .

ECK (*Blank*). All day . . .

All day! It's ten to ten! And I've got a job interview at ten-thirty? And I'm not even dressed . . .

He rushes to the door. The pain hits again.

BOTH. Ooyah!

ECK. Awwww . . . Dad. Dad stand up. Aye, now. Now walk towards me . . .

WILLIE *staggers towards* ECK; *at a certain distance the pain stops.*

BOTH. Aaaaah . . .

WILLIE. Hey, that's good.

ECK. Fine. Just fine. Just as long as we stick together we don't get the Vincent Price appendicitis.

WILLIE *embraces him.*

WILLIE. William and Alexander Dundee. Just like Pinky and Perky, eh? D'you no remember we used tae watch that on the . . .

ECK (*breaking the embrace*). Look Dad, I'm gonna be awful busy the day and . . .

WILLIE. Yes.

ECK. I mean it's em nice . . . a nice surprise an' that . . . but can't you see that with you around . . .

WILLIE. What?

ECK. Well, can't you just . . .

WILLIE. See what?

A pause. ECK *waves his arms about in exasperation.*

ECK. I don't believe this.

Scene Two

At the bus stop.

Music: 'Champ' – The Mohawks.

WILLIE *and* ECK *running for the bus,* ECK *desperately tucking his shirt in and tying his tie.*

WILLIE. A'm sorry but A cannae walk as fast as you . . .

ECK. Here comes the 33 now.

WILLIE. You'll have to walk slower.

ECK. Is my hair messy?

WILLIE. It's no that I'm old or anythin . . .

The bus pulls up.

ECK. We get on now, OK?

They get on the bus.

ECK. Right. 40 please.

Ticket machine, etc. ECK *takes ticket and walks on,* WILLIE *follows closely.*

ECK (*arrested*). What? Oh. You mean you can . . .

He waves his hand around in front of the bus driver's face.

You can see him too? (*To* WILLIE.) I thought you'd be invisible.

WILLIE. Sorry.

ECK. Stt. Another 40 please. (*To Audience.*) Great. Some ghost. I cannae get 15 feet away from him and everybody can see him. What'll I do about the interview? And Roseanne tonight? Aw no.

I mean I cannae just tell him to . . . I mean he's ma father. Hell, I just hope he gets beamed up before tonight . . .

They sit down.

WILLIE. So what's yer interview for then son?

ECK (*smug*). Trainee producer for the BBC, actually.

WILLIE. The BBC? The BBC?

ECK. What's wrong?

WILLIE. Naebody Scottish works for the BBC.

ECK. Plenty do. Plenty.

WILLIE. Like who?

ECK. Em, Mary Marquis.

WILLIE. She's no Scottish. She's just English pretendin.

ECK. Yes, well that's just what I want to help change . . .

WILLIE (*suddenly*). Ma God. Will you look at that.

ECK. What?

WILLIE (*Pointing out of the window*). PT's. PT's isnae there. Patrick Thomsons.

ECK. Aw. The store.

WILLIE. Aye. The store. A bought ma first Viyella shirt in that store. An a lot of ma ties. A grand place for ties, PT's.

He indicates his tie, a particularly horrid kipper specimen.

ECK (*low*). My father. My all too visible dead father.

They smile at each other.

ECK. Maybe I could get him a sack or something . . .

WILLIE. Mind we ayeways used tae sing on the bus. You were a braw singer. We sang . . . (*Sings.*) Roamin in the gloamin, by the . . .

ECK (*mortified*). Dad . . .

Scene Three

At the front desk.

Music: more of 'The Champ'.

ECK *and* WILLIE *dash in through a revolving door.*

ECK. One minute past the time! They've sacked me already . . .

WILLIE. So did you get a golden handshake?

ECK (*high voice*). Hello I'm here for the . . .

Coughs and straightens out.

Hello. I'm Alexander Dundee. I have an interview this morning with Julian Critchley.

WILLIE. Of the famous Scotch Critchley clan ...

AND WHO IS WILLIE?

ECK. Oh him he's here to chum ... he's here to accompany me.

A seat in the foyer is indicated.

ECK. No I really think he should come with me because ... em ...

WILLIE. A've got his pills. He might have one of his turns.

WILLIE *clutches* ECK *supportively.* ECK *smiles and nods. They follow 'the doorman' in a circle into a lift. Lift noises and action.*

ECK (low whisper). What did you have to say that for? They'll think I'm unfit to work now.

WILLIE. Och he's the doorman, he's not Lord Reith.

They arrive.

ECK. Oh. Straight in, eh? Righto.

(*To* WILLIE.) You stay right here. Touch nothing. Do nothing. Don't even think anything.

WILLIE *makes a face. Innocent, who me? etc.*

Scene Four

Talking Turkey

ECK *walks straight in, square and confident.* WILLIE *is shut 'outside'. 'Two* INTERVIEWERS*'. A chair facing them.*

ECK. Good morning. Mr Critchley and ... pleased to meet you, Mr Guiles.

The chair is indicated.

ECK. Thank you.

But the chair is too far away from WILLIE. *As he sits in it* ECK *contorts and fights to conceal his suffering. Off-stage/outside is heard a howling, like a dog in pain,* WILLIE.

ECK. What? Em ... no I ... I can't hear anything ... Well, now you come to mention it ... I expect it's a hoover. A loud hoover. Ha ha. (*Under his breath.*) Come closer you old sod ... (*Aloud.*) Now. What can you do for me? Well ... Well it's more of a question of what I ... what I can do ... em do ...

WILLIE *and* ECK*'s agony starts to rise towards a climax.*

ECK. ... Me? No I'm not ill. I'm fine. Just a bit of a frog in my throat ... and eh my stomach ...
Now I think ... I think I'm suitable for the training you offer because ... because oh God.

WILLIE *bursts in and falls on the floor.*

BOTH. Aaaah ...

ECK *looks at* WILLIE. *Both look at the* 'INTERVIEWERS'.

WILLIE. Eh. Hello.

Maintenance.

I've come for the maintenance. A unnerstan youse have a problem with yer radiators.

WILLIE *is satisfied.*

ECK (*whisper*). There aren't any radiators.

WILLIE. There aren't? There aren't. That's just the problem. Accordin to ma plans youse should have some.

(*Indicates* ECK.)

Sharp-eyed youngster you have there. What are you young man, Director-General perhaps? Oh – you're not employed here yet?

Wellll (*To* INTERVIEWERS.) *take ma tip* ...

He nods towards ECK *and gives thumbs up, A1, etc.* ECK *glowers and coughs.*

WILLIE. Well don't mind me, carry on, carry on. A'll just investigate this radiator crisis in an unassuming manner. A'll blend in. A'll be as quiet as a wee mouse. Yez won't even know A'm here.

He wanders round knocking walls, bending over, etc. ECK *opens his mouth to re-continue the interview but ...*

WILLIE. I'm totally invisible.

ECK *tries again*.

WILLIE. Jist you carry on.

ECK (*finally*). Yes. As you said, why me? Well, I'll tell you. I think as my CV shows . . . as my journalistic and creative work shows, I have a great interest in and ability to work with culture.

WILLIE. My boy. Culture. That'll be why he's talkin in that funny accent.

ECK. Mm. OK. Well take for instance Scottish culture. Not the haggis and tartan variety, not the Harry Lauder tourist stuff . . .

WILLIE *shrugs and softly sings 'Roamin in the Gloamin'*.

ECK. . . . But what's actually happening in Scotland now. Like the way we've got some of the longest dole queues in Britain. And the most substandard housing. And the fact that the New Wealth just isn't arriving in Scotland. But also that people are doing something about it, getting together . . . if you look at my programme proposal . . .

A QUESTION.

ECK. Em no. I've never actually been a member of any political party.

WILLIE. Just as well. Ayeways catches up wi you in the end.

ECK. Mm. Organisational structure. Well for me the most important thing is to get together a team of people who can all work together and trust each other enough to share ideas . . .

WILLIE (*looks concerned*). Sounds like a holiday camp.

WILLIE *crawls over to behind* ECK*'s chair*.

ECK. Well, yes, as producer I'd be the boss ultimately . . .

WILLIE (*whispers*). Tell them you'd no take ony lip.

ECK. . . . but I'd take a strong . . . a strong line if anyone got out of em line. The unions? Mm. The unions . . .

WILLIE (*whispers*). Nothin but trouble . . .

ECK. Well yes I believe there is overmanning . . .

WILLIE (*whispers*). Tell them you'd smash 'em.

ECK. But on the other hand . . .

WILLIE (*whispers*). Other hand nothin, tell them yer Dad wis a Rotary Club member.

ECK. On the other hand you have to protect the job security of the tradesperson. (*Forcefully to* WILLIE.) Even those who claim to be in radiator maintenance.

They face each other for a moment. Then WILLIE *about-turns and crawls away in a sulk. Occasionally over this next sequence he glowers over his shoulder.*

ECK. Yes . . . Look, could we talk about my programme proposal? . . . yes, well I think a lot of what I'm saying will become clearer if we do. Thank you.

He takes a deep breath and looks at WILLIE, *who is busy listening to a wall.*

ECK. Right. What I propose is this. A programme about what people in this country have to say now. Young people, the people who get spoken for, the voice that's not heard. That's why it's called (*Proud.*) 'It's No Ma Accent, It's Your Ears' . . .

A QUESTION.

ECK. Em from Scotland. Scottish people. That's what it's about. Hence the title, 'It's no ma accent . . .'

A series of objections on the topic of how unviable, uninteresting and unwanted regional programmes are. ECK *looks from one* INTERVIEWER *to the other, a bit harassed, shrinking.*

ECK. . . . em 'parochial', what do you mean by . . .

   . . . well, local, yes, but . . .

   . . . yes, I realise of course you're aiming at a national market . . .

   (*Finding his principles again.*) But still, what about people here, what about what they want . . .

WILLIE (*aside*). A good kick up the backside's what they want . . .

ECK (*to* INT). So your priority is entertainment . . .?

WILLIE (*aside*). The guy's right by the way. A bit of song and dance. A bit of fun.

ECK (*to* INT). Well that's where I think you're wrong. I don't think ordinary people are stupid.

WILLIE. You've just no been lookin. (*He begins to whistle 'There was a Soldier'.*)

ECK. I think they can take the facts, and they want hard-edged material and . . .

A QUESTION.

ECK (*aggressively*). Well no, I must say, coming from a working-class background myself . . .

WILLIE *stops whistling and looks across aghast.*

ECK. I think you're entirely wrong to suggest that folk all want to . . .

WILLIE (*walking slowly across*). What did you say?

ECK (*a little alarmed*). . . . to escape the truth . . .

WILLIE. Who tellt you we wuz working-class?

ECK (*definitely alarmed*). . . . so I . . .

WILLIE. We wuz never working-class.

ECK (*whisper*). Yes we were. Shut up.

(*Aloud.*) Now . . .

WILLIE *puts his hand over ECK's mouth.*

WILLIE. Scuse me gentlemen, spot of sortin out tae do wi the wain.

What do you mean working-class? Eh? A sold hoovers. A had trainin. A voted Tory. That's no working-class. Now yer Auntie Bella, her and that sailor man, livin in their single end, that's working-class. But no you.

(*To* INTERVIEWERS.) How would A ken? How would A ken? Cos A'm his bloody faither, that's how A ken.

ECK (*innocent*). Em. Who is this man? I've never seen him before in my life . . .

WILLIE. Oh aye . . .

ECK. Is this some sort of psychological technique? To see how I hold up under stress?

WILLIE. A'll give you stress awright. Course A'm his faither. Otherwise how would A ken that he's Alexander Dundee, he's let me see now, aye 24, he wis born in Renfrew, he went tae

Thistlebrae primary, he ... well, A'm a bit fuzzy on the last twelve year like ... but A ken he suffers fae hayfever, an he's got a mole the size of a thruppenny bit on his bahookie.

ECK (*after a moment*). Father!

He flings himself around WILLIE.

ECK. Is it really you after all these years? Mr Critchley, Mr Guiles, you must excuse my emotion, but to find my dear old Dad, William Dundee, after we thought we'd lost him so long ago in that ... that whaling accident ... that ...

(ECK *sits down again*.) Aw, what's the point, eh. Yes. He's my father. Yes ... well, no I didn't invite him here. No, certainly not for moral support. (*Sighs*.) Look, you might find this a little hard to believe. But I'm being haunted. This is a ghost. Aren't you?

WILLIE *nods reluctantly*.

ECK. So you see all this isn't my fault.

Now. Can we talk about my programme a bit more ...?

Scene Five

Post Mortem

Music: 'Can't Quit Your Love' – Bobby Thurston.

ECK *and* WILLIE *on a park bench.* ECK *not facing* WILLIE.

WILLIE. Well they made you an offer ...

ECK. Suggesting I apply to 'Story Time' is not an offer.

Pause.

WILLIE. Och, you were too good for them.

ECK. Aye, right. I'm too good for a 12-K salary. I shouldn't have lowered masel.

Pause.

WILLIE. Look, A'm sure there'll be plenty more ...

ECK (*faces* WILLIE). Plenty more what? Eh? Plenty more what? Plenty more good jobs naw. Plenty more time tae be shit poor

yeah. I mean don't you see what happened in there? What you
... I mean why did you have to ... I mean ...

He looks at WILLIE. WILLIE *looks hurt.*

ECK. ... aw hell family, bloody saintly untouchable family ...

ECK turns away. A pause. Then WILLIE *delivers the following speech.
Lights narrow to him, and we hear 'Abide With Me' on the soundtrack.*

WILLIE (*hurt, tearful and pious*). A woulda thought, son, that you
would welcome the chance tae spend time wi yer old Dad.
That you'd see it as a gift, as a wee present fae the Almighty,
a chance for us to say hello and how're you doin?

You see, A'm as scunnert as you are as tae why A'm back, but
A reckon it's this – that when you were young, A wis
ayeways ower busy, sellin ma hoovers, tryin tae turn an honest
penny. An' we never had the time tae share, well, the things a
man can only share wi his son.

But A think Our Lord heard ma last words on this Earth, as
you aw gathert roon ma hospital bed. D'you no mind them,
Alec? A know A'm goin, and A don't know where, but if A
can be with yez aw, A will.

End with WILLIE *in a saintly pose; for a moment* ECK *looks like he
might say sorry, but then ...*

ECK. Shite. Your last words were, and I quote, 'Och, ye ken A
dinnae like orange juice, and can ye no sneak me in some
Embassy Regal?'

An' then you snuffed it, mid-moan.

ECK stomps off. But at the appropriate distance.

WILLIE. Oooyah! Where you goin?

ECK. Somewhere extremely gloomy.

Scene Six

In a pickle.

Music: 'Long Gone Lonesome Blues' – Hank Williams.
ECK and WILLIE *come in through a set of spin or double doors.* ECK
leads purposefully, in his bad mood.

WILLIE. The museum? Why've you come here?

ECK. This is where I come to think, awright?

WILLIE. Could you no have stayed doon the park and thunk? It's aw dark and dingy in here.

ECK. Aye it's dark and dingy. And that's the whole point. This is where I come to do what Scots are best at.

WILLIE. Shinty?

ECK. Moping. It's a need we've got. And we're experts. Now most folk when they're depressed, after Scotsport and that, they make do wi cryin into their last lonely can of special. But I come here to see history gummed up, life stuck on a pin. To see the elephants wi the wrinkly ears, and the dusty fish, and the big whale skeleton hanging from the roof, and sometimes, when I'm feeling really miserable, when I really want to reassure masel that life is utterly terrible, I come to the pickle room. You go up here, up through the insect's gallery, wi the Diseases Preying on Man section, and up the back stairs through the spiky crabs bit and the blown-up jellyfish, and you're here: aw the pickles in jars in glass cases, aw white and still. Brilliant. Aw the things that didnae live, hangin in jelly.

Hail Caledonia! I'm fed up wi it.

ECK *sits down, moping.* WILLIE *explores the specimens.*

WILLIE. Section of Indian Elephant's Trunk. Eeeeurgh. Young of the Crab-Eating Opossum. Oh dear . . .

(*Turns to* ECK.) This is a guy dreich place, son. Why don't we go and get oursels somethin to . . . (*Catches sight of a pickle and feels a little ill.*) . . . well, get a wee cuppa anyway, eh?

ECK. Donald in London's laughin now. He's roarin his heid off. You winnae get a decent job in Scotland, he said. Not unless you've got an Italian suit, he said, and an English education; they dinnae want what's on their doorstep.

And Donald was right.

WILLIE. Who's Donald?

ECK. Who's Donald . . . ? I'll tell you – Donald's that empty jar over there. He's slipped his pickle and buggered off to the land of gin and tonic.

WILLIE. Oh.

ECK. While the rest of us hang on here. Like there's you – the fatherly tortoise.

WILLIE (*looking*). Yon beastie's cut in half.

ECK. Extra slow that way.

WILLIE. And which wan are you then, smartie?

ECK (*pointing*). That's me there – wide-eyed, wi ma tongue hangin out.

WILLIE (*reads*). West African Chameleon. Hey. A thought chameleons were meant tae change. Colour an that. Blend in wi their backgrounds. That wan's aw white.

ECK. It's aw white because it's deid. Blends in pretty well here.

(*Sighs.*) Deid as a dodo, wi nothin to do, and nothin' to look forward to, and . . .

(*Stops and thinks.*) Hmmn. Well. No quite. No quite.

ECK *looks at* WILLIE.

ECK. Dad, how long are you going to be here?

WILLIE. Oh A don't know son. It's in the hands of the Lord.

ECK. Right. That settles it. If you can't change it, gie it a polish.

WILLIE. Oh aye, right. What?

ECK. Dad, I'm meetin someone tonight and it's dead important. And if, as seems likely, you are gonna to be lookin over ma shoulder when I meet her . . .

WILLIE (*gleeful*). Oh. A woman. You wee devil . . .

ECK. . . . we don't want a repeat of this morning's . . . unpleasantness. So there's something we've got to do first.

WILLIE. Aw. Get her a box of chocolates?

ECK. Naw. Get you a haircut.

NB *In between scenes six and seven, seven and eight, eight and nine – i.e. the sequence where* WILLIE *and* ECK *are out and about – they do an exaggerated 'walking about town' dance or routine as they set up each scene.*

Recurrent Music: 'Magic Moments' – Perry Como.

Scene Seven

In the Barbers.

WILLIE *in the chair.* ECK *standing parentally next to the invisible* CUTTER, *overseeing the job. From time to time* WILLIE *moves his head, as if manoeuvred by the* CUTTER.

WILLIE. A'm surprised at you, Eck. A stopped comin tae smokey wee barbers like this years ago. A went tae Helena's Boutique. Dead nice. Some wee girl strokin yer heid.

ECK. How unpleasant for her. Short at the sides. And the back. Trim it on top, but watch an no take too much. Dinnae want him lookin like a monk.

WILLIE. A've still got a fine heid of hair . . .

ECK. Oh yeah, and the sidies. Definitely off wi the sidies.

WILLIE. You've got sidies . . !

WILLIE'*s head switches side to side as the sidies are razored off.*

Eck. Aw. An' you dinnae. (*To audience.*) There now. That's a much more acceptable vision of parenthood.

Scene Eight

'At William Lows the price is always way down.'

ECK *is picking up items off the shelves and putting them in a mime trolley which he wheels in front of him.* WILLIE *is looking about him nervously and clutching his newly denuded head.*

WILLIE. S'an awfy breeze in here. A could catch ma death of cold.

ECK. Onions. Chick peas. I cannae mind – d'you like brockley?

WILLIE. Brockley. Whit's that again?

ECK *holds some up.*

WILLIE. Is that no just unripe cauliflower?

ECK *puts the broccoli in the trolley.*

ECK. It'll put hairs on yer chest.

WILLIE. Well at least A'm allowed some there.

ECK. Can you see the cream? (*He moves off.*)

WILLIE. Brockley. Cream. A thought you were on the Parish.

ECK. The . . . oh aye. I am. (*Meaningfully.*) Still.

WILLIE. Yez dinnae act poor.

ECK (*stops*). Dinnae act . . .? What? This morning you were busy telling the world and his uncle about how affluent and respectable we were. Now all of a sudden it's hodden grey you're wanting.

WILLIE. We never lived beyond wur means. That's the thing. You just shouldnae act rich if you're no.

ECK. So who wants to act poor? I dinnae. Nobody acts poor these days. Everybody acts rich. You winnae get a job unless you act rich and successful. Ah, milk.

WILLIE. But you widnae need a job if you were rich and successful. That's cock-eyed. A tell you, you should do the auld clathes and parritch routine. Cap in hand. Respectful. Worked a treat for me efter the war.

ECK. Wholegrain or Italian? (*He looks at* WILLIE.) OK, sliced pan.

Look Dad I dinnae make the rules. Things've changed. It's just no fashionable tae be hard up right now.

They reach the cash desk and ECK *begins to unload the shopping.*

WILLIE. Aw those poor folk you were so keen tae talk aboot earlier on must be helluva unfashionable then.

ECK. Who? Oh them. Yes. And a carrier bag, please.

WILLIE. Em . . . Eck . . .

ECK. Will you take a cheque? Actually, could I cash one for twenty pounds? No. Oh. I see.

WILLIE. Eck, you forgot something.

ECK. What? I dinnae see.

WILLIE. You forgot the meat.

ECK. Oh that. Oh I never have any of that.

WILLIE. That's no poor? Hell, that's just like back in the thirties . . .

Scene Nine

Teatime Fun.

ECK *and* WILLIE *walking in after shopping.*

WILLIE. . . . and that was in 1978, eh? Man A'm glad A
  didnae live tae see that. A never trustit that MacLeod
  character, what did he ken aboot fitba anyway?

ECK. Hiya Carol. Dad, this is my flat-mate Carol. This is my
  Dad. He's eh staying for a little while.

WILLIE. Pleased to meet you Carol.

He shakes hands with her and moves over to ECK, *who is unloading
the veg, etc.*

WILLIE. Is she eh . . . is she . . .?

ECK. Naw, Dad. She's someone else. Carol's my flat mate.

WILLIE *looks puzzled.*

ECK. As in we happen to live in the same flat. The girl I'm
  meetin later is called Roseanne. Everything entirely clear now?

WILLIE. Oh. Aye.

ECK *gets a knife and chops the veg.*

WILLIE (*hovering*). What're you doin?

ECK. I'm making a model aeroplane. Naw really I'm chopping
  carrots. What'd you think?

WILLIE. Oh.

He continues to watch ECK, *half aimless, half mesmerised.* ECK *gets a
mime wok and puts it on the cooker, pours oil in, turns on the gas, etc.*

WILLIE. What's that then?

ECK. That, Dad, is a wok.

WILLIE. Well A hope it's no a long walk cos A'm starvin . . .

He doubles up wheezily at his own joke. ECK *rolls his eyes unamused.*

WILLIE. It's just funny ken, odd like, tae see you cookin.
  Listen, is there anythin' A could dae to . . .

ECK (*suddenly*). Look Dad I cannae do anything with you keekin
  over ma shoulder all the time. Now why don't you sit down,
  read the paper, watch some TV, anything, eh?

They face each other for a moment. Then WILLIE *about-turns on his heel and walks penitently to a chair. An empty one beside it.*

WILLIE. You were ayeways such a nice wee boy too.

WILLIE *looks about him and finds a newspaper. He picks it up.*

WILLIE. What is this? Is this a joke? (*He looks at front of paper.*) Daily Record. Is this a joke?

ECK (*distant*). What?

WILLIE. This. 'Prime Minister Margaret Thatcher today celebrates eight years in office.'

Slight pause.

Who's she then?

ECK. You dinnae ken?

WILLIE. Naw.

ECK. Course. Twelve years. You wouldnae. Lucky you. I think there's a Sunday Post around there. You'll like that better. The news'll be familiar.

WILLIE (*picks it up*). Aw aye. The Sunday Post. 'Danger of Radiation Veg'. Hey Eck, you'd better watch out.

Skip the religious poem. Hustle through tae the results ... aw, the Fun Section. Aw. Hey Eck, mind you ayeways jumped up and doon beggin for the Fun Section while A read the football. An A would say, Awright Wee Eck, Oor Wullie'll let you read his comic.

ECK (*unimpressed*). But then Oor Wullie kicked the bucket and Wee Eck got big.

The phone rings. Sound effect: ECK. *He keeps this effect up until he actually answers the phone.*

CAROL *sits down in the vacant chair next to* WILLIE. ECK *strolls towards the phone.*

WILLIE. Oh hello eh Carol. Doin yer homework are you? Oh. A see. What is it you work at then?

ECK *remembers the vegetables, the noodles are boiling over, etc.*

ECK. Hell. The noodles ...

He dashes back to the cooker and sets things to rights during which ...

WILLIE (*shocked and impressed*). Oh. Oh. Mechanical engineering, eh? Great Scottish trade that. Eck's got an uncle did that. In the merchant navy, like. Changed days, eh? Hard to see a pretty lassie like you bein a grease monkey down in the boiler room ...

ECK (*finally getting to the phone*). Father dearest ...

He picks up the phone.

(*Sharp.*) Yes what? Oh. Hi Roseanne.

Lights focus in on ECK.

Oh out and about. Yeah. How're you? Good. Mmm ... a wee bit earlier tonight. What then? Nine. OK. Look forward to it ...

He looks at WILLIE.

WILLIE. An you're sayin there's lotsa lassies doin it. No. No reason why not, A suppose.

ECK (*looking at* WILLIE). Hey em Roseanne, when I come along tonight, there might be ... well ...

WILLIE. Well anyway, your mum an dad must be proud of you ...

ECK. Aw nothing. No. Nothing. I'll see you later, OK? Bye.

WILLIE. Course it'll no be long afore you get married ...

ECK (*coming back across*). Dad, I'm sure Carol ... (*Suddenly sniffs and turns to the cooker.*) It's burning!

WILLIE. A thought that gas wis too high.

ECK. You've let it burn!

WILLIE. What is it anyway?

ECK. Brockley stir-fry wi cream.

WILLIE. Disnae sound very filling.

ECK. Naw. But it'll keep your mouth occupied for a while.

Interlude – *Dumb-show*

Music: 'The Captain Scarlet Theme' – Barry Gray Orchestra.

WILLIE *and* ECK *at the table, eating the stir-fry.*

WILLIE *is not keen on it. He eats fussily, making euurgh faces, feeling hard done by.* ECK *eats in a temper, looking at* WILLIE *and sighing.*

ECK *drops a bit of food on the floor. He leans over to pick it up, that is he looks away.*

WILLIE *immediately shovels the food down hungrily.*

ECK *returns.* WILLIE *goes back to being fussy again.*

Scene Ten

'Oh no'.

ECK *and* WILLIE *are just finishing the last of the meal.*

WILLIE. Well that was awright. Coulda done wi some mince in it, but it was awright.

ECK. Right. Dad. I've got some stuff to do, to get ready for tonight an' all.

WILLIE. Well don't mind me, just you carry on, glam yersel up.

ECK. Aye well that's just it. I want a bath. So you'll just have to park yerself outside, awright?

WILLIE (*picking up the Sunday Post*). Suits me. A havenae finished reading The Honest Truth about Prince Edward's marriage prospects yet.

They walk round to the bathroom. ECK *closes the door while* WILLIE *turns his back and stands outside. Reading the paper,* ECK *walks towards the bath. But they hit the stomach pain distance.*

BOTH. Ooooyah!

ECK. Aw no.

WILLIE. What is it?

ECK. I cannae reach the bath wi you out there.

WILLIE (*opens door nonchalantly*). Well son, it's no as if A've never seen it before ...

ECK (*to audience*). I'm a grown man ...

WILLIE (*to audience*). Ma wee boy ...

ECK (*to audience*). I'm a grown man ...

Scene Eleven

Bathtime.

ECK *in the bath, embarrassed.* WILLIE *sitting facing him, reading the paper.*

ECK. This is embarrassing. I wish we had some bubble bath.

WILLIE. Och A'm no lookin.

A pause.

WILLIE. A havenae eaten prunes fer years ...

ECK. Shut it.

WILLIE. Heh. Ma wee son in the bath. Aye. Aye. D'you no remember when you wuz really wee, on hot summer days we'd go out tae the back green and A'd blow up yer old paddlin pool an' you'd go splashin around like a mad thing. Eh?

ECK *is silent.*

WILLIE. Naw, d'you no mind? When the weather was really hot ...

There is a 'Change of State': a Home-Movie sequence.

Music starts: 'Two Little Boys' – Rolf Harris.

WILLIE *as Dad.* ECK *as four-year-old* ECK.

WILLIE *blowing up paddling pool.* ECK *leaping around, encouraging him.* WILLIE *puggled. Pouring in water.* ECK *trying the water. Running away. Jumping in, splashing.*

The sequence should be full of flicker and cuts and starts and blinking in sunlight consciousness to camera.

Music lowers: Dialogue Sequence.

WILLIE. Watch where you're puttin that water! A'm no goin in tae get any more.

ECK (*splashing him*). Nut! Nut!

WILLIE. Hey you, less of that. A'm drookit. A'm no jokin, you drown me and A'll drown you.

ECK *plays with his boat thoughtfully*.

WILLIE. Stt. Ma clean shirt.

ECK. Daddy.

WILLIE. Aye. What?

ECK. Can we go the seaside? Can we?

WILLIE. Aye, we'll go soon, we'll go on to the Bank Holiday. That's soon. We'll go tae Largs. Would you like that?

ECK. Aye. Ken why?

WILLIE. Not ken why, son. Do you know why.

ECK. Aye bit, ken why?

WILLIE. Why then?

ECK. 'Cause at the seaside, ye've got the water, and the water disnae go away.

Return to normal state. ECK *in the bath,* WILLIE *in the chair as before.*

WILLIE. A thought that wis rare. 'Ye've got the water an' the water disnae go away ...' Rare. Course you didnae unnerstan about tides or anythin then.

ECK. If you say so.

WILLIE. What's that supposed tae mean?

ECK. It means I don't remember all that stuff.

WILLIE. Aw course you do ...

ECK. Look, what do you want?

WILLIE. What d'you mean what do A want?

ECK. A mean what do you want fae me?

WILLIE. Nuthin. Nuthin. Did A ask for anything? A'm seein ma own wee son. That's aw A could ask for.

A pause.

ECK. I'm gettin out.

ECK *stands up to get out of the bath.*

WILLIE. Sling it ower your shoulder an' go as a . . .

ECK. Just read the paper, eh?

Scene Twelve

All Dressed Up.

Music: 'Patsy Cline' – Crazy.

ECK*'s bedroom.* ECK *wet – shaving at a sink.* WILLIE *prowling around the room looking at things.*

ECK (*whispers confidentially to the audience*). This is all I bloody need. As if I wisnae gonna be nervous enough about tonight, ma first real date wi Roseanne, the first actual time I've asked her and she's said yes, as if I wisnae gonna be quakin in ma boots anyway . . . and now I'm lumbered wi him on a Down Memory Lane trip . . .

WILLIE. S'an awfy dust in here. Do you never . . .

ECK. No. I don't.

WILLIE *goes on poking around.*

WILLIE. You wuz ayeways so tidy too.

ECK (*to audience*). Diggin up aw that stuff from the past. I dinnae need that. Makin me feel like a three-year-old. That slippy-slidey in the gut family feeling. That's today to a tee. No hope. No change. No nuthin. Hell, that's this whole place to a tee. Well, screw that . . .

(*A thought.*) Donald. That job . . .

WILLIE. Heck are these aw your records? What a money you musta spent on these. (*He flicks through them.*)

ECK. Give up, Dad. You winnae find Jimmy Shand.

WILLIE. More's the pity.

ECK *has finished shaving. Now he poses with clothes in front of a mirror.*

ECK. Well, Roseanne, do you like me in ma green shirt, or ma stripey shirt or ... hm.

Aw hell, neither.

WILLIE. Hud on though but ...

ECK. Maybe wi the red tie ...

He pulls a model pose.

Smart but casual. Mr 1980's. (*Smoothie.*) Hi ...

Drops pose, deflated.

Aye well, they cover up yer body.

WILLIE. Patsy Cline. Yez like some old stuff then.

ECK. What?

WILLIE. A says yez like some old stuff. Patsy Cline.

ECK. Oh. Aye. She's awright.

WILLIE (*sings*). A go tae pieces ...

Hey wait a minute. (*Reads from the back of the album.*)

23 Springvalley Avenue. This is ma record. What're you doin wi ma record?

ECK. You didnae take it wi you.

WILLIE. Imagine. You likin Patsy Cline, eh?

ECK (*under his breath*). I expect it's your terrific influence ...

WILLIE. What?

ECK. Is ma tie straight?

WILLIE. Aye, but you've got egg on your chin. Hell, button flies wi pleats and cuffs. A coulda worn them to the dancin 30 year ago.

ECK *mouths 'I coulda worn them to the dancin ... and then stops, and walks around* WILLIE, *inspecting his tragic seventies suit.*

ECK. Is that so? Is that so?

WILLIE (*nervous*). Aye. Wi a good jacket, mind.

ECK. Well Dad. Tonight we relive your glorious past.

WILLIE. How d'you mean?

ECK. I mean there's a spare pair in the cupboard. 'Cause if you think I'm goin out wi you the night lookin like Earth, Wind and Fire meets Sidney Devine, you've got another think comin.

WILLIE. This is ma best! A wis buried this way!

ECK. An I'll die if any of ma friends clock me wi you. Drop them.

WILLIE. Awww . . .

Music: 'The Avengers Theme' – Ron Grainer Orchestra.

Choreographed sequence as ECK *changes* WILLIE's *clothes. Room for gags as* WILLIE *objects to undressing and can't believe what he is forced to wear. Eventually he wears trendy trousers, shirt, tie and jacket, possibly an American Airforce bomber jacket, covered with badges for effect – or whatever is currently fashionable and therefore ridiculous for* WILLIE *to wear.*

Music ends. WILLIE *looks in mirror.*

WILLIE. A look a proper tookit.

ECK. You look twenty years younger.

WILLIE. But A'm no young Eck, A'm old.

ECK. Better old than unsightly. Get yer zimmer, it's time we were goin.

Scene Thirteen

On the way.

Music: 'Walkin' After Midnight' – Patsy Cline.

ECK *and* WILLIE *walking to the pub.*

WILLIE. And you say she designs clathes? A thought machines did that.

ECK. She's a designer. She makes designer clothes.

WILLIE. For other designers tae wear, like?

ECK (*sighs*). Look Dad, this is important tae me, right? When we get in here, and when we meet Roseanne, you're gonna be on yer best behaviour. Just drink yer beer and keep quiet, OK?

WILLIE. OK.

BOTH (*to audience*). Some date.

Scene Fourteen

In the City Cafe.

Music in the background: 'Bop' or 'Bossa Nova'. (Continues through the scene.)

WILLIE *and* ECK *enter the pub,* ECK *first, they weave tortuously through a tight crowd. On the way* ECK *says hello to an alarming number of people.* WILLIE *begins to join in behind him.*

ECK. Hi. Hi Darryl. Hiya Lindy. How's it goin. Good. Hi Mark.

WILLIE (*nods*). Mark.

ECK. Hiya Roz. How're you? Oh I'm fine.

WILLIE. I'm fine too.

ECK. Richard. David.

WILLIE. David. Richard.

At the bar.

ECK. Got here. (*To* WILLIE.) Well, what're you wantin?

WILLIE. Oh A'll have a . . . a . . . (*He studies the bar taps closely.*) . . . a pint of Special, Eck.

ECK. Hey Michelle. Hiya. Bottle of Pirroni and (*Coughs.*) a pint of Special please.

ECK *looks in his wallet and then at* WILLIE.

ECK. I wish you'd got buried wi your chequebook.

Well, Michelle, how's the paintin goin? Aw you got a show? Good. Great. Who? Oh em him. He's my eh, he's my Dad.

ECK *gives* WILLIE *an enforced shoulder-hug.*

ECK. Just showin my old Dad the hip scene, y'know. The City Cafe shuffle. Heh.

WILLIE. Everything's cool. A'm groovy.

ECK (*for the drinks*). Thanks.

ECK looks around for ROSEANNE.

WILLIE. Is the dame here yet?

ECK. She's not a dame. And she's no here yet. Let's find a seat.

WILLIE. Suits me.

They manoeuvre their way across the bar – ad lib: 'Sorry', 'Excuse me', etc. Frustration.

ECK. Och there's nowhere.

WILLIE. Aye there is. There.

ECK. But there's folk awready sitting there . . .

But WILLIE *has gone ahead.*

WILLIE. Excuse me, mister.

No response.

WILLIE (*more forceful*). I said excuse me mister.

Still no response.

WILLIE (*shouting*). Hoy mister.

GETS A RESPONSE.

WILLIE. Aye, you wi the poncy-lookin hat on. Are yez expectin sumdy or have yez just got a wide erse? Aye, well, just shift up a bit, eh, let folk sit doon.

(*Shouts to* ECK, *very loudly.*) Here you go, Eck!

ECK crawls across, affronted, nodding embarrassedly to those people who have turned to watch the commotion.

ECK. Hello. Tom. Jane. Heh. (*To himself.*) I will not go red . . .

ECK sits down, stiff.

WILLIE. Cheers!

After a little while.

WILLIE. Guy funny pub this, Eck.

ECK. How?

WILLIE. Well it's . . . it's. Well. Aw these folk in black. And those funny lights.

ECK (*tense*). It's a brasserie. It's meant to be hip. There's a lot of them in Scotland these days. It started in London.

WILLIE. Oh. Aye.

Still. Feels funny tae be drinkin Special in a paper mashy spaceship.

ECK. Look will you cheer up? God.

ECK *looks around for* ROSEANNE.

WILLIE. Aw A get it. You reckon A'll stop you gettin a lumber.

ECK. I am not getting a lumber.

WILLIE. So what d'you keep lookin out for? Santa Claus?

ECK. Look, Dad. This is my life. This is my time. This is my night. If things seem a bit strange to you, just a bit different from Barrowlands Ballroom, then just do as I do, OK?

ECK *looks around*. WILLIE *apes him*.

A pause.

WILLIE. S'awfy smoky in here.

ECK (*looks at his watch*). Where is she?

WILLIE. Poooo. Woulda thought young folk'd ken better.

ECK. Ros . . . aw. No her.

WILLIE. A says it's awfy smoky in here.

ECK. What? But you always smoked like a chimney. Embassy Regal sent a wreath tae yer cremation.

WILLIE. Naw son naw. A gave up.

ECK. When?

WILLIE. In Heaven.

ECK. Is it no allowed up there?

WILLIE. Oh aye it's allowed. It's a terrible money though.

A pause.

ECK *looks around again.*

WILLIE. Awful crowded in here.

ECK. Come on Roseanne . . .

WILLIE. Hey what's that on the flair? Is that a fiver?

ECK (*looking beneath the table*). Naw it's just a . . . hey, maybe that's no a fiver but we're in luck anyway. That's a free pass tae the El Mocambo club.

WILLIE. Aw too bad.

ECK. Too bad nuthin . . .

ECK *crawls beneath the table.*

Simultaneously:

ECK. . . . that's where we're goin later on. This ticket'll save me three quid of ma hard signed dosh . . .

And:

WILLIE (*budged into*). Hoy, watch it doll, watch it . . .

A further budge and a spill. WILLIE *stands up.*

WILLIE. Aw will you look at that, aw doon ma nice troosers . . . aye, aye well, just kindly be a bit more careful in future, eh? What's a wee girl like you doin on licensed premises anyway? Does yer mother ken yer oot?

ECK *emerges. A shock.*

ECK. Em. Hi Roseanne.

A moment.

ECK *looks mortified.* WILLIE *looks panic stricken. Suddenly:*

WILLIE. Och they were just an old pair . . .

ECK. Why don't you sit down.

WILLIE. Look, A'm awfy sorry if A spilt your . . .

ROSEANNE *sits down next to* ECK. *All budge up.*

ECK. I thought you'd never get here . . .

WILLIE. Aye, he's been waitin.

ECK. But I knew you would. So . . . who? Oh.

He looks at WILLIE *and then back to* ROSEANNE.

ECK. Roseanne, this is em . . . this is my . . . I'd like you to meet . . . that is, he's my . . . em . . .

ECK *is paralysed. He cannot bring himself to admit that* WILLIE *is his father. But then* WILLIE *leaps in.*

WILLIE (*arch-cool, offering his hand*). Gimme skin, chick – A'm an old, old friend of the family, dig? A'm in culture, an artist, ken, what the people are really sayin now an that. A wis respectable, but now A'm workin class. The name's Critchley. Willie. Pleased tae meet you.

He looks at ECK. ECK *gapes in astonishment.*

WILLIE (*rapidly*). Oh yes, you're a very lucky girl. Young Alec here, whose family A've known a long, long time you know, he's a fair hot shot wi the voice that's no heard, he's hip ken, too bad about the job, you woulda thought they would need somebody, what wi Fyffe Robertson bein deid. A tell you he was robbed. (*Winks at* ECK, *whispers.*) Do like you do, eh?

ECK (*stunned*). Em yes. Yes. No. I didn't get the job. I was eh robbed.

ECK *looks back at* WILLIE.

WILLIE. Well, dinnae let an auld codger like me keep you young love-birds fae enjoyin yourselves. Just you carry on. A've got lots to do. A've got a whole bundle of culture tae think about.

WILLIE *adopts an artistic thinking pose.* ECK *smiles weakly at* ROSEANNE.

ECK. So, did anything interesting happen to *you* today . . . ?

Scene Fifteen

Gettin' a lumber.

In the pub as before.

ECK. So the collection went down well in London? Oh good . . . really? Excellent. I mean it's the place to sell, isn't it?

WILLIE (*aside*). He never tellt me she wis English. Quite posh like. Mind you, maybe it's no her accent, maybe it's ma ears.

ECK. Yeah I know, the me generation, the selling culture – but it's kind of inevitable, isn't it, having to go to London.

WILLIE (*aside*). Oh inevitable, inevitable.

ECK. As a matter of fact, I'm thinking of applying for a job down there.

WILLIE *sits bolt upright.*

WILLIE. Whit?

ECK. Yeah sure, the hills and the glens are awful pretty – but they don't pay the rent. Anyway, that's easy for you to appreciate. You've lived in London and now you're here . . .

WILLIE (*aside*). She jist kens which side her bread's buttered . . .

ECK. But I need . . . out, I reckon. And eventually it's money. Money beats principle. I can't do what I want to do here without starving for it.

WILLIE (*aside*). He should eat some meat.

ECK. Well not immediately, I'll still be here for a while you know . . .

WILLIE (*sings volubly*). Mony a hert will break in twa
    Should you no come back again . . .

ECK (*under the above*). . . . and even when I go there are, well, particular people I know I'll want to keep in close contact with . . .

ECK *stops and looks at* WILLIE.

ECK. Yes?

WILLIE (*innocent*). Nothin.

Music louder for a moment:

A little later, ECK *and* WILLIE *at the bar.*

ECK. You didn't have to make such a fuss about helping me. There's only three drinks to carry.

A pause.

WILLIE. Well. London, eh?

ECK. Yeah. Maybe.

A pause.

ECK. Don't look at me like that.

WILLIE. Like what? What way am A lookin?

ECK. Like I'm doin something wrong.

Look, just do us a favour tonight, Dad. Shut it.

ECK walks away with his drinks. WILLIE stays by the bar. ECK reaches the pain barrier, winces, and turns infuriated.

ECK. Yes?

WILLIE. You forgot tae get the peanuts.

Music louder for a moment. A little while later, sitting down as before. ECK is getting on smoothly with ROSEANNE. WILLIE, *peeved, is muttering aside.*

ECK. Yes, I suppose my accent is quite easy to understand . . .

WILLIE (*aside*). They'll no tell him that down south.

ECK. It sort of changes depending who I speak to.

WILLIE (*aside*). Surprise . . .

ECK (*inching closer*). You know, yours is a nice mix. Very . . . well, I could listen to it for a long time, you know . . . what? Oh

ECK looks at WILLIE. WILLIE looks at ROSEANNE *and joins the conversation.*

WILLIE. Naw. Naw lassie, yer tootin. Mine's no a nice accent. A mean, it's the best accent in the world an' that – but it's just no nice.

ECK (*to* ROSEANNE). Certainly not as nice as yours . . .

WILLIE. Course, you shouldnae trust someone just cause he speaks like a namby-pamby Embra toff . . .

ECK glares at WILLIE.

ECK (*whispers*). Shut it. Remember?

WILLIE. Oh. Aye.

But as ECK turns back . . .

WILLIE (*all innocence*). Though A hear that some of them are positively supercharged in the trouser department . . .

ECK (*unbelieving*). Gosh. I feel like dancing. Don't you, Roseanne?

Cut: Bossa Nova

Music: 'Walkin after Midnight' – Patsy Cline.

Later, on the way to the Club. ECK walking along, arm around ROSEANNE. WILLIE *scurrying behind.*

ECK. Oh, I'm glad you like him. Yeah he em seems to have invited himself along. It's just a pain when what I really want is to talk to you . . .

What? Oh yes . . . (*Looks back.*) I'm sure he'll want to go home fairly soon.

At the door of the club.

ECK. Ah. The bouncer. Hold on a sec, Roseanne.

ECK *goes back to* WILLIE.

ECK. Dad, huckle yer collar up and hide yer face a bit, eh? If the bouncer sees how old you are we'll never get let in.

WILLIE *pulls a face and complies.*

WILLIE. Who am A? Methuselah?

They file towards the door.

ECK (*to* WILLIE). Just duck in quick, eh?

ECK *smiles ingratiatingly at the* BOUNCER *on the way through.*
WILLIE *tries to dart in but is stopped.* ECK *rushes back in a panic.*

WILLIE. Eh . . . what's up, man?

ECK. Him . . . he's with me . . . it's OK . . .

But WILLIE *has pulled down his collar and stretched out his hand to the* BOUNCER.

WILLIE. Charlie! Charlie Forrest! A havenae seen you since the day yer faither chopped his hand off in a printing press . . . How's he doin anyway? No so good at the darts these days A suppose . . .

WILLIE *is ushered into the club as an honoured guest.*

Music. 'Love Boat' – Jack Jones.

In the Club.

Music louder. Very packed. Moving through a tight crowd.

ECK. Yeah? So it is – hi! How're you?

(*To* ROS.) What's his name again?

WILLIE. This isnae the dancin. This is the black hole of Calcutta. (*To an invisible* PUNK.) Will you get yer hair outta ma face dear? (*The* PUNK *turns round.*) eh Mister.

ECK. Yeah, I'll have a can of Red Stripe.

WILLIE. What? Oh – a pint of Special, thank you love . . .

BOTH. Are you not . . .

What?

Are you not drinkin awful much?

In the club.

ECK *and* ROSEANNE *dancing.*

ECK. It's trendy to be Scottish in London right now? Why's that?

WILLIE *cha-chas across the floor.*

ECK. Yeah, I suppose we did vote the right way . . .

WILLIE *dances back with a partner.*

WILLIE. Naw, A dinnac come here often either.

ECK. I wish we'd stayed near the edge of the dance floor . . .

In the Club.

ECK *mimes necking with* ROSEANNE. WILLIE *stands close by, drains his glass, rolls his eyes, etc.*

ECK (*laughs*). No . . . I mean yes, yes . . . it's just funny. I was about to propose the very same thing to you.

WILLIE *smacks his lips, rubs his tummy.*

ECK. Oh I see. And your sister's actually staying in your room. So your place is out. Yeah well that's fine. We can go back to mine. Yeah. Just the . . . just the two of us.

WILLIE (*catches* ECK'*s arm*). Hey, Eck – is there a chippie on the way home?

Scene Sixteen (a)

Back at Eck's flat.

Music: 'My son calls another man daddy' – Hank Williams.

Semi-dark. A bit drunk, ECK *and* ROSEANNE *are giggling.* WILLIE *finishing a poke of chips is behind them.* ECK *unlocks the door to his flat.*

ECK. Shshsh ... I don't know, maybe he wants a cup of coffee or something ...

He looks back at WILLIE.

Yeah. Yeah I know. But it's cool. I'll deal with him. You go on into my room and I'll sort him out, OK? I'll be in in a moment.

He lets her go, then measures distances around his bedroom door.

ECK (*smiling*). Yeah. We should just about reach.

WILLIE. Cannae get used tae this broon sauce stuff.

ECK. Look Dad, we're going into my bedroom now ...

WILLIE (*starts in*). Fine ...

ECK. So you're stayin out here, okay? You'll be awright.

WILLIE. Oh.

ECK. Thanks Dad, you're a pal.

ECK *walks through bedroom door and closes it.*

Scene Sixteen (b)

Dad at the door.

A pause.

Lights slowly down on WILLIE. *He looks a bit melancholy and put out.*

WILLIE. Hmph. He's in there. Wi her.

Pause.

Well, A remember. A remember. A wouldnae huv stuck ma faither ootside in the cold, but A remember.

Pause. He makes a face.

Come tae think of it, A probably wouldn't huv invited ma faither in either. Mind. A didnae get up tae this sort of shennanigans wi Maisie.

He sits down with his back to the door.

Maisie. I wonder how Maisie is. Auld probably. Hasnae had the advantages of preservation like me.

At least A dinnae think she's deid. Aye, A mean it stands to reason, ma ain wife would come and meet me, say hello an that. That's how it happens.

Pause.

A dinnae think she's deid. Stupit, A never even asked him. Y'know, how she was keepin. Maisie. It'd be nice tae see her. Have a chat an a cup of tea. Eejit, it never even crossed ma mind, comin back an no seein her . . . maybe A could get him tae phone her. A never even asked him how she was . . .

He looks round at the door. A pause.

S'awfy cold oot here.

Pause.

S'no nice. A mean it's hardly like the thing is it, shuntin me oot here while he . . . A mean it's no nice is it. It's no like family. It's no like family at all.

(*Aloud.*) A says it's no like . . . och. Hell mend him. Get some sleep. Just close yer eyes and, aye. Forget it. Forget it.

A short pause. Eyes closed. Then open again.

Maisie. She canna be deid can she? A mean she'd no pass on an no come an see me would she? A mean she wouldnae just avoid me would she, never even say hello like . . .

He looks around, a little desperate.

Son . . . A never even asked him. Oh God. A've got this terrible feelin inside . . . She wouldnae just . . . would she . . . A never asked . . .

He has stood up.

Aw no . . . aw tell me . . .

He bursts in the door. ECK is in some embarrassing position on the floor.

WILLIE. Son.

ECK. Dad.

WILLIE. Is yer mother deid? Tell me – is yer mother deid?

Scene Seventeen

Saying goodbye.

Music: 'Magic Moments' – Perry Como.

ECK *at the front door.* WILLIE *skulking as far behind as he can get.*

ECK. Please Roseanne ... look I'm sorry, I'm really sorry ... I didn't think that ... no look, it's not like that, he's not a friend, he's my ...

(*Shouts after her.*) Look, I'll call you ... I'll ...

She's gone. ECK *turns and glowers at* WILLIE, *then stumps past him to a chair (one of two) at a 'table'.*

ECK. Why d'you have to do that, eh?

WILLIE. A just wanted tae know.

ECK. Why?

WILLIE. A wis worried about yer mother. How she is.

ECK. She's fine. She's just fine. You could've just asked. Better still, you could have fucked off to bother her, no me.

A pause.

ECK. Bloody ghost of ma bloody faither.

(*An idea.*) I ken what tae do wi you.

He takes his chair round the other side of the 'table' and sits down, square. Throughout ECK *is prickly with a sarcastic anger.*

ECK. Put yer hands on the table touching mine.

WILLIE. Is this a gemm?

ECK. Aye. It's called Bugger off Dad.

WILLIE. Oh aye.

ECK. Aye. Go on. Touching mine. Unless you find the thought of huddin hands wi yer son a wee bit poofy.

WILLY *complies.*

ECK. We make a circle see ...

WILLIE. S'no much of a circle.

ECK. The shape's no material. You apparently came from (*He coughs.*) the other side. So what we'll do, you listening?, what we'll do is we'll call them up and get them to take you back.

WILLIE. Oh A seen this at the pictures wance . . .

ECK. Well you'll ken aw about it then. OK. Is there anyone . . .
is there . . . Maybe I should switch the lights out.

He rises. WILLIE *sniffs. The lights go dim.*

ECK. Well at least yer good for something. Right. is there
anyone there? Is there anyone there?

A pause.

WILLIE. Maybe they're no in.

ECK. OK. Let's stop mucking about. Awright God. Or Fate.
Or whoever. You sent ma Dad back to me this mornin. It's
worked really well, he's totally ruined ma day, in fact I think it
could honestly be said he's spoilt life for the foreseeable future,
mission accomplished, now would you kindly come and
remove him, eh?

A pause. Then a funny gurgling noise from WILLIE.

ECK. Dad?

WILLIE (*booming voice*). Alexander . . .

ECK. Dad are you awright?

WILLIE. Alexander . . . this is John MacLean . . .

ECK (*incredulous*). Really . . . ?

WILLIE. Alexander . . . the historical process requires that we
understand the past . . .

ECK. Aye but I'm sick fed up of him. Now . . .

WILLIE (*cheery voice*). Hello Alec, Sir Harry Lauder here . . .

ECK. Aw naw . . .

WILLIE. A bit of old, a bit of new, that's always been my
formula . . .

ECK. Aye, an look where it got you . . .

WILLIE (*gruff Glasgow*). Look Eck, life's a gemm of two
halves . . .

ECK. Jock Stein . . . ?

WILLIE. Me an' the Board don't think Willie's quite ready for
a re-transfer as yet . . .

ECK. Aw please, I'm goin spare ...

WILLIE (*smooth, odd*). Hello. The name's Chic. Chic Murray.

ECK. I didnae know you'd died ...

WILLIE. You were never at the Alhambra on a Saturday night ...

ECK. Aw you're just makin this up.

ECK *breaks contact. Lights up.*

WILLIE (*giving himself a shake*). Makin what up?

ECK. Aw that stuff. Aw those old bufties sayin you cannae go back yet.

WILLIE. Did they say that? Did they say that?
Aye well, it's a funny business death.

ECK. Well ha ha ha I've had enough. Understand?

I've had enough of you interfering and expecting me to do stuff, to be somethin for you. I don't owe you anything. Got that? Nothing. You disappeared a long time ago. I'm someone different now. I'm not the wee boy you could moan to and shout at and play with and push around.

No more. OK?

A slight pause.

WILLIE. Is that aw you think there is? Is that aw? So you can shut me out and dress me up and ponce me about, an squeeze me intae yer high-falutin arse lickin cultural schedule. Some thanks A get.

ECK. It's ma bloody life.

WILLIE. A'm your bloody faither.

ECK. You're bloody dead. Now stay bloody dead.

A pause.

ECK. And don't do the doleful holy eyes at me. There's nothing sanctified about death. I should've had done wi all that weepin an' quiet voices an' no speaking ill of you shite a long time ago.

A long pause.

WILLIE. You were ayeways the affectionate one too. Didnae like anyone leavin. So much as a sniff of sayin goodbye – pow – floods of tears. An' the thought of anyone dyin. Well. There was one time. There was this one time . . .

ECK. There was always a bloody occasion . . .

WILLIE (*firm*). There was this one time . . .

ECK. I don't need this.

WILLIE. Aye you do. You were four.

ECK *is silent.*

Another memory sequence. Lights change to give, if possible, a flickery black and white effect.

WILLIE. You'd been watchin the telly. A was sittin readin the paper when you came in and said

ECK (*four years old*). Daddy . . .

WILLIE. Mm?

ECK *bursts into wailing tears.*

WILLIE. Aw what is it son? What is it, eh? Did ye hurt yersel? Tell Daddy, eh?

ECK. He's deid, he's deid.

WILLIE. No one's deid silly . . .

ECK. He's deid.

WILLIE. Who's deid?

ECK (*gathers himself.*) Captain Scarlet's deid. (*More tears.*)

WILLIE. Aw Eck, no he's no . . .

ECK *nods yes he is and leads* WILLIE *round to the TV. On the way:*

WILLIE. A thought that guy wis indestructible . . .

They sit down to watch. ECK holds WILLIE's hand and points, frown-faced.

WILLIE. Aye well he's in the hospital right enough. But maybe the doctor'll make him better, eh? Maybe . . . aw hell.

A fresh flood of tears from ECK.

WILLIE. A cannae believe they'd put this on a kid's show. A funeral an everything. What do they think they're up tae? Look, Eck, it's only a story son, it's only a thing on TV, it's . . .

Look, hey look, Eck – he's there! He's alive! Look – Captain Scarlet's alive! He's walkin about an' . . . aw A get it. Look, there's wan of the eh . . . the Angels? Right – an' she fell asleep an' had a bad dream, right, an' she dreamed that Captain Scarlet wis deid, an' that's aw this wis about, it wis a dream this week Eck. Aw a dream, eh?

Sequence ends and lights return to normal. ECK is caught in present time on WILLIE's knee, being comforted by him.

ECK (*a little embarrassed*). So what're you saying? Are you sayin I didnae miss you? I didnae cry over you? (*Gets up.*) Well I did. And I didn't. You were a pain, Dad. You were a wheezing, complaining, sick, old-fashioned pain in the arse by the time you kicked it.

WILLIE. You were ayeways a right trouble. Wi yer moods an' yer demands an' yer rotten temper. An' yer fancy big ideas. A tell you, A've had peace since.

A slight pause.

ECK. OK.

WILLIE. Aye, OK.

A slight pause.

ECK. And now I've seen you again. And you've seen me. So we won't, well, we won't forget. An' I'll probably manage to survive what's happened today. Probably. But now it's time to go. I want you to go.

WILLIE *stands up and finds his original clothes. He begins to change back into them.*

A long pause.

WILLIE. Do you no mind that song we used tae sing when we wuz goin home fae holiday in the old Victor, fae Rothesay or yer gran's or whatever. That just popped intae ma heid the now. What was . . .

He whistles the first line of 'The Quartermaster's Store'.

WILLIE. D'you no mind?

ECK *is silent.*

WILLIE. Naw, d'you no mind?

ECK. Yeah, OK I remember.

WILLIE (*sings*). There was eggs, eggs
Would gie you . . .

What did the eggs gie you again? Go on. For me. A cannae
mind the now.

ECK. Bandy legs.

WILLIE. What?

ECK. The eggs gave you bandy legs.

WILLIE. Looks like you had too many.

ECK. Watch it.

WILLIE (*sings*). Would gie you bandy legs
In the store, in the store
There was eggs, eggs

BOTH. Would gie you bandy legs
In the quartermaster's store

My eyes are dim I cannot see
I did not bring my specs wi me
I did not bring my specs wi me.

WILLIE. And then?

ECK (*sings*). There was cheese, cheese

BOTH. Would gie you knobbly knees
In the store, in the store
There was cheese, cheese
Would gie you knobbly knees
In the quartermaster's store.

While WILLIE *sings the chorus,* ECK *hums and wanders over to one
side, with his back to* WILLIE.

ECK. I've got a wee drop whisky here. D'you want one for the
road?

ECK *joins in on the end of the chorus.*

ECK. I did not bring my specs wi me.

There was ham, ham . . .

He holds out a bottle of whisky.

Alas poor snifter . . . hey, did you want some?

ECK *turns round. But* WILLIE *is gone.*

ECK. Dad? Dad?

A pause. ECK *feels his stomach. Nothing.*

Oh.

ECK *sits down. After a while.*

Some day. Ma Dad here. Ma Dad gone.

Pause.

London. Bed. Both maybe. Aye, maybe.

End music: 'Lovesick Blues' – Patsy Cline.

End

RONA MUNRO was born in Aberdeen in 1959. After studying history at Edinburgh University she worked as a cleaner and later as a receptionist before getting her first professional commission for *Fugue* at the Traverse Theatre, Edinburgh, in 1982. Since then she has written for stage, radio, television and several community theatres. Her work includes *Watching Waiters* and *The Dirt Under the Carpet* for BBC radio, *Hardware* and *Biting the Hands* for television and *The Way to Go Home* which was commissioned and performed by Paines Plough Theatre Company. She travels as much as she can, including trips to Nicaragua, Turkey and South America. She also appears with Fiona Knowles in a feminist double act called the Msfits, who perform their show in Aberdonian and have toured all over Britain. At the time of going to press, she is writing a full-length stage play for 7:84 Scottish People's Theatre, who commissioned and performed *Saturday at The Commodore* as part of *Long Story Short: Voices of Today's Scotland* (1989).

Saturday at the Commodore was commissioned by 7:84 Scottish Peoples' Theatre as part of *Long Story Short: Voices of Today's Scotland*, and first performed at Isle of Skye on 28 February 1989 at Sabhal Mor Ostaig, with the following cast:

LENA, a woman of about thirty.   Patricia Ross
Speaks with an Aberdonian accent.

Directed by Finlay Welsh
Designed by Colin MacNeil
Lighting by Alastair McArthur

LENA. Saturday night, the Commodore Hotel, Stonehaven.
A'body cruisin' aboot looking at a' the folk they saw fae one
end o' the school week tae the ither like they're going tae turn
intae David Essex or Racquel Welsh (I've jist pit a date on this
story for you hiv I?) like they're gonny turn intae Bryan Ferry
or Suzi Quatro just wi' wishing. An' they pit on Lynnard
Skynnard, *Free Bird*, an' you hud a' the slow bit tae get off wi'
someone afore the guitars went crazy and you'd tae get your
tounge oot their mou' if you'd ever got it in and get the
dandruff flying wi' fitever it wis you cried dancing: playing an
invisible guitar or daein that wee sideways shuffle fae side tae
side treading a wee trench for yoursel' on the flaer. The maist
boring dance in the world that wis, and we a' did it tapping
oor tottery wee platforms fae side tae side ahint oor handbags,
like pygmy carthorses. Aw God d' you mind they shoes? Fit
wey did we ever get aboot eh? I was gaein wi' this loon,
Kenny Morrison, six foot four wi' six inch platforms.
Could've tied a torch tae his head and planted him in the
groond at Dunnottar as anither lighthoose.

They were great times though eh? You never think at the time
dae you, these are the laughs that've to last you your life. Och
but they were some laughs I had. Some pals.

Nora was my pal.

School sports, 1974, a wee dreich day wi' the haar in a'ready,
in fae the harbour tae hing aboot the playing fields and turn
your knees purple wi' damp and cauld 'cause you're in the
summer sports kit 'cause that stupit bastart Ma Hockey
reckons we actually *get* a summer in Stoney. Telling you, you
couldnae see one hale race, jist fitever bit was closest tae you.
Lethal, javelins and shot puts flying oot o' the fog, Tavvy
Nichols putted his shot intae the stovie bucket, naebody
noticed, that wis school mashed tatties for you. Aye and that
was school catering for you, if it wis the Christmas dance, the
concert or the sports it wis aye the same, stovies on a wee
paper plate, iron brew or cauld pale broon coffee, that's fit
they cried a celebration.

Nora wasnae great at running, but we were best pals and I
hud some idea o' mysel' as an athlete, Christ kens fit wey, I've

aye hud ideas that were ahead o' their time, maybe I'll come
back in anither life as Daley Thompson, this time roon I'm
lucky if I can run doon the street wi'oot tripping oer my lungs.
I've aye been great at panting. It was my chief athletic skill,
I'd lie aboot the finishing line wheezing and mopping my heid
like I'd seen the marathon runners dae in the Olympics.
Flopped oot waiting for Tanya Caie to run by. Tanya Caie got
three toes chewed aff by a stirk oot its brain on bad silage. She
was aye last in the cross country.

Aye well Nora wasnae much better than me but we baith went
to the lunchtimes athletics. I practised wheezing, Nora
practised running. She must hae pit something intae it. She
qualified for the two hundred metres that year.

Did I tell you fit Nora looked like? Nae much. She was blonde.
That's aboot a' you'd notice aboot her. I took up wi' her first
because she was quieter than me. She was a great audience
Nora, but fan I'd kent her a while I kent tae listen, she aye
made sense, jist at that time you're trying tae make sense o'
a'thing, Nora'd pit it a' intae words in her quiet wee serious
way. Jist at that age you're a' biling intae big steamy messes
wi a' your feeling, you could talk tae Nora and she hud wee
cool words tae calm you doon . . .

She cam fleeing oot the fog wi' her hair streaming, she
must've been growing it an' I never noticed. She wasnae first.
She was fourth, fifth, something like that, I canny mind. She'd
gone a' broon, dinny ken far she'd found the sun tae get
hersel' a tan, an' she was grinning, running her wee legs aff
an' grinning a' o'er her face. She'd a wee twisted grin Nora,
made her look like a cat trying tae yawn. I went running up
tae her pit baith arms tight roon her neck and says 'Aw well
done Nora, you nearly got a ribbon', gied her a hug. An'
Susan and Mingo were gaen past and they gaes 'Aw lezzies!
Lezzies!' An' Nora walked awa fae me. No like she was cross.
Like she was feart o' me . . . for me.

You just didnae hug folk much in Stoney ken? Wasnae the
way you carried on.

So . . . Saturday night . . . Commodore Hotel . . . Och fit am
I trying tae tell you here?

Och see they aye used tae gie you a hard time, onything aboot
you they could get their teeth intae. Well Mingo did it, it wis
her pit the names tae folk, och she's a wee bit coorse Mingo

but she's aye been far the party is eh? Och I wis a bit feart frae her then, well . . . naebody got the wrong side o' her but you aye had laughs wi' Mingo, that's a' it wis, laughs, we were pals. Your best pals are the ones from fan you were wee eh? I reckon Nora jist didnae . . . och she never tried tae fit in ken, doon the bogs, haein a smoke, a blether, she didnae ken fit wey to dae it. Naebody would've ca'd her names if she hadnae let on she bothered . . . I aye telt her that . . . I did. They ca'd Kenny the Jolly Green Giant, did you see me bothered? Though mebbe it wis worse mebbe it . . .

There was this party see the weekend afore *that* Saturday, the Saturday nicht doon the Commodore I mean . . . Is ony o' this makin' sense? Och I'll tell you onyway. Parties see, parties were a problem roon Stoney cause if you didnae live in the toon you probably lived on a farm at the back end o' beyond, halfway tae Drumlithie or Laurencekirk . . . folk said a' the bairns fae Laurencekirk hud nits, I never believed it . . . Anyway if you wanted a party you hud tae get somebody wi' a car and a licence tae drive it that'd round you a' up fae Maryculter tae Auchenblae and drive mebbe a forty mile circuit, cramming you a' in the car till you were a' on top o' each other, earrings and perfume an' fresh sprayed hair a' mixed in wi' each other, till you piled oot the car at Arburthnott or farever it wis, a do in somebody's barn or milking room. You'd pick your way in your new platforms slipping and sinking in the sharn, get oot your brain on cider and stuff yoursel wi' birthday dumpling, fresh oot the pan wi' a soggy biled crust on it. They were great those parties. This een, this een I'm telling you aboot was oot at Fourdoun, in the front room, no' the barn, 'cause it wis only ten o' us that nicht. Onyway. Half ten, lights oot, same as usual, I'm sitting on Kenny's knee makin' een kiss last through the hale o' the second side o' Pink Floyd's 'Meddle' an' this wee voice pipes up . . . I'd swear it wis Mingo but she said she never . . . this wee voice, 'Nane o' you lassies snogging wi' Nora is there?' Och a'body laughed. When the record was o'er an' they pit the lights on Nora wis awa.

Now, foo dae you get hame fae Fourdoun at eleven o'clock at night fan you've nae car and your lift's snogging his mou aff wi' Corrinne Murray? Did she walk it? Fourdoun tae Netherley? Twenty odd miles in the dark wi' the rain driving in aff the sea an' even the coos sleeping ahint the dyke oot o' the blast of it? She never said. I never asked. I should've.

Saturday nicht, the Commodore Hotel, Stonehaven. It wis
some disco that nicht. I wis desperate for Nora tae cam oot wi'
me. I thocht it wis just for the company cause Kenny was in
the hospital wi' a broken ankle ... Aye it wis dancing did it
... Ken the Rolling Stones, Brown Sugar? Ken that bit in the
middle fan they gae 'I said yeah, yeah, yeah Woooh'. (*Spoken
hurriedly*.) Ken the bit I mean? Kenny's idea o' flash dancing.
His only attempt at flash dancing was tae wait till the 'Wooh'
and jump up in the air and clap his hands o'er his heid. You
try daein that in six inch platforms. Onyway I reckoned that's
fit wey I was desperate tae gang wi' Nora, you couldnae gang
tae a disco on your ain. But fan it cam tae it Tavvy and Sheila
were giein me a lift ...

We came by the steading tae pick her up. She was oot by the
kiy, wasnae dressed up, naething, just standing there in her
wee red kagool letting the calves suck on her hand. She was
looking at the calves, she wouldnae look at me. 'Come on
Nora, cam oot wi' us.' She jist shakes her heid. 'Aw come
on Nora' Naething, then, I dinny ken fit wey I wis jist
blazing at her, 'cause we aye did fit I wanted, we aye went
far I led us an I wis wanting her oot wi' me just ... 'cause I
did ... I wanted her tae cam oot ... Dinnae ken fit wey
... I says, 'Right Nora are you my friend or no?' She
looked at me, maybe ten seconds, felt like forever, staring oot
o' her wee pinched up kitten's face, one o' the calves made
another grab tae sook on her jaiket, she jist shoved it off then
she says, 'Aye I'll be wi' you in a meenty', gacs awa intae
the hoose.

A' body was there that nicht. It was great boppin' ken.
Hadnae hud such great bopping since I got myself in love
wi' Kenny ... Nae since it wis jist me and Nora, trying oot
different ways o' dancing in the loft over the byre, Nora
teaching me fit wey tae move, a' the ways she was aye too
shy tae dae hersel' fan we were in the disco. We played
Bryan Ferry, 'I'm in wi' the in crowd' thirty seven times one
nicht till I kent a' the moves she could dae, till the loft was
dark and we could see oor breath in the cauld an' the
shooting stars sliding past ootside the cracked skylight. That's
foo we danced that nicht, doon at the Commodore. And
Nora moved like that even though a' the folk were roond us,
she danced like it wis jist her and me in the loft, danced like
she ran, wi' her hair flying an' her wee twisted cat's smile on
her face ...

Went tae the bogs, giggling wi' each other, Nora was aye that clever, the sly wee things she said aboot folk, naebody could mak me laugh like Nora. I'm in haein a pee, hear the door, Nora awa oot I thinks I says 'Wait on me ya cow' cam oot, Mingo's there, airms folded that look on her face, trouble. I'd jist got in on Mingo's crowd then, jist a bit, they were the only crowd, the rest were jist trying tae get there, Mingo'd been there for years. Ken fit its like, you stick in far your weel in, I wanted to stick in wi' Mingo. She says, 'That Nora, she's a lezzie'. I says naething for a bit then I says 'She's a'richt', jist quiet, mumbling it. Mingo says 'Haw so you're a lezzie tae?' I says 'Naw!'. She moves in on me, richt intae my face, naebody should wear pancake wi' freckles like Mingo hid but fa'd tel her? She says, 'Then fit wey are you gaein aboot wi' her?' I swallowed, I says, 'Aye well ken fit it's like, she used tae be my pal, I'm sorry for her'. And Mingo grinned, and I grinned back and she gaes 'God's sake you're fiel, you're saft, get rid o' her and cam away for a smoke, we're gaein doon the back o' the swimming pool'. And Mingo's awa oot the door back to tell the rest o' them the shape o' the world an' I turned roond an' there's Nora, 'cause she'd been in the bog a' the time an' she's jist looking at me again. Jist looking. I tried a grin but it wouldnae stay put. I said 'God . . . that Mingo . . .' She didnae even blink. I says 'Och . . . sorry Nora ken . . .' She walked awa.

Nora wasnae my pal after that, till we left school she jist kept tae hersel', folk left her alane . . . maist o' the time, she jist kept oot the road. She got her highers went awa tae Aberdeen.

Kenny and me never lasted either, couldnae be bothered after a whiley, it wis boring being in love, too much hard work tae keep makin' the Jolly Green Giant intae Ben Murphy, och you grow oot o' a' that stuff dae you? 'Less you get lumbered wi' the hale thing. Kenny's married up by Alford, twa bairns . . .

I never fancied ony o' that, och you're better yoursel' eh? Naething but trouble. I went tae teacher training in Aberdeen, noo I'm back at the auld school, teaching Maths, Ma Hockey's still here, an' they still mak stovies for the school concert . . . I jist live mysel', up by . . . och I've heaps o' pals, och well you can tell I fair like a blether eh? We get some good nichts oot, jist the girls . . . course a'body's got their ain families noo so it's nae so often we get thegether . . . Och I canny be daein wi' a' that . . . you're better jist yoursel' eh? I mean I've had my good times . . . back then . . .

Aye but . . . fit I'm telling you. I saw Nora in Union Street, Saturday. She was running, I mean she's the same age as me ken? Thirty years auld an fleein' aboot like a bairn, dressed like een o' the lassies in my class. I'd be affrontit charging aboot like that. She comes fleein' roon the corner o' Marks and Sparks racin' this ither lassie, baith o' them laughing like they're fiel or fou . . . crashes richt intae me. She jist gawps. She gawps twa seconds then she says 'Lena?' like she's half feart I'll say aye. 'Lena I'd never have kenned it wis you.' She looked jist the same.

Och we had a wee blether, caught up on the news ken. It wis a bit awkward ken 'cause this ither lassies hinging aboot. Nora pit her arm roon her an' telt me her name, canny mind fit it wis, I didnae ken far tae look. Och but they looked happy right enough. They looked happy.

Nora said she'd gie me a ring and hae a proper blether . . . but I've no heard yet. I wouldnae mind a wee blether, you can tell I've a lot tae say for mysel' eh? Onyway . . .

I'll tell you fit it is, fit I canny mak oot . . . I'd been telling her a' I'd been daein aboot Stonehaven these days a' that, I mean I keep busy ken? . . . So she's listening, she's smiling but . . . Onyway. Jist as she's awa and the other lassie's walked on a bit she turns back to me, looked straight at me, jist straight intae me like she aye could . . . She says . . . 'I'm sorry Lena.' Jist that. I'm sorry Lena.

Noo, fit did she hae tae say sorry tae me for?

TONY ROPER made a living as a miner, shipbuilder and brickie's labourer before studying at the Glasgow College of Music and Drama. His acting credits include BBC-TV's *Naked Video* and *Scotch and Rye* (Scotland's answer to the Morecambe and Wise Christmas Show), the video of which outsold that of the Royal Wedding! A request to write a play resulted in *The Steamie*, which to his astonishment ran for six months, winning the Glasgow Mayfest Award. It was later produced in Oldham and Nottingham. He adapted it for Channel Four Television, and it attracted the highest viewing figures in Scotland. It was seen in London as *Talk of the Steamie* in autumn 1989 at Greenwich Theatre. He is currently writing a play entitled *Paddies* for the Tron Theatre, Glasgow, in 1990 and doing a series for the BBC called *Rab. C. Nesbitt*.

The Steamie was first staged by Wildcat Stage Productions at the Crawfurd Theatre, Jordanhill College of Education, Glasgow on 1 May 1987 with the following cast:

ANDY	Ray Jeffries
DOREEN	Katy Murphy
MAGRIT	Dorothy Paul
MRS CULFEATHERS	Ida Schuster
DOLLY	Elaine C. Smith

Directed by Alex Norton
Designed by Malky McCormick
Songs by David Anderson

The play was subsequently presented as *Talk of the Steamie* at the Greenwich Theatre, London on 16 October 1989 with the following cast:

ANDY	Graham de Banzie
DOREEN	Emma Dingwall
MAGRIT	Judy Sweeney
MRS CULFEATHERS	Julia McCarthy
DOLLY	Myra McFadyen

Directed by Alex Norton
Designed by Sally Crabb
Songs by David Anderson

ACT ONE

Date: December, 31st. Time: 7 pm

Music playing 'Jingle Bells', 'a guid New Year', 'White Xmas', voices saying 'cheerio', 'Happy New Year when it comes', etc.

Curtains open or lights up to reveal MRS CULFEATHERS. *She is finishing off the last pile of washing. She mops her brow and gives a huge sigh. She is in her late sixties and 'does for people'. Her stall is the far left, No. 57, one of four. She pushes the trolley full of clothes out of the way and starts to load the washing from the pram to start the next load. Voices are heard off right. They come from* MAGRIT *and* DOREEN.

MAGRIT *enters first. She's in her late thirties. She shouts off.*

MAGRIT. Whit stall are you in Doreen?

DOREEN (*off*). Fifty nine.

MAGRIT. Where the hell da pit that ticket. (*She searches her pockets.*) Hullo Mrs Culfeathers.

MRS CULFEATHERS. Hullo Magrit . . . can ye no find yer ticket hen? (DOREEN *enters also with pram. Looks at numbers and goes to 59. She is about 19.*)

MAGRIT (*still searching*). See it's been like this aw day.

DOREEN. Can ye no find yer ticket? Oh hello Mrs. Culfeathers.

MRS CULFEATHERS. Aye Doreen.

MAGRIT (*still searching*). Trying tae dae too many bloody things at the wan time. What the hell did ah dae wi' it? . . . ah've loast it . . . ah think ah'm gaun aff ma heid.

DOREEN. Ye were right in front of me so it's probably that wan (*She points to No. 58.*) . . . jist take it anyway.

MAGRIT (*she starts to unload*). Wait tae ye see this ah'll jist get startit and someb'dy'll come up and say 'excuse me is that your stall?' Well they'll get a mouthful fae me.

They are now starting on the washing procedure. The large tub is turned on. Washing is sorted. Coloureds in large tub, whites in boiler, blankets

in lower tub, gel in boiler, washboard in large tub. Blankets steeping.
During this Mrs Culfeathers is working at loading her machine; she is
efficient, but the others are quicker because they are stronger. During this
DOLLY enters. She is in her late fifties and could be described as a
bachle. She also has a pram. She is a quick alert wee woman and she
looks at all the numbers then says:

DOLLY. Magrit, zat your stall? (*There is a small silence.*
  MAGRIT *turns.*)

MAGRIT. How?

DOLLY. You left your ticket at the desk.

MAGRIT. Oh, zat what happened? Thanks Dolly (*She holds her*
  hand out for the ticket.)

DOLLY (*studying ticket*). It's just that according tae this you're
  number sixty see, an' ah'm fifty.

MAGRIT *stares at her coolly.*

MAGRIT. Ur ye wantin' me tae shift Dolly?

DOLLY. I thought maybe you wantit number sixty? (DOLLY
  asks this quite innocently. She likes to be friends with people.)

MAGRIT. How? Is there something special aboot number sixty.

DOLLY (*looks at 60*). Ah don't think so Magrit . . . but if you
  want it ah don't mind lettin' you have it.

MAGRIT. Ah think ah'll let you have it.

DOLLY. Aye OK save ye startin' aw ower again. Hullo Doreen.

DOREEN. Dolly.

MRS CULFEATHERS. Aye Dolly.

DOLLY. Mrs Culfeathers, workin' away?

Dolly takes off her coat, hangs it on the stall, puts her apron on the
ground. Sits on it, removes her shoes and puts on her husband's boots.
She stands up, puts on the apron and starts on the wash procedure.
There is a sign saying prominently 'NO OVERALLS OR GREASY
OBJECTS TO BE WASHED IN THE STALL'. DOLLY makes
sure no one is looking and packs in three pairs of dungarees. DOREEN
and MAGRIT have the same business at the Director's discretion
beforehand. They wash after a suitable time.

DOLLY. Doreen, did you know Cissy Gilchrist?

DOREEN. Ah don't think so.

DOLLY. Aye you dae, stays oot in Garngad noo, but came fae here originally.

DOREEN. When did she leave here?

DOLLY. Oh she's a long time oot this district, she'd be ages wi'me or yer grannie.

DOREEN. Ah'll ask ma Mammy, maybe she knows her.

DOLLY. Aw yer Ma'll remember her. Fine big woman, her husband was the wee society man here for a long time . . . he was a right wee messen.

DOREEN. Oh.

DOLLY. Aye . . . he wisnae liked . . . naw . . . good tae her mind ye, but he thought he wis something, he'd wan o' yon awffy toffy voices. (*She imitates him.*) Eh think Mrs Johnson, you should maybe consider changing your poalicy . . . aye naebody liked him. He applied fur a joab on the wireless as wan o' they announcers.

DOREEN. He never did.

DOLLY. Aye . . . stupit wee swine, but she wisnae like that, me an' her had some rerr terrs thegither when we were younger. (*Shouts.*) Magrit did you know Cissy Gilchrist?

MAGRIT. Aye, she used tae be pals wi' ma Ma.

DOLLY. Well her Man's died.

MAGRIT. His he?

MRS CULFEATHERS (*stops what she is washing and comes to* DOLLY*'s stall. To* DOLLY). Ah couldnae help overhearin' ye hen. Did ye say the lassie Gilchrist's man's died?

DOLLY. Aye Mrs Culfeathers. It wis in the paper this mornin'.

MRS CULFEATHERS. She'll miss him.

DOLLY. Aye.

MRS CULFEATHERS. Ah knew them well. She's younger than me of course. They were a happy couple. He was awful good tae her.

DOLLY. Aye he was that.

MRS CULFEATHERS. Aye ... he wisnae liked hisself though ... wisnae liked.

DOLLY. Naw ... he wis a wee messen ... How's Mr Culfeathers?

MRS CULFEATHERS. Ah! he's no the man he was ... it's a terrible time o' the year this, Dolly.

DOLLY. Aye ... a lot o' deaths at this time of the year. Ma mother always said that ... ma Uncle Harry died on a New Year's Day.

MRS CULFEATHERS. Wis he ill for long?

DOLLY. Naw. He was drunk and fell doon the stairs.

MRS CULFEATHERS. Oh.

DOLLY. Aye. What's fur ye'll no go by ye ... will ye be celebratin' yerselves the night, you and Mr Culfeathers?

MRS CULFEATHERS. Naw. We never bother wi' Hogmanay noo hen, wi' the family away ... it's no the same.

DOLLY. Ye're welcome tae come up tae us ye know.

MRS CULFEATHERS. That's awful nice of ye.

DOLLY. It's no formal or nuthin' Mrs Culfeathers, jist a wee terr in the hoose wi' the neighbours n'at ... come up ... it'll be a wee break fur ye.

MRS CULFEATHERS. Tae tell ye the truth Dolly, ah've been here since wan o'clock the day, and by the time ah finish the night, ah'll jist be ready for ma bed.

DOLLY. Well if ye change yer mind ... yer welcome Mrs Culfeathers.

MRS CULFEATHERS. Ah better get back. Ah'm awful sorry tae hear aboot wee Gilchrist, she'll miss him, I suppose she liked him.

DOLLY. If yer needin' a wee hand noo ... jist gi'e us a shout.

DOREEN. Whit did he die o'?

MAGRIT. Lack o' breath.

DOLLY. Aye something like that. It never said in the papers jist said he'd passed away leaving a grievin' wife.

MAGRIT. Nae money?

DOLLY. Naw. Jist a grievin' wife. 'Course it's awkward dyin' at this time o' the year for the family.

DOREEN. Aye wi' everybody else celebratin', be kinna strange right enough.

DOLLY. It's no so much that hen, it's jist they've goat tae lie a long time . . . wi' the hoaliday's n'at . . . he could lie fur a week afore he goat buriet.

DOREEN. In the hoose?

DOLLY. Ah think Catholics have them in the hoose.

DOREEN. Dae they?

DOLLY. Ah think so . . . Magrit.

MAGRIT. Whit?

DOLLY. When wan o' youse die, dae they stay in the hoose tae they're buriet.

MAGRIT. Sometimes, sometimes no, but definately no fur a week.

DOLLY. They'll probably cremate him . . . or he'd smell.

MAGRIT. Can ye no talk aboot something else?

DOLLY. Ur ye goin' first fittin the night?

MAGRIT. We were supposed tae be, but he's lyin' up there drunk already, oot the game, sick o' o'er the carpet, pig. His breath's like a burst lavy, ye could strip paint wi' it.

DOLLY. Aye he likes a drink your Peter. Did ye have a nice Christmas? Oh ah never wished ye Merry Christmas. Merry Christmas Magrit.

MAGRIT. Merry Christmas Dolly.

DOLLY. Merry Christmas Doreen.

DOREEN. Merry Christmas Dolly. Merry Christmas Magrit.

MAGRIT. Merry Christmas Doreen.

DOLLY. Merry Christmas Mrs Culfeathers.

DOREEN. Merry Christmas Mrs Culfeathers.

MRS CULFEATHERS. Merry Christmas Doreen . . . Merry Christmas Dolly.

MAGRIT. Merry Christmas Mrs Culfeathers.

MRS CULFEATHERS. Merry Christmas Magrit.

DOLLY. Aye Merry Christmas Magrit ... did ah wish you a Merry Christmas Doreen?

DOREEN. Ah think so.

DOLLY. Ach I'll wish you it again in case a didnae. Merry Christmas hen.

DOREEN. Aye Merry Christmas Dolly.

DOLLY. Did yet get nice presents?

DOREEN. Aye. Ma Ma and ma Da gave us a lovely table lamp and John gave me a dress and money tae get ma hair done.

DOLLY. It's lovely ... where d'ye get it done?

DOREEN. Francinis, up in Sauchiehall Street ... it was 7/6.

DOLLY. But they've made a lovely joab o' it ... it's beautiful ... zat a bubble cut?

DOREEN. Aye.

DOLLY. Wee Angela wants wan o' them.

DOREEN. Is that your wee granddaughter?

DOLLY. Aye ... she's just twelve though, she's too young for it ... she's champin' at the bit though, she canna wait tae be a teenager, ye should see her in the hoose, aw dressed up wi' her Mother's lipstick and make-up oan, she thinks she's a right wee glamour girl. It's a bloody shame ... oor Helen clatters her if she catches her an aw.

DOREEN. Aye?

DOLLY. Nae wonder but, she ladles it oan somethin' terrible, she's goat the lipstick aw o'er her face she uses it for rouge y' know ... oan her cheeks 'n' she tries tae pit shadin' oan wi't like the big lassies dae ye know, roon her eyes 'n' at. Her faither says she looks like an apache.

MAGRIT. Does she wear her Mother's shoes tae? I used tae dae that.

DOLLY. Naw she doesnae dae that ... her feet are too big.

MAGRIT. Whit size are her feet?

DOLLY. She's a size six. Oor Helen's a four and a half.

DOREEN. That's big for a lassie o' twelve isn't it?

DOLLY. She's sweatin' blood in case they get bigger. She hates goin' tae get new shoes in case she's tae get a bigger size since the last time she went. Her faither torments the life oot o' her 'n' aw cause ye know how she's awful like him.

DOREEN. Is she?

DOLLY. Oh, she's his double yon red red hair, blue eyes an' she's even goat his nose 'n' aw and he keeps tellin' her she takes after him . . . well he takes a size eleven. He says he's gonnae leave her his sannies when he dies 'n' he's goat her name doon tae jine the polis when she leaves school. 'S a bloody shame. He has her in tears, 'n' the mer she gets mad the mer he torments her, he telt her no tae hing up her stocking at Christmas, 'cause it wisnae fair tae the rest o' the weans. She says tae me the last time I was up in the hoose that aw the rest o' the lassies in her class were always measurin' their busts 'n' she says 'I'm no worried aboot ma bust Granny, it's ma feet a keep measurin'.

MAGRIT. Christ. Oor Teresa's aye measurin' her bust, she's daein exercises for it, ah caught her the other night aboot a week ago staunin in front o' the lobby mirror wi' her hands oot in front o' her like this (*She demonstrates.*) 'n' she's whisperin' tae herself 'Ah must, ah must, ah must increase mah bust, ah must, ah must, ah must increase mah bust, a bigger size is the prize fur dacin this bloody exercise. Ah must, ah must, ah must increase mah bust'. Oh ah nearly wet masel, so wait tae ah tell ye, she comes in fur a cup o' tea about half an hoor later, 'n' she's sittin' drinkin' her tea y'know so . . . there was just the two o' us in the hoose, Peter an' the boys were away tae the pictures, so, ah says tae her 'Is your chest no gettin' bigger?' She says 'Ah don't know.' 'n' ah says tae her 'We'll mebbe need tae think aboot gettin' you a bra'. Oh 'n' she jumps 'n' she says 'Can I get wan for ma Christmas Ma?'

DOLLY. Oh, the wee soul.

DOREEN. Did ye get her wan Magrit?

MAGRIT. Aye, oan Christmas mornin' ah took her aside and gave it tae her privately, she was nearly greetin she was that happy she says tae me 'Mammy that's the best Christmas present I've ever had'. I was near greetin masel. She says 'Ah cannae wait tae get back tae school 'n' show aw ma pals'.

MRS CULFEATHERS. We used tae use bandages when I was a lassie, jist tied roon aboot tae support ye. It wis great, ye felt that secure.

MAGRIT. Ah think ah'd need a bloody hammock.

DOLLY. Aye you're big that wey Magrit.

MAGRIT. Peter says it was the first two things he noticed aboot me, the funny thing is ah'd me back tae him at the time.

DOLLY. Oh yer' a helluva terr Magrit. Mrs Culfeathers d'y' want a wee hand doon tae the wringer wi' them?

MRS CULFEATHERS. Ur ye no too busy hen?

DOLLY. Naw they can lie steepin' there tae ah get back. (*She crosses over and loads* MRS CULFEATHERS's *first load on to a trolley helped by* MRS CULFEATHERS.)

DOLLY. Oh, that's a lovely bedspread Mrs Culfeathers.

MRS CULFEATHERS. It's the doctor's wife's. (DOREEN *and* MAGRIT *give them a hand as well*.)

DOLLY. Wee McInness?

MRS CULFEATHERS. They've goat a lovely hoose, lovely stuff in it, look at this tablecloth . . . it's Irish Linen, that embroidery's all hand done.

DOLLY. N'at lovely Doreen.

DOREEN. Ah'd be feart tae pit that doon in case ah spilt somethin' oan it.

MAGRIT. He's bloody useless him, no matter whit you go tae him wi', he tells you it's yer nerves.

DOREEN. Ah think he's creepy, ah hate gaun tae him. They're nice curtains them, ah'd like a pair like that in ma big room.

MRS CULFEATHERS. They're a lovely colour, aren't they?

DOLLY. Is he no homeopathic?

DOREEN. Ah think he's homeo something, ah don't know aboot pathic.

MAGRIT. Merr like homeo-pathetic, he gave me tablets the last time ah went, fur mah leg. Ah said 'Ye gave me these before and they never did any good'. He says 'These are different ones'. So ah went hame and looked, same bloody tablets.

DOREEN. Did ye go back tae him?

MAGRIT. Aye. Ah showed him the two bottles and ah says 'You tell me is that or is that no the same tablets'. Know what he says? 'These last ones are a different strength'. Ah says 'Well they look exactly the same tae me'. And he just gave me one ae they stupid wee smiles o' his, ye know thon wey as if tae say yer no right in the heed, so ah says tae him 'Well ah'm no wantin' them 'cause as far as ah'm concerned they're the same and they're no helping me'.

MRS CULFEATHERS. Did he give you something else?

MAGRIT. Bloody right he did. He says 'Well you're obviously not happy Margaret, so we'll try you on these see if they're any better. Come back and let me know how you get on with them'. He's a plausible wee swine.

DOREEN. Aye so he is.

MAGRIT. Ah let him have it. Ah telt him. Ah says 'Hey d'you think ah'm a bloody guinea pig? Am ah a bloody test case or something?' Excuse ma language Mrs Culfeathers.

MRS CULFEATHERS. It's aw right hen.

MAGRIT. Ah says 'Cause if ah'm ur, I want tae be tested by somebody competent, ah could dae what you're daein, haundin oot pills and sayin' try that and if they don't work we'll try something else'. Any stupit bugger could dae that. N'en he says tae me 'well maybe you should think about registering with another Doctor'. Ah says 'listen you, ah'm here wi' a sore leg ah cannae go traipsin' two mile tae the next Doctor'.

DOLLY. Is that Bell? 'S that Doctor Bell?

DOREEN. Aye. Ye cannae get on his books, he's smashin'.

DOLLY. Is his wife no a Doctor as well?

DOREEN. Aye. She's good n'aw.

MRS CULFEATHERS. What happened Magrit?

MAGRIT. He gave me an appointment for tae see some big cheese in the hospital. He should have done it long ago.

DOREEN. What did he say's up wi' your leg?

MAGRIT. He says it's ma nerves.

DOLLY. Zit sore?

MAGRIT. Of course it's bloody sore.

DOLLY. Naw ah mean is it sore the noo.

MAGRIT. Naw, it comes and goes. It's thrombosis.

DOREEN. Is that no a clot?

MAGRIT. Aye ... 'n' so's that bloody Doctor.

MRS CULFEATHERS. Well ah'll away ... and see if there's a wringer free, just noo.

DOLLY. Ah'll gie ye a wee hand tae load them in.

MRS CULFEATHERS. You're a saint hen. (*They exit.*)

MAGRIT. Christ there they go Saint Dolly and Blessed Molly Culfeathers.

DOREEN. It's a shame but though i'n't it?

MAGRIT. D y'e want a cigarette?

DOREEN. Aye. Takin' in washing at her age.

MAGRIT *searches in her coat for cigarettes.*

What age wid she be?

MAGRIT. I cannae find the bloody cigarettes noo. See if that wee swine Peter's taken them, I'll bloody murder him. Oh, here they are.

DOREEN. Have ye caught him smokin'?

MAGRIT. Naw no yit, but see if you go intae the lavy after him the place is reekin' and there's aye a wee dout in the pan, 'cause they'll no sink ye know. Ah aye know when he's been at it cause he keeps flushin' it tae try an' make it go away. Here, look at that, there was seven in there before I left ... there's only six noo.

DOREEN. Ye should tell his faither.

MAGRIT. I will ... the first time ah catch him sober. (*Lights cigarette.*) What were ye sayin' aboot Molly Culfeathers?

DOREEN. She said she's been here since wan o'clock. Imagine havin' tae take in washin' at her age. Y'ed think her family wid help her oot.

MAGRIT. Ah know. It's a disgrace, she'll no hear a word against them either.

DOREEN. She must feel it herself though. Two sons she had?

MAGRIT. Aye. Christ they wantit fur nothin' they two. Of course the old fellah had a good joab, ah don't know what he did, but he'd good money. Ah mind ma mother sayin' she'd aye a big bag o' messages every Saturday n'aw paid fur. Never ony tic. N'a lovely hoose tae. She's still goat a lovely hoose. Ma mother goes up noo'n'again. She says it's spotless, s'auld fashioned of course . . . no oor taste.

DOREEN. Ah think it's terrible, ah'd never treat mah mother like that, she charges one and six a washin'. I mean she's been here since wan o'clock, what is it noo? Efter seven . . . that's say six hoors . . . three washin's that's four and six, nae wonder the old soul's no celebratin' the New Year, she's goat nuthin tae celebrate, the auld fellah's no long fur this world either.

MAGRIT. Oh when he goes, she'll no be long behind him.

DOREEN. Aye, an' wait ye see the two hert broken sons at the funeral, they're in England aren't they?

MAGRIT. Ah think so.

DOREEN. John wantit us tae go tae England after we goat merrit, but ah didnae fancy it. I mean ye widnae know anybody. Would ye?

MAGRIT. Right enough.

DOREEN. I cannae stand the wey they talk aw yon ya ya ya.

MAGRIT. Oh. They're a pain in the airse, see yon bloody British pictures.

DOREEN. Ah know, they're loupin i'n't they?

MAGRIT. We went tae the Rex aboot a week ago tae see . . . eh whit wis it called eh Fred McMurray and eh . . .

DOREEN. 'Double Indemnity'.

MAGRIT. It was great wint it?

DOREEN. It was marvellous.

MAGRIT. But did ye see thon thing that was oan wi' it?

DOREEN. Aye, Ron Randell leanin' up against a lamp post smokin' a fag.

MAGRIT. He tells ye the bloody story before ye've seen it.

DOREEN. Aye'n'en he flicks the fag away, supposed tae be tough. 'N' says 'It was moorder'. They cannae fight right either, know how in the yankee pictures they belt wan another dead hard wi'their fists n'at see if there's a fight'n' the British wans, they wrestle aw the time.

MAGRIT. So they dae, it's like an auld fashioned waltz.

DOREEN. They never touch wan another. I mean in the yankee pictures they actually dae hit wan another. You can see them daen it.

MAGRIT. Oh aye. Jimmy Cagney's a rerr wee fighter. Can ye imagine Jimmy Cagney in wan ae they British pictures. He'd murder the whole lot o' them.

DOREEN. Aye. Nae bother. Have ye ever seen Tony Curtis?

MAGRIT. Naw. Ah've heard ae him though.

DOREEN. Oh he's beautiful.

MAGRIT. Is he a fine boy?

DOREEN. Oh whit . . . oh ye want tae see him. He's goat a fantastic haircut, and beautiful eyes 'n' a dead low voice, but his eyes though oh they go right in tae you. 'N' he wears smashin' clothes tae. John 'n' I went tae a picture he wis in. It was the first time ah'd seen him . . . I just sat there . . . I'm no kidding ye Magrit I was actually droolin', ma insides were aw going', see when the lights came up I didnae know where tae look. I was dead embarrassed . . . John says tae me 'Are you aw right ye're aw flushed. What's the matter?'

MAGRIT. Whit d'ye say?

DOREEN. I just telt him it was women's troubles, well so it was in a way.

MAGRIT. Did he believe ye?

DOREEN. Aye . . . he bought me an ice-cream tae help cool me doon. (*They laugh*.)

MAGRIT (*still laughing*). An did it?

DOREEN (*still laughing*). Naw. It was aw meltit by the time he goat back.

MAGRIT. He should've goat ye an ice lolly ... at least it would've been the right shape ... oh ah've drapt ma fag ... that's God punishin' me. Ah'm terrible so ah ahm sometimes.

DOREEN. Will ye need tae tell that when ye go tae confess?

MAGRIT. Naw. It would be too complicatit trying tae explain it aw tae the Priest, I'll stick in something else. That'll make up for it.

DOREEN *sings 'The Big Picture'.*

DOLLY *comes back.*

DOLLY. That's her loaded up in the wringer.

MAGRIT. Have you ever seen Tony Curtis, Dolly?

DOLLY. Naw. Does he come fae roon here?

MAGRIT. Naw. He's an actor. Doreen wis sayin' he's a right fine body.

DOLLY. Ah huvnae been tae the pictures fur years. We used tae go afore we were merrit, mah hero was George Raft. 'S'a marvellous dancer.

DOREEN. I thought he was a gangster.

DOLLY. Aye, but he's a marvellous dancer tae. The tango was his speciality, mah favourite dance. I was good at it when I was younger. Ah was never away fae the dancin'. (*She sings 'The Big Picture.'*)

DOREEN. Where wis it ye went?

DOLLY. The Playhouse, the Albert and the Barrowland.

DOREEN. John and I met there.

MAGRIT. So did Peter an me ... it's goat a loat tae answer fur that place ... ah liked the quickstep and the foxtrot.

DOLLY. They don't dance noo though Magrit, it's aw that jitterbuggers they dae the noo. Naw there was nothin' tae beat the tango. Ma partner was aye Big Agnes Gillespie.

DOREEN. Did ye no dance wi' men?

DOLLY. Aye, whit ah meant wis big Agnes 'n' I aye went the gither.

DOREEN. Tae get a lumber?

DOLLY. Och, we never bothered wi' that, we went fur the dancin'. If somebody asked ye up ye went up tae dance, no for a click. There was plenty o' time fur aw that later oan. Andy Wilson aye goat me up fur the tango, he used tae say ah wis good 'cause I'd bowly legs.

MAGRIT. Ye should have warmed his jaw fur him.

DOLLY. Naw, he meant they came in handy when I leaned back.

MAGRIT (*looks at* DOREEN *and looks back at* DOLLY). Aye right enough so they wid.

DOREEN. How d'ye mean Dolly?

DOLLY. Well it meant when we were daen the lean-back he could get his leg in atween mine faster than usual.

MAGRIT. Nae fool Andy Wilson eh?

DOLLY. C'mere an' I'll show ye what I mean Doreen.

DOREEN. I don't know how tae dae a tango.

MAGRIT. I can dae it, show us what ye mean.

DOLLY. Right Magrit, gies yer haunds. (*She starts to hum.*) Ta rum tum tum tum . . . tar rara ra ra rum tum tum tum. Right here we go.

They tango

Noo ah'll dae the lean-back, right stick your leg in.

MAGRIT *does so and* DOLLY *does the lean-back. They stop in this position,* MAGRIT *looks at* DOLLY *and says:*

MAGRIT. Ah think this is us engaged. (*They stand up.*)

DOREEN. Oh that's rare. You're good right enough Dolly.

DOLLY. Ah can still pick up a hanky aff the grund in atween ma teeth.

DOREEN. Can ye?

DOLLY. Aye . . . c'mon Magrit we'll show her.

MAGRIT. Ah'm supposed tae be daein a washin'.

DOLLY. Ach tae hell it'll soon be Hogmanay, c'mon.

MAGRIT. Aw right ye daft wee bugger.

DOLLY. Right ah'll get a hanky. (*She rummages in the washing but can't find one.*) Ach I'll jist use this.

DOREEN. Zat no a semmit?

DOLLY. Aye but he's hardly worn it c'mon. (*She drops the semmit on the floor.*) This is actually easier than a hanky, but tae hell it'll gie ye an idea. Ye ready Magrit?

MAGRIT. Ah must be aff mah heid, but c'mon then.

They do it again, and at the appropriate moment DOLLY does the lean-back and picks up the semmit in her teeth. During this the wash-house mechanic enters and watches them. He is called big ANDY. He is a friendly big fellah.

ANDY. Not *the* Fred Astaire and Ginger Rogers?

DOREEN. She should have done it wi' a hanky.

ANDY. Fae what ah saw . . . she should've done it wi' a yankee, ye know there's nae drunks allowed in here.

MAGRIT. How did you swing it then?

ANDY. Whit the hell are y'es daein?

DOLLY. We were showin' Doreen the tango. Can you dae it Andy?

ANDY. Aye, but I never knew ye had tae eat a semmit during it, where have ye'se goat aw the drink stashed? (*He does a mock search.*)

DOREEN. We're just havin' a wee laugh.

MRS CULFEATHERS *enters.*

MRS CULFEATHERS. Andy, there's something wrong wi' the wringer, its no goin' right, son.

ANDY. I'll away an sort it. Do you know where they're gettin' the drink fae Mrs Culfeathers?

MRS CULFEATHERS. What drink's that son?

MAGRIT. Pay nae heed tae him Mrs Culfeathers.

MRS CULFEATHERS. I don't know nothing aboot it son.

ANDY. Did ye know Magrit and Dolly are havin' a wee affair?

MRS CULFEATHERS. Aye . . . Dolly asked me up tae it, but I'm too tired. I'm just gonnae spend a quiet night in the hoose.

ANDY. I think I'll come back and start again.

DOLLY. Stay and gie's yer patter Andy.

ANDY. Aye, aw right. (*Condescending.*)

They are all busy washing again.

ANDY. Zat a new haircut ye've goat Doreen?

DOREEN (*smiling*). Aye. (*She carries on washing.*)

ANDY. Good. You and Peter goin' first fittin' the night Magrit?

MAGRIT. Naw. (*She carries on washing.*)

ANDY (*to* DOLLY). Hoh! ye've no goat any greasy overalls in there have yez?

DOLLY. Naw.

DOREEN. Naw.

MAGRIT. Naw.

ANDY (*to* MRS CULFEATHERS). I'll go and fix the wringer.

He sings 'The Big Picture'.

ANDY. I think the conversation's flagging doon the bottom end, I'll just away doon and liven things up.

MRS CULFEATHERS. Aye.

He exits.

DOLLY *sits down, takes her boots off, hitches her skirt into her knickers.*

DOLLY. Doreen hen?

DOREEN. Aye.

DOLLY. Gonnae gie's a wee shoodery intae the sink tae ah dae the blankets.

DOREEN. Aye. Jist a minute tae a finish this aff.

DOLLY (*studies her feet*). Ah think ah'm gettin' another wee corn in there. Naw, it's just a bit o' hard skin.

DOREEN. Ye right Dolly?

DOLLY. Aye thanks hen. (*She gets up in the sink. She tramps the blankets after a while.*)

DOLLY. This'll save me washin' ma feet the night.

MAGRIT *and* DOREEN *do the same almost simultaneously.* MRS CULFEATHERS *also does it just after* MAGRIT *and* DOREEN. *They are all tramping firmly almost on the spot marching.*

DOLLY. It fairly gets the dirt oot them this.

MAGRIT. Whit . . . yer feet?

DOLLY. Naw the blankets . . . 'Roses are shining in Picardy' (*She sings the song.* MAGRIT *and* MRS CULFEATHERS *join in.* MRS CULFEATHERS *gives it her heart and soul with sincerity.*)

DOLLY. It's a lovely song isn't it Mrs Culfeathers?

MRS CULFEATHERS. Lovely Dolly, lovely.

DOREEN. Where is Picardy?

DOLLY. Oh, don't know, is it no in London?

MAGRIT. Naw. You're thinkin' aboot Piccadilly.

DOLLY. Aye . . . so ah um . . . do you know where it is?

MAGRIT. Nae idea.

DOLLY. Mrs Culfeathers, d'you know where Picardy is?

MRS CULFEATHERS. Naw . . . I know there's a Pickfords in the Coocadens, it wouldnae be nothin' tae dae wi' that wid it?

DOLLY. Naw . . . ach it doesnae matter it'll be somewhere probably . . . it's a nice song anyway. (*She pulls the plug and lets the dirty water drain away, sitting on the top sink the while paddling her feet. The others do the same.*)

MAGRIT. It's amazin' where the dirt comes fae intit?

DOREEN. Aye . . . I can understand sheets gettin' dirty, but no blankets.

DOLLY. It comes aff the men.

MAGRIT. Aye right enough . . . he's mingin when he gets home especially if he's been workin' wi' the boiler scalers he's covered in rust.

DOREEN. Aye John's the same, but he always has a good wash though, and he goes tae the baths twice a week.

MAGRIT. Peter's a bit like that, except he has wan twice a year
... see the boys ... they'll no wash themselves. It's a fight tae
the death every night. Ye want tae see their shirt collars, ye
could plant tatties in them.

DOLLY. Aye men are aw clatty in their persons.

DOREEN. That's what ah want eventually. A hoose wi' a bath.

MAGRIT. Ah like the sprays better, ah never have a bath in
here, ah always go tae the sprays.

DOLLY. Naw ah like a bath.

MAGRIT. Ah always think you're lyin' in yer ain dirt wi' a
bath.

DOLLY. But it is yer ain Magrit, it's naebody else's.

MAGRIT. Naw ah prefer the sprays.

DOREEN. See in America, they've aw goat them in the hooses
but they call them showers.

DOLLY. Is that no jist in the pictures they have them?

DOREEN. Naw. Aw the hooses have goat sprays, and washin'
machines and aw.

MAGRIT. And thon refrigerators, and they've aw got
telephones as well.

DOREEN. And televisions tae.

DOLLY. Mah sister's Jenny's daughter's husband's bought wan
o' them.

DOREEN. Whit a television? Have ye ever seen it?

DOLLY. Naw, but Jenny's seen it. She says it's great.

MAGRIT. Ah know some ae the big hooses in Dalmeny
Crescent have them, ye can see yon big things sticking oot the
chimney pots.

DOLLY. They cost a fortune.

DOREEN. Aye, but ye'd save money, ye'd never need tae go
oot.

DOLLY. Oor Jenny says that, says they never go oot, cause they
used tae visit her quite a loat but they never come near her
noo.

DOREEN. See that's what ah mean, ye'd save a fortune.

DOLLY. She's goat tae go roond there noo, and she says naebody talks while it's oan.

MAGRIT. Christ, that wouldnae suit you Dolly eh?

DOLLY. Naw ... I like tae hear people talkin'. Mah Alex says it's a wonder mah lips are no' frayed at the edges, ah'd be as well talkin' tae maself as tryin' tae haud a conversation wi' him though.

DOREEN. Whit kinna things dae they see on the television?

DOLLY. Ah couldnae tell ye hen.

DOREEN. That's mah dream, a hoose in the country wi' a television, a bath, and a phone, an' a garden as well.

MAGRIT. Christ yer no wantin' much are ye?

DOREEN. Ah'll get it eventually Magrit, ah've put ma name doon fur a hoose in Drumchapel.

DOREEN *sings 'Dreams Come True'*.

DOLLY. Oh she'll not be talkin' tae us Magrit eh?

MAGRIT. Between being oot in the gairden, watchin' the television and havin' baths, she'll no have the chance tae talk tae anybody.

DOREEN. Course ye's could aye phone for an appointment.

MAGRIT. Aye right enough, eh ... wait a minute. (*Crosses to DOLLY's stall, she mimes dialling on an imaginary telephone.*) Bring, bring, bring, bring, she's no in Dolly.

DOLLY. She might be oot in the garden Magrit. Keep trying.

DOREEN (*affected voice*). Hello-o ... Drumchapel 3776.

MAGRIT. Oh hello, this is Magrit McGuire here. I was wondering if I could perhaps have a word with Mrs Doreen Hood.

DOREEN. I am her maid. I think Mrs Hood is in conference with the workmen who are putting in the new *terrazo marble* floor in the big room.

MAGRIT. Well I don't want to disturb her. If you could just say that one of her old friends from the Carnegie Street Steamie called I'd be most grateful.

DOREEN. Oh just a moment, I think you're in luck, Mrs Hood has in fact just entered through the *French windows*. I'll see if she's free.

MAGRIT. Thank you you're very kind.

DOREEN. Hello-o.

MAGRIT. Hello-o is that Doreen Hood of the Willows, Drumchapel.

DOREEN. Yes this is her speaking to you *personally*.

DOLLY. Is it her? We were lucky we goat her in.

MAGRIT. This is Magrit McGuire, we used to be friendly . . . *in the old days*.

DOREEN. Oh yes. (*Non committal.*)

MAGRIT. I don't suppose you'll remember me?

DOREEN. No-o.

DOLLY. Ask her if she minds o' me, she'll remember me.

MAGRIT *gives her a quizzical look*.

DOREEN. Eh. Do you have an appointment?

MAGRIT. I'm afraid not.

DOLLY. Gie it tae me, let me speak to her.

DOREEN. Is there someone with you?

MAGRIT. Yes, another chum of yours, a Mrs Dolly Johnson.

DOREEN. Dolly Johnson . . . Dolly Johnson, now just a moment, eh does she have bowly legs?

MAGRIT *is starting to laugh*.

DOLLY (*serious*). Ah tell ye she'd mind o' me, gies the phone.

MAGRIT. There is 'nae wan.

DOLLY. Ah know that, ah know that (*Excitedly.*) . . . but gies it anyway.

MAGRIT *and* DOREEN *are both astonishedly amused, or laughing*.

DOLLY. Hello Doreen, are you up to yer ears in it hen?

DOREEN. Oh goodness me yes. What with the workmen being in and everything.

DOLLY. Aye they'll cause an awful stoor.

DOREEN. Well it's been one of those days, Mrs Johnson.

DOLLY (*fully into it*). Mhmm mhmm.

DOREEN. You see, John and I are going to the opera tonight, and I went and dropped my tiara on the bathroom carpet, and of course the *pile* on the carpet is that *thick* that it took me ages to find it.

DOLLY. Zat right hen.

MAGRIT *is in silent torture trying not to laugh.*

DOREEN. Oh yes Mrs Johnson and of course this *terrazo marble* just arrived from *Italy* this afternoon and when the workmen were carrying it in they nearly broke the *television set.*

DOLLY. Oh.

DOREEN. But fortunately the *display cabinet* got in the way.

DOLLY. Aye oh aye.

DOREEN. And they only just missed the *radiogram* too.

DOLLY. Oh that was lucky eh?

DOREEN. I've just sat them all down in the kitchen, and told them to help themselves from the *refrigerator.* I just hope the noise from the *washing machine* doesn't disturb them too much.

DOLLY. Aye. D'ye no mind o' Magrit McGuire Doreen? Her maiden name's Docherty, but she goat mairied oan tae Annie McGuire's boy Peter.

DOREEN. I don't think so. (*She can't believe this.*)

DOLLY. Ye must know Annie McGuire, her uncle used tae work in the fish shop at the coarner o' Balshagry Crescent.

DOREEN (*to* MAGRIT). Ah cannae keep this up.

MAGRIT (*holds an imaginary phone up to her ear*). Hello-o is that Dolly Johnson?

DOLLY. Is zat you Magrit? (*Incredulous.*)

MAGRIT. Yes . . . I would just like to say that if you don't get off that phone ye'll never get your washin' done the night.

DOREEN *collapses laughing.*

DOLLY *gets off the sink and says to* MAGRIT.

DOLLY. Christ I got right carried away there, ah actually thought ah wis phonin'.

MAGRIT *and* DOREEN *are still laughing.*

I enjoyed that, I wouldnae mind havin' wan o' them in the hoose Mrs Culfeathers.

DOLLY *goes to her stall. During this* MRS CULFEATHERS *has been very busy washing.*

Mrs Culfeathers, did you hear me phonin' there?

MRS CULFEATHERS. Naw, I was busy hen, I never knew they had a phone in here.

DOLLY *is about to reply when:*

Enter ANDY.

DOLLY *goes back to her stall.*

ANDY. That's the wringer awright noo Mrs Culfeathers.

MRS CULFEATHERS. Thanks son . . . Andy where's the phone in here? (*Looking round the stall.*)

ANDY. Phone? In here? (*Also looking round the stall.*)

MRS CULFEATHERS. Dolly Johnson's goat wan in her stall, is there no wan in this stall son?

ANDY. No that I know of.

MRS CULFEATHERS. . . . Ach it doesnae matter, there's naebody would be phonin' me anyway. (*She exits to the wringer.*)

ANDY. Has she been at the bevvy as well?

MAGRIT. Your mind's obsessed wi' drink so it is.

DOREEN. Andy d'ye want a wee drink?

ANDY. Ye's have been at the bevvy.

DOREEN. Naw we haven'y . . . but . . . John asked me tae bring some back wi' me fur later oan like, in case we ran short. It's in ma message bag . . . d'ye want a hauff?

ANDY. We're no supposed tae touch it oan duty . . .

DOREEN. Oh ah see.

ANDY. But seein' it's Hogmanay . . . I'll no insult ye . . . but just a wee wan mind.

DOREEN. Right. (*She goes to her bag. There is the sound of clinking. She returns with a bottle and a glass.*) See ah've even got a glass as well. My mother gave us some o' hers in case we ran short. (*She pours him one.*) Wid ye like wan Magrit?

MAGRIT. Naw I cannae stand whisky . . . just the smell o' it makes me sick.

DOLLY. Ah'll take a wee wan Doreen . . .

DOREEN. Right y'are Dolly . . . ah'll get ye a glass. (*She does so.*)

DOLLY. Very good health hen . . . are ye no havin' wan yersel?

DOREEN. Naw, ah don't like whisky either, Dolly. (*She comes with glass.*)

MAGRIT. Ah don't mind a sherry, but I'm no fond o' that stuff.

DOLLY. Wid ye like a wee sherry then Magrit? Doreen would you like a sherry?

DOREEN. Have ye goat some?

DOLLY. Aye ah've goat plenty. (*She goes to her bag. There is a lot of clinking. She pulls out various bottles, Pale Ale, Export, Wee Heavy, whisky, sherry.*)

ANDY. Fur Christ's sake, it's like a bloody shebeen in here. Watch what yer daein, somebody could see ye.

MAGRIT. Aye right enough . . . but you're the only wan wi' a glass in their haund.

ANDY. Oh Christ. (*He leaps inside a stall.*)

DOLLY (*holding up two sherry bottles.*) D'y'es want sweet or dry?

DOREEN. Sweet fur me Dolly. (*She goes to get two more glasses.*)

MAGRIT. Aye me tae.

DOLLY. There ye's are then, haud oot yer glasses. (*She pours.*) Well here's tae next year.

ANDY (*agitated*). Fur Jesus sake, will ye's come in here oot the road.

DOREEN. Aye we better right enough. (*They all go into DOREEN's stall.*) Ah'll stand in the sink and keep a look oot.

DOLLY. Ah need a wee drap water in this. (*She turns on a tap.*)

ANDY. Well here's tae us.

DOLLY. Wha's like us.

DOREEN *and* MAGRIT. Gey few and they're aw deed. (*They drink.*)

MAGRIT. S'a nice sherry that.

ANDY *is keeping a lookout.*

DOREEN. So it is. It's lovely.

DOLLY. S' only three and elumpence a bottle.

DOREEN. It's nice an' sweet.

DOLLY. Oh. It's good sherry . . . it's South African.

ANDY. Ye've left the bottle oan the flerr. (*Whisky.*)

MAGRIT. Zat a hint ye want another wan?

ANDY. Somebody might see it, wan o' y'es better go oot an' get it.

MAGRIT. Christ. What d'yer last servant die ae, or were ye too tired tae ask him? . . Get it yersel.

ANDY. Fur fuck sake.

MAGRIT. Heh. Language you . . . there's ladies present.

ANDY *makes sure there is no one coming and creeps out to the bottle. He looks about to make sure no one is looking, and bends down. He is just about to pick it up when* MAGRIT *shouts in a low voice.*

MAGRIT. Andy . . . what are you doing there?

ANDY (*shouting in fear*). It wisnae me . . . it's no mine . . . I found it.

The women are laughing.

ANDY. Aye aw right, very good, the joke's oan me. (*He goes back to the stall.*) Jist fur that I'll have another wan.

DOREEN. Help yourself Andy . . . Dolly d'ye want another wan?

DOLLY. Naw. Ah've still goat some left. D'y'e's want mair sherry?

MAGRIT. Naw Dolly.

DOREEN. Naw thanks Dolly.

MAGRIT. It goes tae mah heid awful quick.

DOREEN. Aye me an'aw.

ANDY. Right girls. All the very best tae ye's. (*Drinks.*) Oh, that's lovely, that's jist pit the taste in ma mooth fur later oan the night.

MAGRIT. Are ye gaun oot the night . . . at the bells?

ANDY. Aye. We're first fittin ma mother, and then we're gaun tae a party in Partick, some pal o' Jeans that she works wi'. I don't know them masel.

DOLLY. That's what ah like aboot this time o' the year, ye meet people ye've never met before.

MAGRIT. Aye . . . an usually ye hope ye never meet them again.

ANDY. Ah'll see ye's later.

MAGRIT. Aye c'mon ah'm aw behind.

ANDY. Ah widnae say that Magrit, ye've a good bit in front as well.

MAGRIT. Ach, away an' play in the traffic you.

DOREEN. Right everybody oot. (ANDY *exits.*)

DOLLY. Ach it'll no take us long tae catch up.

They all breenge into the washing. There is great activity as they go through this, during which MRS CULFEATHERS *comes back from the wringer and pulls out the donkey and hangs the clothes on to dry.*

MAGRIT. Right. Ah'm away to see if ah can get a wringer.

DOREEN. If you spot another wan gie's a shout.

MAGRIT. Right you are.

DOLLY. Gie's a shout as well will ye Magrit?

MAGRIT. OK Dolly. (*She exits with trolley of washing.*)

MRS CULFEATHERS. It's awful busy . . . she'll be lucky tae get wan.

DOLLY. It always is this time of the year.

DOREEN. The week before Fair Fortnight's the same, ye're lucky tae get a stall it's awful stupit though, they should pit mer wringers in the place.

MRS CULFEATHERS. It's aye been the same hen. Ma mother used tae go tae the wan in Glesca Green.

DOLLY. Was that no the first washhoose they built?

MRS CULFEATHERS. I think it wis Dolly, but ah might be wrong. It was enormous, ah know that. It was open fae seven in the mornin' tae nine at night every day except a Sunday. Ah kin aye mind, as a wee lassie, gaun wi' ma mother, and d'y'e know whit was lovely? Seein' Glesca Green wi' aw the washin' hingin fae the lines. Yon was a marvellous sight.

DOREEN. Doesnae sound aw that marvellous tae me.

MRS CULFEATHERS. Ach, ye should have seen it hen, especially in the summer time. Of course we had real summers then, fae May right ontae September. It was that hot the tar used tae stick tae yer feet, and the whole of Glesca Green was like a sea of colour, sheets and mattress covers and the men's shirts. White as snow as far as ye could see, and lovely coloured silks and woollens, aw dancin' in the dryin' wind.

At that age ah always thought they looked kinna happy, it sounds daft ah know hen, but it was the men's shirts and women's dresses. Ye see, they aw have arms and when the wind blew them aboot, they aw seemed tae be wavin' tae each other. It wis as if the claes had a life o' their ain. Ah aye mind o' that, and underneath them the women were aw movin' aboot, laughin' and jokin' wi' wan another ... it was noisy but tae me then, somehow ... thrillin'. We just went once a week, but ye could go and have a wee blether anytime ye felt like it, anytime except a Sunday. The men used tae play the fitba on a Sunday, but it was a great meetin' place. There was never any loneliness in *that* place, *naebody* seemed tae be lonely then.

DOLLY. That's what ah like aboot the steamie, yer aye busy and there's aye somebody ye know tae talk tae.

MRS CULFEATHERS. Aye that's true, but mind ye the best o' it's gone. It's mer enclosed noo, ah don't know what ah mean, but it's smaller somehow, and when yer finished yer oot and hame, but in thae days when ye came oot, ye'd aye Glesca Green tae look forward tae, sort of round off the day, you know what ah mean Dolly?

DOREEN. They're closin' aw the steamies doon, they say launderettes are gonnae take over.

DOLLY. Oor Jenny has wan o' them next tae her. She doesnae like it.

DOREEN. They save ye a lot o' work though Dolly.

MRS CULFEATHERS. What are they Dolly?

DOLLY. They're awful wee. There's only aboot ten machines and they only take aboot seven or eight pun o' washin. Jenny says when she goes in she never knows anybody. Aw ye dae is sit and stare at the machines. Naebody talks tae wan another except maybe 'it's a cold day', or 'have y goat change o' a shillin''. Kinna conversations that never seem tae get anywhere, ye know thon wey everybody's helevah polite tae wan another.

DOREEN. Is that her wi' a daughter that's goat a television?

DOLLY. Aye, she's comin' up the night for a wee terr. She says she's awful bored.

DOREEN. Ah don't see how she's bored. Ah think it would be great tae just pop round and watch a television set, and have aw yer washin' done fur ye by a machine. Ah kin see your point aboot Glesca Green Mrs Culfeathers, but you're just rememberin' it when it was summer. What was it like in the winter when it was freezin' and soakin' wet?

MRS CULFEATHERS. Aw, ye didnae hing oot yer washin' in the cold weather hen.

DOREEN. That's what ah mean.

MRS CULFEATHERS. But ye aye had the summer tae look forward tae. Ah'm no clever or brainy hen, and ah know ah'm auld fashioned, but it seems as if people are no aw-the-gither, as they used to be.

DOREEN. But we're the gither the noo, how can ye say that?

MRS CULFEATHERS. Aye, but when we leave, we aw go awa hame. Ah know it's New Year's Eve and it'll be nine o'clock at night, but even if it was twelve o'clock on a lovely summer's day, as soon as we were done in here, we'd still aw go different ways. And in these launderettes they don't even speak tae wan another right? An' when the machines are in the hoose, we'll no need tae go oot at aw. Ah think friendship wi' a lot of people is gonnae be impossible. Friendly, wi'wan or two is all we can hope for.

DOREEN. Naw, ah think we'll aw have a loat mer leisure time.

DOLLY. What's that? ... what's leisure time?

DOREEN. It's like spare time, just time tae dae anything ye want. Listen tae the wireless, or go tae the pictures, or if ye'd a television watch that, ah don't know, just relax.

DOLLY. Oh, I couldnae be daein wi' that, that's no what d'ye call it ... leisure time ... that's just hingin aboot, that's aw that is.

DOREEN. How is it?

DOLLY. Cause yer no daein something, yer jist watchin' other people daein something. Naw I'm like Mrs Culfeathers, I like tae be busy and in amongst people.

DOREEN. But ye can go oot in yer leisure time and meet people if ye want, in fact ye'd have mer time tae meet other people and stand an' talk if ye want, while the machine's daein the work fur ye. Can ye no see that?

DOLLY. Aye ... I can see what ye mean Doreen, I'd still rather be busy and talkin' at the same time, but I'll no be here tae see aw that anyway, so it'll no bother me.

DOREEN. Well I fur wan am lookin' forward tae it.

MRS CULFEATHERS. Och aye hen, everybody's goat their ain wey that suits them.

DOREEN. Mrs Culfeathers, I hope you don't think I'm cheeky, I don't mean tae be, but it's jist that the way yer talkin' ... are you feelin' lonely? ... if it's none o' my business just tell me tae shut up. I just wondered if I could maybe help.

MRS CULFEATHERS. Doreen, that's awful kind o' ye. I'm no lonely here hen, but, when I go back tae the hoose ... well ... Harry's no too good, an mebbe ah jist ... (*She is almost in tears.*)

DOREEN. Oh Mrs Culfeathers.

MRS CULFEATHERS. I'm sorry. I jist feel as if I'm finished.

DOLLY. Naw yer no. There's many a young wan couldnae get through the work you dae.

DOREEN. That's true Mrs Culfeathers. Yer smashin' fur yer age.

MRS CULFEATHERS. I'm healthy enough, it's jist when yer family's moved away, and ye don't see them, it's awful empty. D'ye know, I've got three great grand weans . . . and I've never seen them.

DOREEN. Are they in England Mrs Culfeathers?

MRS CULFEATHERS *nods her head.*

DOREEN. How d'ye no go doon and see them?

MRS CULFEATHERS. They've never asked me . . . but I'd like tae see . . . (*She breaks down.*)

DOREEN (*to* DOLLY). That's a bloody shame.

DOLLY. They want their buckin' airces kicked. (*To* MRS CULFEATHERS. *Sits beside her.*) Never mind ye've goat friends aw roon ye here. Wid ye like a wee drink Mrs Culfeathers? Steady yer nerves a bit.

MAGRIT. It's like the January sales doon there (*Entering.*) wi' the queues at the wringers, ah've jist left mine tae keep ma place . . . whit's happened?

DOREEN. Mrs Culfeathers is jist feeling a bit sad. (*Whispering.*) She's missin' the family.

MAGRIT. It's this bloody time ae the year, that's whit it is.

MRS CULFEATHERS. I'm sorry Magrit.

MAGRIT. I aye greet at this time . . . so does ma Maw.

DOREEN. So dae ah.

MRS CULFEATHERS (*still crying*). I just feel . . . I keep rememberin' . . .

DOREEN. I think ah'm gonnae greet as well. (*She sits beside* MRS CULFEATHERS *and consoles her; she is tearful now.*)

DOLLY (*on the other side of* MRS CULFEATHERS, *looks at* DOREEN). Aw don't hen ye'll start me aff an' aw . . . don't worry (*She starts.*) Mrs Culfeathers.

MAGRIT. Aw fur Christ's sake (*She starts.*) . . . ah aye feel awful stupit when I greet.

DOLLY. . . . it does ye good, gets it oot yer system.

DOREEN. Are ye feelin' any better Mrs Culfeathers?

MRS CULFEATHERS *nods her head and pats* DOREEN's *hand.*

MAGRIT (*recovering*). See this time ae the year ... I bloody hate it. It's memories that's what it is ... memories. Dolly could ah have another sherry? ... would ye mind?

DOLLY. Not at all Magrit, Doreen would you like wan?

DOREEN. Aye mebbe ah will, dy'e want another whisky Dolly?

DOLLY. Aye why no it'll mebbe cheer us up.

DOREEN. I don't suppose ye'd like a wee sherry Mrs Culfeathers?

MRS CULFEATHERS. Naw hen ... I'll take a whisky though.

DOLLY. That's the spirit. (*She pours the drink and sits beside them.*) Aw the best tae ye's. (*They drink.*)

MAGRIT. Ye know ah never touch this fae wan year tae the next.

DOLLY. Me an aw, unless it's an occasion. It's a man's thing really i'n't it?

DOREEN. John hardly touches it though.

MAGRIT. Ma Peter wid drink it oot a shitty cloot.

DOREEN (*laughing*). You make him sound like an alcoholic.

MAGRIT (*laughing*). He no only sounds like wan, he looks like wan.

DOLLY. I never thought tae ask ye, wid ye like some water in that Mrs Culfeathers?

MRS CULFEATHERS. Naw thanks Dolly ... is that McInlays Whisky?

DOLLY. Ah couldnae tell ye (*She looks at the bottle.*) aye ... it is. (*They all look at her.*)

MAGRIT. How did you know that?

MRS CULFEATHERS. Ma faither was a tester and he used tae bring them home wi' him ... every kinna whisky ye could mention, and he used tae teach me how tae tell the difference ...

MAGRIT. Whit age were ye?

MRS CULFEATHERS. Och I was only young.

DOLLY. Did ye no get awful drunk?

MRS CULFEATHERS. Oh, I never swallied it, neither did he. Ye jist pit it in yer mooth, and spat it oot. (*She starts laughing.*) There was aye an' awful smell o' whisky in the hoose, and there was not wan ae us drank it.

MAGRIT. Ye'll need tae tell us the secret, and I'll pass it on tae Peter. He's the opposite. He drinks it and never tastes it.

They're all happy.

MRS CULFEATHERS. This time for the first time, I'm gonnae drink it, tae toast you three . . . for being ma pals . . . To pals.

MAGRIT. Pals.

DOREEN. Pals.

DOLLY. Pals.

They sing 'Pals'.

ANDY *enters.*

ANDY. It's pandemonium at they wringers . . . *aw fur Christ's sake*!

Blackout

ACT TWO

DOLLY *sings 'Cry'*.

The scene opens with MRS CULFEATHERS *and* DOLLY *hanging up their blankets, sheets in the donkey or horse (dryer). They do this so that the blankets and sheets will be dry by the time the last washing is finished. This washing is never dried, but taken home and ironed semi-dry.*

DOLLY. Ah aye like when I get tae this stage Mrs Culfeathers.

MRS CULFEATHERS. Aye ye know yer half-way through it Dolly.

DOLLY. Are ye needin' a wee haun there?

MRS CULFEATHERS. Naw . . . I'm managing fine Dolly.

DOLLY. Ach I'll gie ye a haun anyway. Ah'm finished here. (*Crosses to* MRS CULFEATHERS*'s stall. Helps her.*) They're a bloody ton weight these things when they're wet in't they? (*Loading the top of the donkey.*) Huv ye ever been up at the Whiteinch Steamie Mrs Culfeathers?

MRS CULFEATHERS. Naw Dolly, I havenae. I hear they're nice baths though.

DOLLY. Oh they're beautiful. Ma other sister Agnes goes there. She lives up there noo.

MRS CULFEATHERS. An awful nice lassie, Agnes.

DOLLY. Aye she's been up there aboot six years noo. She's in the sandstone flats. They're lovely, hellovah clean lookin' so they ur, an' the closes are aw well looked after . . . they're aw tiled closes where she is . . . they look as if it was doctors that lived up them at wan time ye know thon wey.

MRS CULFEATHERS. Aye, be lovely Dolly, and were ye in the wash-house?

DOLLY. Aye, ah go there during ma holidays at the summer. They're lovely. The stalls are aw thon bakelite, beautifully white ye know, and the wringers are aw chrome.

MRS CULFEATHERS. Be lovely.

DOLLY. Aye . . . tends tae make yer washin' look shabby though.

MRS CULFEATHERS. Does it?

DOLLY. Aye . . . and when ye have a bath they're scentit.

MRS CULFEATHERS. What d'ye mean Dolly?

DOLLY. There's a smell aff them.

MRS CULFEATHERS. Be comin' fae the drains mebbe.

DOLLY. Oh ah don't know how they dae it, but ye can have yer choice, ye can have . . . oh what is it again noo, ah think wan o' them's pine . . . and then . . . the other scent's . . . oh aye . . . medicinal peat . . . that's fur rheumatism. Ah had that, Agnes had the pine wan.

MRS CULFEATHERS. Peat? Is that no the stuff that ye burn?

DOLLY. As faur as ah know Mrs Culfeathers.

MRS CULFEATHERS. Does it no make the water awful dirty?

DOLLY. Oh aye, it was. 'S is black as the Earl O' Hell's waistcoat. Ye need ah right bath efter yer finished. 'S a lovely smell though.

MRS CULFEATHERS. Ah aye remember ma Mother's Mother used tae burn it. It was a lovely smell right enough, but I never knew ye could wash wi' it.

DOLLY. Naw ye don't wash wi' it Mrs Culfeathers, ye just lie steepin' in it. It's mer fur curin' rheumatism.

MRS CULFEATHERS. Ah never knew ye had rheumatism Dolly.

DOLLY. Ah havenae goat rheumatism, it was jist a wee notion ah took, 'n'ah thought ah'd try it y'know. Pamper masel.

MRS CULFEATHERS. Ah don't think ah'd like that Dolly. Is it no awful hard tae drain it doon the plug hole?

DOLLY. . . . Ah couldnae say . . . ye jist leave it there and somebody comes in an' cleans it up efter yer finished.

MRS CULFEATHERS. Oh . . . and dae you fill it up when ye first go in?

DOLLY. Naw . . . it's already filled up fur ye.

MRS CULFEATHERS. Well how dae you know it's cleaned oot?

DOLLY. Eh.

MRS CULFEATHERS. Well, if it's black water when ye start, and black when ye finish, they'll mebbe no empty it at all. Ye know what some oh them are like Dolly. They might just leave it aw day, naebody would know whether it's clean or no.

DOLLY. Oh Christ, ah never thought o' that.

MRS CULFEATHERS. Ye never know who could've been in afore you Dolly.

DOLLY. I went in at half four anaw.

MRS CULFEATHERS. Ye could catch something fae that Dolly.

DOLLY (*thinking*). Aye . . . ah feel aw itchy noo. (*She starts scratching herself.*)

MRS CULFEATHERS. Ye never know who's been in these places. That's near the dry docks an aw oot there, ah mean, there could be seamen fae God knows where using they baths, ah there's aw they bad women, hangin' aboot there as well. Ah'm no wantin' tae frighten ye Dolly, but ye jist never know.

DOLLY. Ah think ah'll have a bath. Are the baths open?

MRS CULFEATHERS. They'll aw be full up hen. Ye'd never get near wan noo.

DOLLY. Right ah'll fill up a sink and have wan in here.

MRS CULFEATHERS. Ah don't think that's allowed Dolly.

DOLLY. Well ah don't care, ah'll no feel right tae ah've had a wash, Mrs Culfeathers. Would you go and explain the situation to Magrit and Doreen, they're havin' a smoke at the wringers, and tell him tae come back here?

MRS CULFEATHERS. Aw right hen . . . (*Starts to exit.*) Ah hope yer gonnae be aw right Dolly. (*Exits stage left.*)

DOLLY (*filling up the sink*). Ah'm gonnae write a letter tae them . . . them and their bloody peat baths . . . plenty o' hot water here. (*Turns on tap.*) Where's the soap . . . (*She finds it.*) . . . Ah'll need tae get these claes aff and washed . . . Christ ah'll need somethin' dry tae go home in . . . (*She selects some clothes from the first wash and opens the donkey and hangs them up and closes the donkey.*) Ah'll pit mah knickers in the boiler, that'll kill anything that might be in there. (*She removes large bloomers.*)

Christ these have goat a hole in the knee. (*She opens boiler and sticks them in with the boiler stick.*) I'll need a sheet for privacy. (*Opens the donkey and pulls off a sheet, drapes it over one side of the stall.*) I'll need a towel tae dry maself aff. (*Selects a towel, sticks it in the dryer.*) I better stop openin' and shuttin' this donkey or they'll be nae bloody heat left in it.

Enter MAGRIT, DOREEN *and* MRS CULFEATHERS *with washing.*

MAGRIT. Whit's up wi'ye? Ye silly wee bugger.

DOLLY. Did Mrs Culfeathers no tell ye aboot the peat baths?

MAGRIT. Aye, but I'm sure they'll have been cleaned oot, and even if they werenae it was six months ago.

DOLLY. I'm no carin', I'm wantin' tae wash maself.

DOREEN. Dolly, ye cannae wash yersel in here, what if somebody saw ye?

DOLLY. Ah've goat a sheet oot Doreen, we can stretch it across the tap o' the stall.

MAGRIT. They'll wonder what the hell the sheet's daein there.

DOLLY. Magrit, ah feel dirty, ah want tae wash masel, and ah'm gonnae wash masel. (*Loudly.*)

MAGRIT (*pause*). Aw right. Whit d'ye want us tae dae?

DOLLY. Just haud the sheet up while ah get undressed and intae the sink.

MAGRIT. C'mon Doreen. They'll be nae peace tae Esther Williams here has her way. (*They cross to* DOLLY*'s stall and pick up the sheet.*) Mrs Culfeathers, keep a look oot.

DOLLY. Right, hand it up. (*They do.* DOLLY*'s head can be seen plus her feet. She removes her leather apron, throws it on the floor right of the stall, her dress right of the stall and her bra also.*)

MAGRIT. If big Andy comes roon noo he'll get an eyeful.

DOREEN. Can ye imagine tryin' tae explain this.

DOLLY. That's me ready. Can ye follow me intae the sink?

DOREEN. Are ye gonnae take yer boots aff Dolly?

DOLLY. Ah forgoat aw aboot them. (*She does.*) Right, folly me intae the sink (*They do.*) At's me there. Ah'll jist get intae the sink. (*Pause.*) Oh . . . ya messen.

MAGRIT. Whit's wrong?

DOREEN. Ye aw right Dolly?

DOLLY. It's bloody bilin, it's too warm. (DOLLY*'s head above sheet.*)

MAGRIT. It'll be aw right wance yer in. (*There is a sound like someone pissing into a bucket of water from behind the sheet. Looks at* DOLLY.) What are you dain in there?

DOLLY. Ah've turned the cold tap oan tae cool it doon, it's gettin' better noo. I'll no be long. (*She ducks below sheet.*)

ANDY *is singing off,* '*Thank Heaven for Little Girls*'.

MRS CULFEATHERS. Ah think Andy's comin' this way Magrit.

MAGRIT. Doreen, you keep him talkin', while I fix this sheet up.

DOLLY (*behind sheet*). Magrit don't leave me.

MAGRIT. Ah cannae staun here. I'll try and fix this sheet up. (*She fails . . . it falls over* DOLLY *covering her.*)

DOLLY. Whit the hell's happenin'?

MAGRIT. Shut up Dolly.

ANDY (*off. Singing*). Thank heaven for them all, no matter where, no matter who (*Enters.*) without them what would little boys do . . . How's the four stooges gettin' on?

DOREEN (*crosses to him stage left*). Yer a rerr singer Andy. (*Gushingly.*)

MRS CULFEATHERS. Aye . . . a lovely voice. (*Sincerely.*)

ANDY. Thank you very much girls, that was from my latest record . . . songs for swingin' loafers . . . d'ye's no get it, ye know swingin' loafers, swingin' lovers.

DOREEN. Oh aye . . . oh whit a laugh, oh that's good, isn't it Mrs Culfeathers . . . ha . . . ha . . . ha . . . that's awful good.

MRS CULFEATHERS. Ah don't get it hen.

DOREEN. Och aye ye dae Mrs Culfeathers.

MRS CULFEATHERS. Have ye made a record Andy?

ANDY. Naw it's . . . eh . . . it was meant tae be a . . . ach it doesnae matter Mrs Culfeathers.

DOREEN. Oh I thought it was really funny Andy . . . it's the best ah've heard for a long time . . . songs for swingin' eh songs for . . . whit wis it again?

ANDY. Swingin' loafers.

DOREEN. Aye that's it . . . ha ha ha . . . ha ha ha ha hahahaha.

ANDY. Ah didnae think it was that good. (*He goes to move on towards* DOLLY*'s stall where* MAGRIT *has draped herself trying to obscure his view of* DOLLY *who is now under the sheet and resembling a pile of washing.*)

DOREEN *intercepts.*

DOREEN. So how have ye been Andy since we last saw ye? Y're lookin' well.

ANDY. Och aye. Ah huvny changed much in the last twenty minutes . . . still goat aw ma ain teeth . . . and how huv you been . . . since I last saw ye?

DOREEN. Oh just great.

ANDY. Still mairrit?

DOREEN. Aye . . . still mairrit.

ANDY. That's good, and when did ye go aff yer heid.

DOREEN. Eh?

ANDY. Ye's are up tae something i'nt y'es? (*Looking at* MAGRIT.) Right Lilli Marlene, whit's goin' oan?

MAGRIT. Whit d'ye mean? *Whit's goin' oan* . . . see your mind, it's diseased. Dae you cairry oan like this in the hoose?

ANDY (*crosses over to her.*) Noo wait a . . .

MAGRIT. Naw, you wait a minute. You've just inferred that mah friend's no right in the head. Just because she was tryin' tae be pleasant tae you, and let me remind you in case you've forgotten it, that the person you have just accused of being a loony, happens tae be a regular customer here, and in case it's slipped your notice, if it wisny fur her and the rest o' us loonies comin' here, you widnae have a joab.

ANDY. She jist asked how ah've been since she last saw me.

MAGRIT. Well what's wrong wi' that? There's nàe pleasin' you is there? If we're no talkin' tae ye, yer off in the huff and if we dae pass the time o' day, that's wrong an' aw.

ANDY. She saw me twenty minutes ago.

MAGRIT. Oh Christ, is there a set time limit noo tae talk tae you, ye'll need tae instal a wee bell an' n'en we'll aw know it's aw right tae say hello. Wait a minute, you've been drinkin' since ye were last here.

ANDY. Ah have not.

MAGRIT. Aye ye huv . . . ah kin smell if aff yer breath. Right I'm goin' for the Manager.

ANDY. Aw haud oon Magrit, there's nae need fur that.

MAGRIT. How is there no?

ANDY. I didnae mean it the wey ye took it, look I'm sorry.

MAGRIT. Don't apologise tae me, it's that wee soul at the back o' ye ye should be sayin' yer sorry tae . . . she's nearly in tears. (*Looks at* DOREEN.) Sure ye ur Doreen?

DOREEN (*twigs, puts on petted lip*). Ah'll be aw right Magrit. (*Sniff, sniff.*)

ANDY (*crosses to her*). I'm awful sorry Doreen, I honestly didnae mean it.

DOREEN. That's all right Andy, it was jist a joke that went too far. (*Sniffle, sniffle.*)

ANDY. Gonnae no cry Doreen.

She breaks down into MRS CULFEATHER*'s arms.*

Oh Doreen please . . .

MRS CULFEATHERS. She'll be awright, Andy.

ANDY. Will she?

MRS CULFEATHERS. She's jist upset because you said she was aff her heid.

DOREEN *cries louder.*

ANDY (*takes* DOREEN *in his arms*). Doreen, if ye stop greetin, I'll see ye get first turn at the wringer aw next year.

DOREEN *pulls herself together and gives the thumbs up sign to* MAGRIT *over* ANDY*'s shoulder.* MAGRIT *returns it.*

DOREEN. That's a very nice gesture Andy, and if it makes ye feel better, I'll accept your apology . . . and your offer.

ANDY. Thanks Doreen.

MAGRIT. Noo I'd like tae ask, where are *you* gettin' aw the drink fae?

ANDY. Well aw the women are the same as yersels.

MAGRIT. Eh?

ANDY. They've aw goat cairyoots fur their men wi' them. Everytime I pass a stall, wan o' them gies me ma ne'erday. Where's Dolly then? (*He goes to her stall before anyone can stop him. He looks at the sheet with* DOLLY *underneath.*) She's goat a helluvah pile tae get through there. (*He gives it a thump, looking at* DOREEN *who is in front of* MAGRIT.)

DOLLY. Hey, watch whit ye'r dacin.

ANDY (*astonished*). Whit was that? (*Looking around him.*)

MAGRIT. Ah said watch what yer daein, yer haunds'll get grease aw oer thae sheets.

ANDY. Sorry Magrit. (*He is a bit confused.*)

MAGRIT. Well if you've nae work tae dae . . . we have.

ANDY. Aye ah better get oan. (*He crosses back left. As he passes the women he glances round.*) Ah could've sworn that voice came fae . . . (*There is a movement in the sheet over* DOLLY, *which he just catches. He stares at the washing.*)

MAGRIT. Whit's up wi ye noo?

ANDY. Ah thought I saw that washin' . . . move.

MAGRIT *and* DOREEN *look at each other.*

MAGRIT. Are you insinuating that my friend Dolly's washin' is so dirty it's movin'? Have ye no done enough damage wi' Doreen? D'y'e want tae start oan wee Dolly noo?

ANDY. Naw naw I didnae mean it that way . . . ah really did think it . . . it seemed tae . . . (*He describes the movement with his head.*) Ah think I'll need tae stop acceptin' ma Ne'erday fur a while . . . ah'll away fur a wee lie doon . . . clear ma head.

DOREEN. Aye I think ye'd better Andy.

ANDY. Aye . . . (*He exits.*)

MRS CULFEATHERS. Magrit. (*Whispering.*) Ah think I saw it move tae.

MAGRIT. It did move. D'y'e no remember Dolly's underneath it?

MRS CULFEATHERS. Oh . . . I see. (*She doesn't.*)

MAGRIT. It'll aw come oot in the washin' Mrs Culfeathers. Don't worry.

DOREEN. Ye saved the day there, I'm here tae tell ye.

MAGRIT. The best line of defence is attack. Ma mother taught me that. C'mon we better tell Quatermass the experiment's finished whether she likes it or no. Dolly. (*She crosses over.*) Dolly came oot o' there.

DOLLY (*still under*). Is he away?

MAGRIT. Naw he's staunin here wi' a box brownie and a reporter fae the 'News of the World' . . . of course he's away.

DOLLY. Right. Jist pull the sheet up so ah can staun up and dry masel. (*They do.*) Gie's that towel oe'r will ye? (MAGRIT *passes her the towel. She starts drying herself.*) I feel better noo. Magrit, gonnae stick that dress and brassiere in the boiler. Use the stick so ye don't need tae touch them.

MAGRIT. Aw fur God's sake Dolly, ye'd think ye'd had the plague. (*She picks up the garments and puts them in the boiler.*) Ah'll jist take a chance and use mah haunds.

DOLLY. That'll be alright. Ye'll be washin' wi' them anyway. Ye can drap the sheet noo. (*They do. She has the towel wrapped around her sarong-fashion.*)

MAGRIT. Oh Christ, it's Dorothy Lamour.

DOLLY. Right enough. (*She does a wee Hawaiian pastiche and sings.*) 'Moonlight Becomes Me, it Goes with my Hair'.

DOLLY (*comes down and waves to* MRS CULFEATHERS). D'ye like the outfit?

MRS CULFEATHERS. Oh aye. It's lovely Dolly . . . too young for me though.

MAGRIT. Heh Dolly, see the next time I see you in the queue doon there gonnae dae me a favour?

DOLLY. Aye of course Magrit, whit dae you want me tae dae?

MAGRIT. Jist let me know what day you're comin' so I can book up fur another wan.

DOLLY. Aye OK Magrit. (*She starts to get dressed.*)

DOREEN. I've never seen it like this before.

MAGRIT. Naw, an I hope I never see it like this again. I'm no gonnae be worth a button by the time I get oot o' here. (*She crosses into her stall as does* DOREEN ... *after a short pause they are filling the sinks.*)

DOREEN. It was a right laugh though. I'll never forget Andy's face when he saw her movin' under the sheets.

MAGRIT. You done aw right oot o' it eh? First turn at the wringer fur a year.

DOREEN. Aye, we'll see how long that lasts.

DOLLY. Listen lassies, I'll need tae get stuck intae this washing here, so if I don't talk tae ye's for a while, I'm no bein' ignorant, I'll jist be a wee bit busy. I hope ye's don't mind. (*She crosses back.*)

DOREEN *and* MAGRIT *look up heaven-wards.* DOREEN *mouths silently 'Thank you God'.* MAGRIT *crosses herself. The sinks are now full and the last of the washing gets underway.*

DOLLY. Magrit.

MAGRIT. I knew it was too good tae last ... what?

DOLLY. Dae you'se huv tae go tae the Chapel the night?

MAGRIT. Naw ... it's Christmas we go ... tae Midnight Mass.

DOLLY. Ah thought ye's went the night as well.

MAGRIT. Naw.

DOLLY. That's the same as us. We go on Christmas Night as well. Saves ye gaun the next mornin'. Of course you'se have tae go don't ye?

MAGRIT. How d'ye mean?

DOLLY. Well, I was telt it was a terrible sin if a Catholic missed goin' tae Mass.

MAGRIT. Aye ... well it is a sin, but it's no as bad as that. They don't take ye oot and shoot ye, yer jist no supposed tae dae it.

DOREEN. Ye's go and confess it don't ye's?

MAGRIT. Aye.

DOLLY. What's that fur?

MAGRIT. If ye commit a sin, ye tell the Priest aboot it and he forgives ye.

DOREEN. Whit kin o' sins Magrit?

MAGRIT. Och anything and everything. The Ten Commandments like, ye know.

DOREEN. How often dae ye have tae dae that?

MAGRIT. Well in theory ye shouldnae have tae dae it mer than wance, cause ye promise never tae dae it again, but of course it never works oot that wey, so it's usually aboot wance a week.

DOREEN. Is it no awful embarrassing tellin' the Priest aboot aw the things yer no supposed tae be daein'.

MAGRIT. Naw, he cannae see you. There's a wee curtain up between ye's.

DOLLY. I like tae see the weans goin' tae thon thing where they're aw dressed in white. Whit's that called again?

MAGRIT. Their First Communion.

DOREEN. Aw aye. I've seen that. The wee lassies are lovely wi' the white dresses and their wee veils. They're that innocent lookin'.

DOLLY. Does your Peter go tae that Confession thing tae?

MAGRIT. Naw. He does aw his confessin' tae the money-lender and the bookie. The only connection he's goat wi' religion is staunin at Parkhead shoutin' aboot King Billy wi' the rest o' the ijiots.

DOREEN. If there's wan thing a cannae staun it's fitba. John goes on a Saturday, right? Then he buys a late night *Citizen* and reads aboot it, then oan the Sunday he's goat the *Mail*, the *Post* and the *Express* and reads aboot it again. Then he goes doon tae the corner and they aw staun talkin' aboot it till efter five o'clock.

Ah went wi' him wance tae see a game an honest tae God ah don't know whit the hell they aw get tae talk aboot. Wan o' them wid kick the ball *up* the wey and n'en someb'day else kicks it back the *other* wey, and efter aboot hauf an hoor o' this, wan o' them kicked it intae the goal . . . an' they aw went crazy. Ye'd think they'd aw won the pools. N'en tae cap it aw they started *fightin'* aboot it . . . mebbe it's me, but ah don't see the sense in that.

MAGRIT. There isnae any.

DOREEN. N'there wis a wee man runnin' aboot. He wis the referee. N'as faur as ah could see, he did nothin'. He never even kicked the ball, but they aw hated him. He wisnae playin' fur wan team nor the other, but whatever he was daein the crowd didnae like him.

DOLLY. Wid they no be better gettin' rid o' him if naebody wants him there.

DOREEN. That's what I said, but John just telt me no tae be daft.

DOLLY. Well I wouldnae go where I wisnae wantit. They'd jist shout at me the wance and they'd never see me again . . . course mebbe he's goat nae life o' it in the hoose. Mebbe his wife gi'es him a hard time . . . but he'd still be better wi' jist wan shoutin' at him than thousands. Naw, he's no wise him whoever he is. Di'ye hear Maureen McCandlish is getting married?

A stoppage of work is now about to happen.

MAGRIT. Maureen McCandlish? . . . Gettin' mairried?

DOREEN. Who's *she* gettin' merried tae?

DOLLY. I think it's some fellah fae Springburn faur as ah know. Anyway that's whit ah wis telt.

DOREEN. Who telt ye?

DOLLY. Tina Harper in the dairy.

MAGRIT. Christ. N'he'll no have his troubles tae seek him.

DOREEN. It'll no be a white weddin' that.

DOLLY. Naw, they're a bad lot them.

DOREEN. It's well seein' she had tae go oot the district tae find somebody that didnae know her. Has she no had a wean already?

MAGRIT. Aye. She wis away for a long time, aboot two years
ago. Supposed tae be workin' in England . . . but she wis
havin' the wean. Ye could see it before she went. She wis goin'
aboot sayin' she'd have tae go oan a diet n' stop eatin'
sweeties. Must think we all come up the Clyde oan a biscuit.
She wis seen up at Blythswood Square.

DOREEN and DOLLY. She wis not. Was she? (In unison.)

MAGRIT. Aye, Bella McNaughton saw her. Of course ye know
what Bella's like.

DOLLY. Aye, she's a helluvah woman.

MAGRIT. Bella says she seen her staunin aboot wan o' the
corners. Course Bella watched her fur aboot ten minutes, tae
see whit wid happen.

DOREEN. Did somebody pick her up?

MAGRIT. Bella says this fellah went up tae her n'they were
talkin' away.

DOREEN. That's terrible.

MAGRIT. Naw, but wait tae ye hear. Apparently he kept
shakin' his head she must have been askin' too much money.

DOLLY. She's nae oil paintin' right enough.

MAGRIT. Oh. She's goat a face like a coo's airce.

DOREEN. Whit happened.

MAGRIT. Well, eventually this fellah walked away, ye see.
Didnae want nothin' tae dae wi' her.

DOLLY. Oh.

MAGRIT. Aye . . . So the bold Bella saunters up tae her n' says
'Hello Maureen . . . 's a lovely night in't? Ye oot for a wee walk?'

DOREEN. Oh.

MAGRIT. Bella says her face went pure purple. She says tae
Bella 'I'm just waiting for my boy friend. He's a wee bit late
so he is' . . . you know thon voice ae hers an'aw, s'like
Tommy Morgan.

DOLLY. Aye. Clairty . . . clairty.

MAGRIT. Aye, except wi' her it's mer like clatty . . . clatty . . .
anyway she's dyin' tae get Bella oot the road, but of course

Bella keeps talkin' tae her ye know. 'And what does your boy friend work at? And how long have you been goin' out together?'

DOREEN. She's pure evil, Bella, wance she gets started.

MAGRIT. Anyway, the Maureen wan says 'I think I'll just go home. He'll probably turn up later on at my Mother's'. So jist at that this wee coolie comes daunerin up tae them aff one o' the boats ye know!

DOLLY. Oh Christ.

DOREEN. Naw.

MAGRIT. Aye, n'he says tae Maureen 'You come jig-jig on boat?' So the Maureen wan says 'I'm afraid I'm no like that'. N'the wee coolie says 'Same price as last night, but this time you not to be so rough'.

DOLLY. Oh in the name.

DOREEN. Oh help. What did Bella say?

MAGRIT. Oh Christ, Bella got off her mark. She got feart in case anybody saw her, but she met her in the Butchers aboot a week later 'n' she says tae her 'Aye Maureen . . . ye still gaun oot wi' that wee fella wi' the baggy troosers?'

DOREEN. Oh . . . she's a bugger Bella. Imagine that though. I'd heard she was hawkin' herself, but I didnae know it was true . . . that's horrible isn't it. She's filthy dirty as well.

DOLLY. They're aw mingin. The Sanitary's never away fae them.

MAGRIT. The faither works aside Peter. Ye know what they call him? The carbolic kid. When he dies they'll no bury him they'll plant him.

DOREEN. Her brother was at school wi' me. I always felt awful sorry fur him. He'd tae sit by 'iself because he'd beasts in his head, he'd had his head aw shaved, a' that blue stuff dabbed oan it . . . but he was no a bad lookin' boy, y'know if he'd been turned oot right.

MAGRIT. Oh he is a good lookin' fellah. You're talkin' aboot Davy McCandlish?

DOREEN. Oh aye aye . . . no the other wan.

MAGRIT. Naw naw . . . oh no the oldest wan . . . no
Humphrey. Christ ye'd think somebody had sat on his face
while it was still warm.

DOLLY. Aye, him an' Maureen take efter wan another.

DOREEN. When we were wee we aw used tae shout efter him
'where d'ye cum fae Humphrey?' . . . n'en run like hell.

MAGRIT. Have ye even been in the hoose?

DOREEN. Naw.

DOLLY. Oh no me. I wouldnae go in there.

MAGRIT. Oh dear God ye want tae see it. I mean nane o' us
have goat much money, but there's nae excuse fur thon. Ye
can aye afford a bar o' soap can't ye?

DOLLY. Zit as bad as that?

MAGRIT. Ye wipe yer feet when ye go oot o' thon hoose. I
went in fur some reason . . . noo whit wis it fur . . . och it's
went oot ma heid.

DOREEN and DOLLY. It doesnae matter Magrit. (In unison.)

MAGRIT. Aye anyway, noo I'll say it masel ma hoose is nae
palace, but how any woman that calls herself a woman could
let things get intae that state . . . they've goat a cat, supposed
tae be fur mice, but ah think it's rats.

DOLLY. Oh don't . . . I'm helevah feart o' thae things.

MAGRIT. Well this cat had . . . shit oan the flair and she'd jist
left it lyin' there . . . ah cannae tell ye whit the smell wis like.
Ah wis . . . ah wis just aboot boakin.

DOREEN. Ouagh.

MAGRIT. I know, ne'en she asked me if I'd like a cup o' tea.
Well if ye'd a seen the cups, whit ever colour they'd been
originally, ah couldnae tell ye. Ma stomach was heavin'. Ah'd
tae make an excuse and I just left.

DOREEN. I've seen that wee cat. It's a wee black and white
wan i'n't it.

MAGRIT. Aye that's right, it's only goat wan eye.

DOREEN. It's a shame, it never gets fed.

MAGRIT. It must be hoachin wi' fleas.

DOREEN. It's called Lucky.

MAGRIT. Oh but ye know what she said when I was leavin'?

DOREEN. Naw.

MAGRIT. Well, she says n'this ma hand tae God. 'Ye'll need tae excuse the mess, but I havenae goat rooned tae ma cleanin' the day'.

DOREEN *shakes her head as does* DOLLY.

Aye, if she ever makes a start on thon place, she'll need tae get McAlpine's in wi' wan o' yon big bulldozers.

DOREEN. Aye, 'n' McAlpine's 'll need tae burn the bulldozer efter it's finished.

They go back to work, sing 'Pride'.

DOLLY. I'll away and see how Mrs Culfeathers is gettin' oan.

MAGRIT. Aye, aw right.

DOREEN *and* MAGRIT *carry on with the washing.*

DOLLY (*crosses to* MRS CULFEATHERS). Are ye gettin' oan aw right Mrs Culfeathers?

MRS CULFEATHERS (*mopping her brow*). Aye ... thanks Dolly ... s'awful hot in here isn't it?

DOLLY. Aye it is. Have a wee blow and I'll get tore in here while ye cool down a bit.

MRS CULFEATHERS. Thanks Dolly. I could dae wi' a wee rest. I've seen the day Dolly when I could've rattled through twice this, an' thought nothin' aboot it, but I'm gettin' too auld noo.

DOLLY (*getting steamed in*). Oh ye were aye a good worker.

MRS CULFEATHERS. Ah always liked tae be workin', ah always enjoyed it.

DOLLY. Y'know the McCandlish's?

MRS CULFEATHERS. The McCandlish's fae Torphicken Street?

DOLLY. Aye they're at the top end next tae the Butchers.

MRS CULFEATHERS. I don't know them tae speak tae, but I know who you mean. The auld Granny used tae have a stall at

the Jiggy. She used tae sell claes tae the coolies off the boat ...
they always walked in single file tae Paddy's Market, and
when they'd bought their stuff, they'd wrap it in an auld
blanket, and walk aw the wey back fae Paddy's Market tae the
Docks wi' the bundle oan their heads. They always used tae
talk awful fast. It was a common sight that. She was a hard
workin' woman auld granny McCandlish. They say she left
her family quite a lot o' money.

DOLLY. Is that right?

MRS CULFEATHERS. Well that wis the rumour that wis goin'
aboot ... but she aye kept tae hersel. Of course her man died
young, and she'd tae bring up the family on her ain ... that's
a *bought* hoose ye know.

DOLLY. Is it?

MRS CULFEATHERS. Aye ... she bought that hoose ... I
know that. Oh she gave the family a good start, but I think
when she died they stopped sellin' things tae the coolies.

DOLLY. Well fae what Magrit wis tellin' me ah think they've
started again.

MRS CULFEATHERS. Well, I wish them aw the luck Dolly.
Auld Granny McCandlish would be proud o' them.

DOLLY. Well I don't think ... aye ... right enough ... so she
would.

MRS CULFEATHERS. There's nothin' nicer than tae see yer
family aw set up and daein well fur themselves. It's jist a pity
... she's no here tae see it. Eh Dolly?

DOLLY. Aye ... oh aye ... aye ... it's a pity.

MRS CULFEATHERS. But ... ye never know Dolly. Even
although she's deid, she could still be watchin' over them.

DOLLY. Aye ... aye ... she'll certainly get an eyeful if she is.

MRS CULFEATHERS. I don't know them noo, cause I never
go tae that butchers. I aye go tae Galloways ... they've got
lovely butchermeat. Their mince is marvellous ... marvellous
mince ... there's hardly any fat on thon mince Dolly ... have
ye ever tried their mince Dolly?

DOLLY (*humouring her*). Oh ... aye ... aye.

MRS CULFEATHERS. It's very good mince isn't it?

DOLLY. It's very good mince.

MRS CULFEATHERS. I've seen me tryin' mince fae somewhere else, jist fur a change ... but ... naw I aye go back tae Galloways mince ... I've seen me bringing in mince fae another butcher and I'll no say nothin' tae faither, but see when I pit it doon tae him, efter the first mouthful, dae ye know whit he says tae me Dolly?

DOLLY. Naw.

MRS CULFEATHERS. He says ... an I know he's gonnae say it. He says 'where did ye get that mince fae?' Aye he can tell it's no Galloways mince ... ye widnae credit that wid ye Dolly.

DOLLY (getting fed up). Naw that's ... amazin'.

MRS CULFEATHERS. Well that's ma hand tae God Dolly ... and the next time I'll get Galloways mince, and I'll pit it doon tae him ... and Dolly ... this is as sure as I'm standin' here ... d'ye know what he says tae me then?

DOLLY. 'That's Galloways mince.'

MRS CULFEATHERS. Naw Dolly ... he doesnae know I get it fae Galloways. He doesnae know wan butchers fae another ... they're aw jist butchers tae him. Ye know what men are like. Naw he doesnae say it's Galloways mince ... that's no what he says.

DOLLY. Does he say 'that's better mince than the last time'.

MRS CULFEATHERS. Naw ... he doesnae say that either Dolly.

DOLLY (losing the rag). Well what the hell does he say?

MRS CULFEATHERS. He says 'can I have another tattie?'

DOLLY. What does he say that fur?

MRS CULFEATHERS. Ah don't know ... but that's whit he says. Every time it's Galloways mince, he asks for another tattie. Dae you know why he says that Dolly?

DOLLY. Mebbe it's jist coincidence.

MRS CULFEATHERS. Naw. He's been sayin' it since I first bought Galloways mince.

DOLLY. How long ago was that?

MRS CULFEATHERS. When they opened that shop. It's over twenty years noo.

DOLLY. And he's aye said 'can I have another tattie'.

MRS CULFEATHERS. Aye, I think Galloways mince must bring oot the flavour o' the tatties.

DOLLY. I'm gonnae ask Magrit. (*Calls and moves to* DOREEN *and* MAGRIT'*s stall followed by* MRS CULFEATHER.) Magrit . . . Doreen.

MAGRIT. Whit the hell is it noo?

DOLLY (*at their stalls.*) Magrit . . . Doreen . . . have ye ever bought mince fae Galloways?

MAGRIT. Aye.

DOREEN. Aye.

DOLLY. Right . . . noo when ye pit it doon in front o' Peter does he ever say anything?

MAGRIT. Does he ever say anything?

DOLLY. Aye.

MAGRIT. I don't know. I never listen tae him. Whit are ye oan aboot?

DOLLY. Doreen, does John ever say anything?

DOREEN. Aye he does.

DOLLY. What does he say?

DOREEN. He always asks fur sauce. He likes sauce wi' his mince.

DOLLY. Wait tae ye hear this. Tell them what ye telt me Mrs Culfeathers.

MRS CULFEATHERS. Well I wis tellin' Dolly that I aye got ma mince oot o' Galloways because it is lovely mince . . . there's hardly any fat in their mince Doreen ye know.

DOREEN (*slightly mystified*). Aye oh, it's good mince.

MRS CULFEATHERS. D'ye no like their mince Magrit?

MAGRIT. Aye . . . it's awright. (*Looks at* DOLLY.)

DOLLY. Tell them aboot whit Mr Culfeathers says aboot it.

MRS CULFEATHERS. Well . . . I wis tellin' Dolly aboot how I aye get ma mince oot o' Galloways, but sometimes I get it oot another butchers . . . ye know just for a wee change, and I was sayin' that when I get it oot another butchers, Mr Culfeathers can always tell, even though I havenae said whit butchers I got it oot o'. If I pit mince doon tae him, and I havenae got it oot o' Galloways, he aye says tae me 'where did ye get that mince fae'?

MAGRIT (*slight sarcasm*). Does he? . . . (*To* DOREEN.) D'ye hear that?

DOREEN. Aye . . . that's . . . that's . . . that's eh . . . very interesting.

MRS CULFEATHERS. That shows ye what good mince it is.

DOLLY. Oh it is . . . aye it is good mince isn't it Magrit?

MAGRIT. Oh . . . second tae none.

DOLLY. But that's no the end o' it. There's mair.

DOREEN. Surely not.

MAGRIT. Ye mean even mair interesting than that?

DOLLY. Aye . . . wait tae ye hear this.

MAGRIT. Well I don't see how you can top that, but do go on.

MRS CULFEATHERS. Well you know I was sayin' that when I bought the mince fae another butchers Mr Culfeathers . . .

MAGRIT. Aye, we've got that.

DOLLY. Tell them whit happens when ye get the mince fae Galloways.

MRS CULFEATHERS. Well . . . when I don't get it fae Galloways . . . I . . . he says . . . I've forgot what I was gonnae say. Whit was it Dolly? I've lost the thread. You tell it.

DOLLY. Are ye sure you don't want tae tell it yersel'?

MAGRIT. Dolly, I've got a washin' tae finish here, noo fur God's sake what are ye's oan aboot?

DOLLY. Right. I'll make it quick. When she buys her mince oot another butchers the old man can tell it's no Galloways cause he always says . . .

MAGRIT. Where did ye get that mince fae? We've got that.

DOLLY. Right, but if she buys it oot o' Galloways whit d'ye think he says?

MAGRIT. That's Galloways mince.

DOLLY. Naw. (*Pleased with herself.*)

MRS CULFEATHERS. Naw he doesnae say that cause he doesnae know ah get it oot o' Galloways. Aw butchers are the same to him.

DOREEN. Well he must say 'eh . . . that's nicer mince than the last lot.'

DOLLY. Naw, he doesnae say that either.

MAGRIT. What the hell does he say then?

DOLLY. Tell them Mrs Culfeathers.

MRS CULFEATHERS. He always says . . . 'can I have another tattie?'

MAGRIT (*to* DOREEN). Well now that was worth stoppin' for eh?

DOREEN. It's a funny thing tae say right enough. Mebbe it's just coincidence.

DOLLY. Naw, that's what I thought, but he's been sayin' it fur twenty odd years.

MRS CULFEATHERS. That shows ye it's good mince.

DOREEN. But why does he want another tattie? I mean ye'd think he'd ask fur mair mince.

MRS CULFEATHERS. I think the mince brings oot the flavour o' the tatties.

MAGRIT. I don't believe this. This is the stupidest conversation I've ever heard.

DOREEN. Dae ye aye get yer tatties fae the same shop?

MRS CULFEATHERS. How dae ye mean Doreen hen?

DOREEN. Well when ye buy yer mince at Galloways, dae ye get yer tatties fae the same fruit shop that ye always dae?

MRS CULFEATHERS. Let me think Doreen. Noo if I buy ma mince oot o' somewhere else I just get ma tatties oot the nearest fruit shop tae wherever I bought the mince.

DOREEN. Aye but when ye get yer mince oot o' Galloways dae ye always get the tatties fae the same fruit shop?

MRS CULFEATHERS. Aye ... always ... I aye get them fae wee Mr Jackson.

DOREEN. Well, that's it ... it's the tatties fae Jackson's he likes. That's why he asks for another wan ... it's nothin' tae dae wi' the mince.

DOLLY. That's it ... ye've solved it Doreen. D'ye hear that Magrit? ... there ye are Mrs Culfeathers. After twenty years the mystery is solved ... it's no' the mince.

DOREEN. It's the tatties Mrs Culfeathers.

MRS CULFEATHERS (*a bit crestfallen*). I always thought it was the mince.

MAGRIT. I wish tae Christ ye's wid shut up aboot mince and tatties. Ma ears are bleedin wi' ye's.

They start back to the stalls.

MRS CULFEATHERS (*whispering*). Dolly. I'm gonnae get mince oot o' another butchers and tatties oot o' Jacksons and see if he asks fur another wan.

DOLLY. That's a good idea, that'll pit yer mind at rest.

MRS CULFEATHERS. Aye ... (*Beckons her nearer.*) I'm no wantin' tae let Magrit hear me ... I still think it's the mince. I'll see ye later. (*She goes back to her stall as does* DOLLY. *There is a long silence and ... then ... MAGRIT shouts out.*)

MAGRIT. I'm sorry I lost the rag ... I was out of order.

DOLLY. Ach it's awright Magrit. Don't worry aboot it.

DOREEN. Och we never thought nothin' o' it.

MAGRIT (*crosses to* MRS CULFEATHERS). I'm sorry I shouted Mrs Culfeathers.

MRS CULFEATHERS. Ye don't need tae apologise tae me Magrit.

MAGRIT. Oh yes I do ... my mother and father brought me up to respect my elders ... if they deserved it ... and you deserve respect Mrs Culfeathers. Yer a fine old woman and I'd nae right tae shout at ye. So I hope ye'll accept my apology.

MRS CULFEATHERS *grips* MAGRIT*'s arm and nods her head.*

Thanks. (*She crosses back to her stall.*)

DOLLY. Nearly finished noo Doreen. No long tae go.

DOREEN. Aye we'll never get a wringer though.

DOLLY. Gie them a good wring oot wi' yer haunds, and then stick them in front o' the fire or in the oven.

DOREEN. Oh ah did that wance. I nearly set the hoose oan fire. Everything was aw burnt.

DOLLY. It's awright if ye keep the oven door open.

DOREEN. I was mortified. We were only a couple o' weeks mairried. I'd jist got the flames oot, the hoose was full o'smoke, when who comes tae the door but John's mother. She asked me if I'd burnt the dinner and I says naw the washin'. See his shirts when I lifted them oot, they aw fell through ma fingers.

DOLLY. Was he mad?

DOREEN. Naw, we werenae long enough mairried fur him tae be mad.

MAGRIT. I was goin' tae a works dance wi' Peter and I was ironin' his shirt. It was a white shirt wi' wee silk threads through it, like stripes ye know, and the iron was too hot. It was stickin' thon wey, so I went tae lift it off. The back o' the shirt came wi' it. A right big hole it left. Him and I had a hellova rammy aboot it. The rest o' his shirts were dirty, so he had tae wear that wan. I telt him no tae take off his jaiket and naebody wid know. Well I'm no' kiddin', see the hall it was like an oven. The bloody sweat was pourin' oot him and everybody kept sayin' 'ye should take yer jaiket aff'.

DOREEN. Did he take it off?

MAGRIT. I made sure he never took it off. I stuck tae him like glue. Wi were wi' wan another the whole night. They were aw sayin whit a devoted couple wi were . . . if they'd only known.

DOLLY. Oh he's a nice fella your Peter.

MAGRIT. Aye if ye take him the right wey . . . by the throat.

Enter ANDY. *Definitely guttered. Sways unsteadily to centre stalls.*

ANDY. Yes . . . yes . . . (*Whoo, breathes out trying to appear sober.*) Right then. Now . . . (*Deep breath.*) Z'ivrything . . . you know . . . workin' awright.

MAGRIT. . . . Apart fae you dae mean?

ANDY. Cause. (*Glasgow drunk's hand-signals.*) Zat's
here for . . . now then . . . z'ivrything awright?

MAGRIT (*this speech should be done with heavy irony to t*
she sings 'Isn't it wonderful to be a woman'). Isn't it wo   ae
be a woman. Ye get up at the crack o' dawn and get the
breakfast oan, get the weans ready and oot the hoose lookin' as
tidy and as well dressed as ye can afford. Then ye see tae the
lord high provider and get him oot, then wash up, finish the
ironin', tidy the hoose and gie the flair a skite o'er. Then it's
oot tae yer ain wee job, mebbe cleanin' offices, servin' in a
shop or washin' stairs. Then it's dinner time. Well it is fur
everybody else but no us 'cause we don't get dinner. By the
time yer oot and run home, cooked something for the weans,
yer lucky if you feel like something tae eat. I know I don't and
even if I did . . . the dinner hour's finished, so it's back tae yer
work; that is efter ye've goat in whatever yer gonnae gie them
for their tea, and efter yer finished yer work, ye'r back up . . .
cookin' again and they'll tell ye the mince is lumpy . . . or the
chips are too warm . . . then they're away oot. The weans tae
play . . . the men tae have a drink, cause they need wan . . .
the souls . . . efter pittin' in a hard day's graft, so ye've goat
the hoose tae yersel' and what dae ye dae, ye tidy up again
don't ye? Mer ironin', light the fire, wash the dishes and the
pots etc. etc. and then ye sit doon. And what happens . . .
ye've just sat doon when the weans come up. 'Gonnae make
us a cuppa tea and something tae eat' . . . What dae ye's want
tae eat? . . . 'Och anything Ma' . . . D'ye want some o' that
soup? . . . 'Naw' . . . A tomato sandwich? . . . 'Naw' . . . A
couple o' boiled eggs? . . . 'Naw' . . . A piece 'n spam? . . .
'Naw' . . . Well what d'ye's want? . . . 'Och anything at all'.
So ye make them something tae eat then ye sit doon and
finally have a wee blaw . . . a very wee blaw . . . cause it's
time tae go tae the steamie. Ye go tae the steamie, finish at
nine o'clock and get the washin' hame. Ye sort it aw oot . . .
and get it put by and then sometimes mebbe take stock of yer
life. What are we? . . . skivvies . . . unpaid skivvies . . . in
other words we are . . . used . . . but ye think tae yersel', well
even if I am being used . . . I don't mind . . . cause I love my
family and anyway it's New Year's Eve. I can relax and jist
enjoy masel . . . and any minute noo the weans'll be in an ma
friends'll be comin' roon wi' black bun, shortbread,
dumplin's, a wee refreshment and I can forget aw ma worries

even if it's jist for a night and the weans arrive and ye gie them shortbread, sultana cake, ginger wine and there is just one thing missin', the head of the family. The door bell goes, ye open the door, and what is staunin there, ready to make the evening complete . . . that's right . . . your husband, your better half . . . the man who was goin' to make you the happiest woman in the world and (*Gently.*) what does he look like . . . *that*. (*At* ANDY.)

DOLLY. Who were ye talkin' tae?

MAGRIT. Masel.

ANDY. So . . . z'a . . . wis sayin' girls . . . everything aw right doon here . . . know . . . cause . . . that's what I'm here fur.

MAGRIT. Oh is that what your here for? We were wonderin'!

ANDY. Oh don't be like that Magrit . . . I mean . . . it's nice tae be nice . . . n'at right Dolly . . . I mean it is . . . in'tit nice tae be nice?

DOLLY. Certainly is Andy.

ANDY. Dolly . . . this is between you and me . . . I mean this is no fur the management's ears . . . (*Lowers his voice.*) Ah've hid a wee drink . . . but that's between you and me. Y'know (*Still whispering.*) that's eh . . . that's our secret . . . schhhhhhh (*He smiles at everyone. Sings 'The Bells are Ringin' for Me and My Gal'. Continues singing.*)

MAGRIT. He certainly knows how tae keep a secret.

DOREEN. He better watch, he'll get his books.

ANDY. For me and my Gal . . . gee but it's great after bein' out late walkin' ma baby back home. (*They stand not knowing what to do.*) Arm in arm over meadow and farm . . . walkin' ma baby back home. (*He continues.*)

DOREEN. We better do something aboot him.

MAGRIT. Whit?

DOREEN. I don't know, but we'll need tae dae somethin'.

DOLLY. Leave it tae me. Andy. (*He keeps singing.*) Andy stop a minute. (*He quietens down.*) Andy listen tae me . . . d'y know any Jolson songs?

ANDY. Rock a bye your baby with a dixie melody. (*Sings.*)

DOLLY. When you croon croon a tune.

ANDY. From the heart of Dixie. (*They continue.*)

MAGRIT. She's a rare help her.

DOREEN (*laughing*). Take a look oe'r tae yer right.

MAGRIT *does.*

MAGRIT. Oh in the name o' the wee man.

MRS CULFEATHERS *is joining in on her own with a faraway look in her eye.*

DOREEN. Listen.

MAGRIT. What?

DOREEN. Listen.

They listen. There is a faint noise of women singing the Jolson song. It grows and swells till the hall is full of all the steamie women singing. Not raucous, beautiful and melodic.

MAGRIT. Wellll.

DOREEN. Gaun wur selves. (DOREEN *dances with* MAGRIT. DOLLY *with* MRS CULFEATHERS. *They join in. Song continues.*)

ALL. *Big finish with a Dixie Melody.*

ANDY *collapses in a bogey* MRS CULFEATHERS *crosses to him, looks at him.*

MRS CULFEATHERS. He's awful peaceful lookin' isn't he? . . . He's a nice big fella. (*She crosses back to her stall.*)

DOREEN. What'll we dae wi' him?

MAGRIT. Just leave him there oot o' harm's wey.

DOLLY. We'll take him oot wi' us when we're finished and get him home.

MAGRIT. He'll never get home in that state.

DOLLY. He can come up tae ma hoose and stay there tae he comes roon. Ah'm jist aboot finished anyway.

The steamie women could still be singing in the background.

MRS CULFEATHERS. Dolly, could ye gie me a wee haund tae finish up, if y'eve a spare minute.

MAGRIT. How are we gonnae get him past the front door?

DOREEN. No' only that, he's supposed tae lock up.

MAGRIT. We'll have tae waken him up.

DOLLY (*crosses over*). Andy . . . Andy, ye'll need tae get up son. (*She shakes him. No response.*)

MAGRIT. Gie's a haun wi' him.

They lift him and take him over to a sink.

MAGRIT. Turn the cold water oan Dolly. (*To* DOREEN.) I'm gonnae enjoy this . . .

They stick his head under the cold tap.

ANDY. Aaghh . . . Aaghh.

MAGRIT. Aaghh . . . whit?

ANDY. Aaghh, don't want any mer tae drink. Ah've had enough.

DOREEN. Andy . . . ye'll need tae loack up.

ANDY. Oh God, I feel awful.

MAGRIT. Mebbe it was something ye ate.

ANDY. Aye.

DOLLY. Come oan and I'll go wi' ye Andy.

ANDY. Thanks Dolly . . . if ye'd jist gie us a wee walk tae the boiler room, I'd be very grateful.

DOLLY. I'll see he's aw right . . . be back in a minute. C'mon son . . . I'll make ye a wee cup o' tea.

ANDY. Thanks . . . I've goat tea and sugar in ma locker.

DOLLY. C'mon then, yer Auntie Dolly'll see ye awright.

They cross to stage left.

ANDY. I'll no forget ye Dolly . . . I'll see ye get first turn at a wringer aw next year.

DOREEN (*to* MAGRIT). What did ah tell ye.

MAGRIT. Right then, I'm goan hame fur a quiet night.

DOREEN. I'll gie Mrs Culfeathers a wee haund tae finish up. (*She crosses to* MRS CULFEATHERS.) How ye gettin' oan? Ye managin' aw right?

MRS CULFEATHERS. I'm jist finishin' up noo Doreen. (*She loads her pram.*)

DOREEN. I'll gie the stall a quick wipe o'er.

MRS CULFEATHERS. I hope Andy'll be awright.

DOREEN. He'll be fine.

There is a lull while they are working.

MRS CULFEATHERS. That was nice eh Doreen?

DOREEN. What was nice?

MRS CULFEATHERS. Aw the women singing like that, wisn't it?

DOREEN. Aye . . . it was . . . Mrs Culfeathers . . . very nice.

MRS CULFEATHERS. Aye . . . good fun tae . . . (*She has a wee laugh to herself.*) Doreen . . . I'm gonna ask Mr Culfeathers if he'll come up tae Dolly's . . . just for a wee while. She did ask me so I'll no be imposin' will I?

DOREEN. Not at all . . . she'd love tae see ye's.

DOLLY (*enters*). I've made him a cup o' tea. Right I'm goin' hame tae get ma party frock oan.

DOREEN. Ye gonnae get aw dolled up?

DOLLY. Oh definately . . . (*She has loaded up her pram.*) Get aw ma make-up oan, ma curlers in . . . bleach ma moustache, get ma corset oan, and a wee daud o'perfume tae finish it aff. Ye's ready tae go?

MAGRIT. Aye . . . ye right Mrs Culfeathers?

MRS CULFEATHERS. Aye Magrit.

They exit stage right.

MAGRIT (*voice off*). I'll gie ye a haund doon wi' yer pram Mrs Culfeathers.

MRS CULFEATHERS (*voice off*). That's awful good o' ye Magrit.

DOLLY *and* DOREEN *are leaving too.*

DOREEN (*to* DOLLY). Whit a night it's been Dolly eh?

DOLLY. Aye . . . it's no been dull Doreen, eh hen. Ye'd never have a night like this in a launderette eh?

They exit.

DOLLY (*voice off*). Night Andy. Happy New Year when it comes.

Pause.

ANDY (*voice off*). Oohhh.

DOLLY*'s song 'We Wish You All You Wish Yourself'*

The End

The Big Picture 1.

DOREEN.

> When you live in a room 'n' kitchen
> You've done the cooking and the washin'
> And you are young and in the fashion
> And full of passion
> Not hard to please.
>
> You get that old familiar itchin'
> You want a lover strong and tireless
> There's nothing special on the wireless
> He's fast asleep in
> his dungarees.
>
> That's when you think about the Big Picture
> The Main Feature
> Tony Curtis in a chain mail shirt
> and a leather skirt
> A perr of legs you just want tae bite
> I've been too long among the 'B' movies
> I need a lover that's the Big Picture
> I'd give new meaning to 'coming soon'
> With Rory Calhoun
> He would be alright for a night
> A fortnight
> He's a bit of alright
> I'd give him the Big Picture show.

The Big Picture 2.

DOLLY.

You should of seen us at the jiggin'
We never went just for a lumber
We done the foxtrot and the Rhumba
We sang each number
Every fandango.

I used to dance with Jack McGuigan
My God, he thought that he was dashin'
A swagger that wid dry a washin'
But he was smashin'
At the tango.

And me and Jack we were the Big Picture
They gave us Top Billin'
And every time we would stop the show
You should've seen us go
Oh we were a sight for to see
On Friday nights I was the Big Picture
I used to feel I was the Star Attraction
An' every time they would clear the flair
An' staun an' stare
At Rudolph Valentino and me.

The Big Picture 3.

ANDY.

When you spend all day long with women
And you're a normal guy like ah'm ur
It's up to you to give them glamour
Because they clamour
For your attention.

You have to yield-not-to-temptation
When everywhere you look there's lassies
You've got tae body-swerve the passes
And I've had masses
I will nae mention.

I mean you're looking at the Big Picture
The Main Feature
It's down to me to be the cabaret
It changes every day
I make it up as I go along
I hear them say 'Here comes the Big Picture'
The big fella
Here's the boy that's gonnae make you laugh
D'ye want my autograph?
I'll give youse a joke or a song.

It's no' just anybody's racket
A lot of guys they couldnae hack it
I'm lucky, I just seem to crack it
It's just a knack it
'S easy to spot it.

I've got a talent for to natter
The anecdotes they run like watter
Where did I get this gift of patter?
What does it matter?
I'm glad I've got it.

So get your tickets for the Big Picture
The Cat's Pyjamas
An even if they take the piss
Ah'm enjoyin' this
This is what I'm destined to do
I was born to be the Big Picture
An' here's the Grand Finale
I'm sorry but the star of the show

Says it's time to go
But remember darlings, I love you too
Don't miss next week's exciting chapter
'Cos I'm the boy for you.

Dreams Come True 1.

DOREEN.

> Me an' John we got married when
> I was only 17
> And before I'm 21
> I'll be old, if you see what I mean
> By the time I'll have carried all
> Of ma washin' up the stair
> I'll no be a lot of fun
> 'Cos we live on the very top flair
> I'll be good fur nothin' by 12 o'clock
> Waitin' for the first foot with a dram
> As they all get plastered all around me
> I'll be sittin' in a kinna dwam
> 'Cos.
>
> Dreams come true
> If you really want them to
> I'll be livin' in my dream
> In a country housing scheme
> Where all my
> Dreams come true
> I've been waitin' in the queue
> For a house on an avenue
> Where dreams come true.
>
> Out of my kitchen window I'll see
> The kids all round the back
> The street will be dead quiet
> Maybe even a cul-de-sac
> I saw it in a picture called Moonlight Bay
> Lots of pretty houses in a row
> Roses round the door and garden fences
> That's where me and John are
> Gonnae go –
> Where.
>
> Dreams come true
> Surely mine is nearly due
> Four apartments and a view
> and an inside toilet too
> I'm going where dreams come true
> and the sky is always blue
> Me and John will get a new
> House in Drumchapel where Dreams come true.

Dreams Come True 2.

DOLLY.

> Dreams come true
> When you least expect them to
> You'll be movin' out of town
> When they pull your houses down.

MAGRIT.

> And you'll have a TV and a hoover
> And a fitted carpet and a phone.

DOREEN.

> A toaster and a Hotpoint Automatic.

MRS CULFEATHERS.

> And lots of time to spend all on your own.

DOLLY.

> To wonder why your
> Dreams come true
> 'Cos they've got big plans for you
> You'll be livin' in Drumchapel too.

ALL.

> So don't you tell me dreams
> Don't come true.

Pals.

When you've got pals
You've got something so rerr
Tell me what could be as fine as
Passin' time with all your chinas.

When you've got pals
Makes it easy to bear
All the pain and all the pressure
Bless your pals.

There was a geezer
You must have heard about
Julius Caesar was his name
He conquered Europe
But if he'd been without
His pals he might as well have stayed at hame.

But he had pals
Or he never would dare
He was just a wee smout
Without his pals.

Old Winston Churchill
They tell me he won the war
Beat Adolf Hitler on his own
A brilliant speaker
But what was the army for?
He never done it on his Todd Ma-lone.

When you've got pals
You can aye have a terr
If you want tae come and see me
Take a dauner doon the steamie.

Supposin' that your man should start tae belt ye
Who'll sock his jaw
Is it the Law?
Naw, it's your pals
Don't call a cop, remember what a telt ye
They'll say domestic
You had best stick
To your pals.

If he comes hame on Friday, skint, an' seein' double
Who'll pay the rent
The Government?

Naw it's your pals
If some boy should get your lassie in-tae trouble
Who'll help you cope
Is it the Pope?
You've got a hope
Naw, it's your pals.

You need your pals
Or you've no' got a prayer
We've got nothin' tae shout about
But ye huvnae got clout without
You are lower than nowt without
If he knocks ye about, we'll pout
We will call him a lout
We will lend you a snout
We'll be staunch, we'll be stout
You're a chucked-away dout
Without your pals.

Cry (or – 'A Song for Ella').

DOLLY.

> The great big clock on the steamie wall
> Says it's time to load your stuff
> On tae the donkey; but it's you's in the stall
> You that's the donkey right enough.
>
> You'd think that after all these years
> Your workin' days'd be by
> But all your life it's blood, sweat and tears
> Don't let the young folks see you cry.
>
> Every Sunday afternoon
> When Family Favourites is on
> You can hear that black woman croon
> 'Bout how her man has gone.
>
> She's got that stormy weather
> Every time he says goodbye
> And you'll never know how much I miss you
> Sounds so good, you wanna cry.
>
> She hates to see that evenin' sun go down
> An' nobody knows the trouble she's seen
> He was her man, but he done her wrong
> Missus, I know what you mean.
>
> You feel as if she's in your shoes
> Although you don't know why
> Maybe it's jist, women get the blues
> You get the blues, and you cry
> You cry
> But nobody knows that you cry.

Pride.

God knows there's none of us got money
Still and all the things we do have
They were bought and paid for, working
With the fruits of honest labour.

And there's none of us would covet
Any special things that you have
Cos there's none of us are better
Than a good and decent neighbour.

But we never will condone
Those who'd rob and cheat their own
No that's no' the kind you're wantin' on your side.

God knows there's none of us got money
But that's not the way we're goin'
Maybe we've got nothin' much
But we've got pride.

We know it's easy to get beaten
When you've constantly to take it
Bite your tongue and go on graftin'
Hold your head up high whatever.

Oh we've got no time for wasters
Those who think they cannae make it
And they go out on the batter
Might as well be in the river.

Be as well if you should drown
If you've gone and let us down
If your weans are no' looked after, better hide.

If we don't have some self respect we
Might as well be in the ground
If we've got nothin' else at least
We've got our pride.

Isn't It Wonderful To Be a Woman.

MAGRIT.

Isn't it wonderful to be a woman?
Yes, everyday I thank the stars above
I just can't wait to get up in the mornin'
'Cos everyday is such a labour of love.

You get up at the crack of dawn
Get everybody's breakfast on
Make the weans get out of bed
Get them dressed and get them fed
Turn them oot the best you can
Then dae the same thing for your man
You don't even get a cup
Of tea before you tidy up.

Then you've got to go to work
All morning like a flamin' turk
Maybe cleanin' office flairs
Or washin' somebody else's stairs
At dinner time you run back hame
To feed the weans then oot again
And back to work till half past three
That's after you have bought the tea
And did ye think to feed yersel?
There wisnae time – ach, what the hell?
Because your life is just a labour of love.

Isn't it wonderful to be a woman?
Is it no' just a joy to make their tea?
And they'll no' hesitate to criticise you
The mince is lumpy and the plate's too wee
And then they all go out, the weans to play
The men to drink, cos they've worked all day.

This is all the time that you're gonnae huv
to yourself, what are you thinking of?
You wash the dishes and you light the fire
You've got to get on with the labour of love.

You're just about to have a seat
The weans come up, they want to eat
So what d'yes want?
'Well what've you got?'

D'yes want some soup?, it's in the pot
        'Naw'
D'yes want an egg?
        'Naw'
A piece on jam?
        'Naw'
A biscuit?
        'Naw'
A wee bit spam?
        'Naw'
D'yes want some toasted cheese, well?
        'Naw'
So what d'yes want?
        'Ooh, anythin' at a'.'

You run down to the steamie
'Cos it closes up at up at nine o'clock
You bring it hame and fold it up
And iron it, and sort the socks
You tidy everything away
And then you think about your day
And dreamin' willnae get you far
A skivvie, that is all you are
You're just a skivvie in your labour of love.

But still it's wonderful to be a woman
Because tonight we're gonnae have some fun
It's hogmanay an' I feel almost human
Even if my work is never done
I've made some shortbread just for auld lang syne
I'll gie the weans some ginger wine
Wait patiently for the man I love
And who should give the door a shove?
Isn't it wonderful to be a woman
And have a man that's such a labour of love.

All the Best (When it comes)

DOLLY.

> It won't be long before the bells
> Time jist overtakes you
> Like today, it just slipped away
> And old is all it makes you.
>
> We wish you all you wish yoursel's
> Let's put the past behind us
> We wish you health and we wish you wealth
> Though it's no' been known tae find us.
>
> And on the wireless, the pipes and the drums
> All the best, when it comes.
>
> And all the best to you and yours
> Today we'll no' remember
> How you slave to an early grave
> Spring until December.
>
> We'll drink a toast, and sing a song
> Laugh, and hug each other
> Time won't stand still, and we never will
> Be this close together.

ALL.

> Some day we'll say 'What became of the slums?'
> All the best, when it comes
> Here's to the day when we get more than crumbs
> All the best
> All the best
> When
> And if
> It comes.